A TALE OF THREE CITIES

A Tale of Three Cities

Comparative Studies in Working-Class Life

John Lynch
Teaching Fellow
Department of Economic and Social History
The Queen's University
Belfast

Consultant Editor: Jo Campling

MACMILLAN

First published 1998 by
MACMILLAN PRESS LTD
Houndmills, Basingstoke, Hampshire RG21 6XS
and London
Companies and representatives throughout the world

ISBN 0–333–71383–4

A catalogue record for this book is available
from the British Library.

This book is printed on paper suitable for recycling and
made from fully managed and sustained forest sources.

10 9 8 7 6 5 4 3 2 1
07 06 05 04 03 02 01 00 99 98

Printed and bound in Great Britain by
Antony Rowe Ltd, Chippenham, Wiltshire

For Ann
who made things possible

Contents

Acknowledgements

I would start by thanking Ken Brown, Liam Kennedy and all the staff in the Department of Social and Economic History at Queen's. I would like in particular to acknowledge the invaluable assistance of Valerie Fawcett, the Departmental Secretary whose patience is an example to us all. I also express my gratitude to the librarians and other staff of Queen's University, Linen Hall Library Belfast, Bristol Central Reference Library, Public Record Office of Northern Ireland, Bristol Industrial Museum and Bristol Record Office, where the bulk of my research was undertaken. I would also like to record my thanks to the staff of many other organisations and archives whose help was invaluable.

I would like to acknowledge the part played in my return to education by the staff and students of Ruskin College Oxford in the years 1987–9; lectures, debates and conversations at that time did much to shape my view of the world.

Lastly, but by no means least, I thank Jo Campling who acted as consultant editor: her advice and assistance have been both needed and appreciated.

The courtesy, tolerance and kindness of many people has made my research not just a possibility but a pleasure.

1 Introduction

A photograph of a socialist demonstration in the early days of the First World War shows a good-natured crowd, mainly women and children, gathered around a wagon on which are displayed the banners of the local Labour Representation Committee, the Socialist Sunday School and The Independent Labour Party.[1] Such gatherings would have been common in British industrial cities; at this time, however, this demonstration was not taking place on the British mainland but in Ormeau Park, Belfast. Such displays of Labour activism are not considered typical of Irish politics, where the dominant issues of Irish Home Rule and Unionism, remained locked in apparently insoluble conflict as the socialists assembled around their banners in the park.

Belfast is usually perceived as the heartland of Ulster, if not Irish, Unionism. However, there were competing ideals and a wide range of socialist and Labour organizations enjoyed widespread support. The retail consumer co-operative, the great economic expression of working-class solidarity in Britain, was active in Belfast, and only there and in a few neighbouring towns did the movement prosper in Ireland. Throughout this period the Belfast Co-operative Society contained over half the membership in Ireland and by 1931 it had over three quarters.[2] Belfast's prosperity was due to industrialisation, an anomaly in a country normally perceived as rural and industrially under-developed. However, by considering the city's growth in terms of Britain as a whole the economic structure of Belfast appears less distinctive. It can legitimately be said that Belfast was amongst a number of British urban areas which in the nineteenth century underwent a process of growth and industrialisation. We find ourselves confronted by a choice: was Belfast an Irish city and thus exceptional, or a British city and thus more typical of contemporary trends within the larger economy? Certainly in many important ways the developing working-class culture of Belfast had more in common with Glasgow, Manchester or Bristol than with Dublin, Cork or Galway.

There is perhaps a need to compare Belfast with other 'British' industrial cities rather than 'Irish' urban centres where conditions were fundamentally different. Cities do not exist is isolation; like people they are the product of both their own environment and external influences. This is not to say that cities are not distinctive or even singular places, far from it; again as with people the response of

1

any two communities to a given situation or development is never quite the same. The only way to quantify, or even in some cases to recognise, the significance of a development to a city is to compare it with others.

The cities with which I shall compare Belfast in the late nineteenth and early twentieth centuries are Dublin and Bristol. Dublin was the only other Irish city which could compare with Belfast in terms of population and physical size. However, even the most superficial comparison reveals huge differences between the cities in terms of economic and social structure which allow them to be usefully contrasted rather than compared. My choice of an English city may appear rather eccentric; Bristol is not normally considered as a comparison for Ireland's industrial cities. However, in this case Bristol offers the researcher some very distinct advantages.

Bristol lies outside the 'Irish Sea Triangle' and thus, unlike the more conventional comparisons of Liverpool or Glasgow which enjoyed widespread trade and migration links with Belfast and Dublin, can be seen as displaying more independent development which can be usefully contrasted with the Irish experience. In common with the Irish cities it is a port with its industrial development linked to trade and, as in the case of Belfast, the importation of raw materials. All three cities were centres of government, commerce and communications although this was particularly marked in the case of Dublin due to its 'regional capital' status. In addition all three cities saw the development of labour and trade union bodies during the late nineteenth and early twentieth centuries, although this experience varied greatly between them.

Bristol has historical links with Dublin that date back to the medieval period when both cities were centres of manufacturing and trade. In contrast, Belfast was a modern creation whose growth in the closing decades of the eighteenth and the nineteenth centuries was a result of industrialisation. The city of Bristol, unlike Dublin, shared much of the nineteenth-century experience with Belfast experiencing massive growth in physical size and population as well as undergoing large scale changes in economic and social structure. In addition Bristol and Belfast shared a tradition of radical political thought and non-conformist religion which again sets them apart from Dublin.

Why have such comparisons not been a feature of Irish or even, to a lesser degree, British economic, social or labour history? In part at least J.D. Clarkson's comments in his history of the Irish labour movement can be applied to wider historical perceptions.

To those who for every Irish movement seek roots in Ireland's Gaelic past, such an hypothesis (that Irish and English trade unions were fundamentally different) is peculiarly welcome. Repudiating any implication of inferiority arising out of the fact of difference, leading champions of Irish Labour yet see in the Irish labour movement an isolated struggle for the re-establishment of the ancient Gaelic social order, rather than merely a part of the general struggle conducted by the working classes throughout western Europe against the evils of industrial capitalism.[3]

Within Irish history there has been a strong tendency to parochialism; studies in such areas as economic and labour history have tended to concentrate on a single city or at best the whole of Ireland. There has seldom been the comparative aspect needed to place Irish experience in the wider European or world context.

To take labour history as an example of this trend, there is almost always an underestimation of the degree to which Ireland's labour organisations were part of a larger British movement. In the latest study of Irish Labour Emmett O'Connor considers the role of movements in Britain and Belfast in the development of the wider movement. However, the underlying emphasis is still on Dublin based developments and the distinctiveness of the Irish movement:

The foundation of the ITGWU marked the beginning of a long and painful decolonization that, combined with Connolly's industrial unionism modernised the movement and made it relevant to native conditions.[4]

How does the Belfast trade union movement fit into this process except as a deviation from the 'norm'? Although the city can be seen as an extreme case, the nationalist demand for Irish unions for Irish workers was prompted, at least in part, by the fact that many Irish trade unionists belonged to British based unions.[5]

There has been a tendency to link the development of the Irish labour movement with the emergence of nationalistic political identity. However, Belfast workers was often highly unionised and were active supporters of labour representation, yet at the same time were dogmatically anti-nationalist in terms of Irish politics. How do we explain this apparent contradiction? Was Belfast simply 'different' or was the link between Irish labour and nationalism more illusory that is often suggested?

If Irish historians have frequently failed to analyse the full extent of Anglo-Irish links in matters such as trade unionism have British authors been more successful? The answer is on balance no but the reasons for this are rather more complex. In the case of labour history there has been a tendency for an Anglocentric approach with events in Ireland or Scotland being seen as far from the main centres of power and therefore of secondary importance. As an example, even in the most comprehensive works such as the two volume *History of the British Trade Unions since 1889* by H.A. Clegg and his associates there is a tendency for Irish events to become submerged in the wider issues of these years.

While there has been some acknowledgement of the role of the Irish in the development of the British labour movement this has often been grudging or incomplete. Even worse in some early works there were elements of anti-Irish racism. This frequently took the form of treating Irish trade unionists, and the Irish in general, in a patronising manner or simply as a source of humour. In an early history of the Boilermakers when discussing the career of Harry Howard, a long serving official in Belfast, the author indulged in racial stereotyping of a kind unthinkable in today's 'politically correct' unions.

> Like all men of the Emerald Isle, he was impulsive and generous; and though like mankind generally, liable to err, nevertheless his desire always is to improve and benefit his fellow-man.[6]

It was not only trade unionists who were capable of stereotyping when discussing the Irish. Lord Askwith, the Board of Trade mediator who was active in both the 1907 Belfast and 1913 Dublin strikes, had very definite views.

> It says much for the general effect of our education and standards of right and wrong that so little violence follows from wild statements. Remarks in the heat of an oration on Tower Hill that so-and-so should be shot lead to no result, while a similar suggestion, if only insinuated, has been known in Ireland to be taken as a hint upon which action will follow.[7]

Amongst British labour leaders and social reformers Ireland was often seen as quite distinctive from the rest of Britain. All too often Ireland was presented as an economically and socially backward region against which the success of the rest of Britain could be compared. This was aggravated by an insufficient understanding on the part of these commentators of the differences between the Belfast region and the rest of Ireland, which often resulted in misleading generalisations. It has also been unfashionable to consider the Irish labour movement as part of the British for political reasons. The labour movement in Britain were early, if at times grudging, supporters of Home Rule and later opposed the partition of Ireland.[8] Any acknowledgement of possible commonality with the labour movement of Belfast would appear to contradict this stance. To justify the political positions of the TUC and Labour Party on Ireland, it was convenient to accept that Ireland's trade unions were fundamentally different.

However it is not always easy to consider the working-class culture of Belfast in terms of its similarity to that of Britain but rather its distinctiveness. Belfast historically has a reputation for sectarian division that could often take the form of violence and intimidation. There were serious outbreaks of sectarian rioting on no fewer than sixteen occasions between 1813 and 1909.[9] These varied from a one day orgy of window smashing in 1835 to four months of sporadic violence which left at least 32 dead and 371 injured in 1886. They occurred mainly in working-class districts of the city, often instigated or aggravated by the workers of the Queen's Island Shipyards. It is notable for example that the bloody riots of 1886 were triggered by a sectarian dispute between Protestant shipyard workers and Catholic navvies working on the Alexander Dock.[10]

Such outbreaks could be profoundly embarrassing to British trade unionists and labour politicians as can be seen in the response of the unions to the shipyard expulsions of 1920. Some unions have sponsored 'political' histories whose primary function is to present the union in the best possible manner. Thus there is a tendency to 'forget' unfortunate incidents. A prime example of this is the Boilermakers official history by J.E. Mortimer.[11] In relation to Belfast this impressive book jumps from the Articles of Agreement with Harland & Wolff in 1914 to the mid-1930s. This allowed the author to avoid the question of the expulsions in which riveters and other members of the union played a significant role. The histories of other unions involved in the shipyards such as the Shipwrights, Engineers and Blacksmiths are also strangely quiet on the subject of Belfast in these years.[12] The electricians mention the expulsions but mainly as an example of the dangers of disunity rather than in criticism of the actions.[13] Only the Woodworkers give a reasonably complete account of these events, mainly perhaps because unlike most other unions they supported their members who suffered expulsion.[14]

There is an undeniable Janus-faced quality to Belfast in these years. On one hand it appears a modern industrial city similar to those in the rest of the United Kingdom. Conversely, there existed violent divisions on grounds of religion and politics apparently alien to the British experience, although, to a lesser degree, a feature of cities such as Liverpool and Glasgow.[15] This strange mix of the familiar and the alien has long perplexed those who seek to analyse the politics of the Belfast working class. As a result, and to avoid difficult problems of comparison, there has been a tendency to accept that Belfast 'is different' and discuss it in isolation.

What I intend to do is place the Belfast working class and the trade unions and other institutions which they created within the British context in which they emerged rather than the more conventional Irish dimension. I will look at aspects of daily life such as housing, diet, income and employment patterns as a means of assessing if Dublin or Bristol had more in common socially and economically with Belfast. I will also look at the viability of the concept of the 'working class' in all three cities to discover how far religious or political divisions undermined 'class unity'. My basic case study will be the work force of Harland & Wolff, the largest and most diverse employer of unionised labour in Belfast. Conditions and attitudes within this employer will be compared with those of other firms in the city of Belfast and the other two cities. The main objective is to try and establish if there existed a distinctive industrial relations pattern in Belfast created by political or social conditions or if it is typical of other industrial centres?

Was Belfast 'British' or 'Irish', I do not ask this question in terms of the modern unionist-v-nationalist debate but in terms of economic and social development in the second half of the nineteenth and early twentieth centuries. The only way that this can really be assessed is by comparing the city to others and trying to quantify the degree of similarity and difference that exists. Is this really possible? Can such distinctive units as cities really be compared with each other in a meaningful manner? Was Belfast really 'different' or simply unique within an Irish context?

2 Belfast, Bristol and Dublin

In his reminiscences of Belfast at the turn of the century the Irish labour leader Thomas Johnson was critical of many things but admitted, with a certain pride that

> Belfast was prospering in the first decade of the century, and if wages were relatively low there was little unemployment. The city was growing and new areas were being developed on the traditional lines of long monotonously similar kitchen-and-parlour houses.[1]

The city in which Johnson lived and worked was the creation of the Victorian era. In 1815 the town was a port and commercial centre with a small but prosperous cotton industry and a population of about 20 000. By the census of 1841 flax spinning had become a major industry and workers in the new mills boosted population to 70 747. By 1861 the adoption of machine weaving increased the demand for labour and 121 602 were resident in the city. The disruption of cotton supplies caused by the American Civil War created a boom in the Belfast linen industry and population reached 174 412 by 1871. By 1901 with the linen, shipbuilding and engineering trades expanding Belfast's population reached 386 974.[2]

Between 1880 and 1925 over a third of those employed in Belfast was engaged in manufacturing industry; in turn this sector was dominated by three industries, linen, engineering and shipbuilding. This level of manufacturing employment was considerably above the UK average and almost four times the figure for Ireland as a whole.[3] The industries were themselves very different in their employment patterns. Linen, as with all British textiles, was dependent upon a large and relatively unskilled workforce, 70 per cent of which was female. Wages in this industry were low and working conditions poor, and thus while a significant employer, it would not have made Belfast prosperous, except perhaps for a few brief years when demand reached exceptional levels during the American Civil War.[4] Engineering although important, employed only relatively small numbers, although these included a considerable number of skilled tradesmen. Initially based upon the manufacture of textile machinery, the industry later diversified into a wide range of production.[5] In general engineering was organised in small or medium sized units and there was little specialisation. Limited in terms of potential employment engineering, like linen, it would not generate the wealth to make Belfast prosper. It was shipbuilding, where up to 70 per cent of the labour force in this period were skilled that created a well paid skilled working class.[6] In 1880 the shipyards employed some 5000 men; by 1911 this had risen to 20 000 and by 1920 there were 35 000 employed.[7]

This demand for labour with varied skills working for differing wage rates was to prove the basis for the economic success of Belfast. As early as 1889 it was reported that 'There is now much competition for female labour, and some complaints of its scarcity.[8]

Another industry which was of great significance in Belfast in these years was fuelled by the growth of the city itself. The vast increase in population created a huge demand for housing which the building industry expanded to meet. Between 1870 and 1900 the housing stock of Belfast quadrupled; in the peak years between 1880–1900 some 50 000 houses were built.[9] The building industry thrived and by 1898 there were 174 building firms in the city and by the 1890s there were thirty-three brickworks in the Belfast area.[10] By 1890 the Belfast Branch of the Operative Stonemasons was twice the size of any other in the union.[11]

The experience of Bristol was similar to Belfast, although the city's building boom was less dramatic. Between 1880 and 1925 Bristol's housing stock increased by 158 per cent. Much of this occurred in outlying areas of the city: Horfield, Stapleton, St George and Bedminster. As in Belfast, the industry was a major employer of skilled and perhaps more importantly unskilled labour. Employment in the industry peaked in the early twentieth century: in 1901, 201 building contractors were employing 11 300 men. This represented 12 per cent of the male labour force in the city. Decline followed and by 1911, 184 firms were employing 9.1 per cent of the male labour force.[12]

Although Dublin's building industry was a major employer of unskilled labour it was never as prosperous as those of Belfast or Bristol. Mary Daly notes that no identifiable street of first class housing (ten or more rooms) was built in the city in the second half of the nineteenth century, and that the industry suffered from prolonged depressions.[13] Unlike Bristol and Belfast there was little construction of working class housing, as the homes of the wealthy, who abandoned the city for the suburbs, were converted to tenements. Much of the building work in Dublin therefore comprised public buildings, civil engineering projects or the construction of suburban housing.[14]

Employment patterns in Belfast between 1881 and 1911 show some significant changes.[15] The proportion in domestic service declined from almost 16 to below 6 per cent and the proportion in commercial activities was to double. However, in most sectors, these years represented a period of continuity within the city's employment patterns, this is what might be expected from a mature industrial city. As population and the labour force grew, the existing industries expanded to absorb the increase. Thus, although some industries declined in overall importance, with the exception of domestic service, where employment dropped from 19 492 in 1881 to 10 273 in 1901, none of the major employment areas suffered an absolute decline in numbers. Conversely, due to rapid population growth, relatively small increases in the proportion of the labour force employed in any sector could conceal a substantial increase in the actual numbers employed. Between 1881 and 1901 employment in the retail and food processing sector increased by only 0.5 per cent of the total labour force, but employment increased from 10 353 to 15 688. Other similar examples would be government employment where a 0.1 per cent increase represented a 49.6 per cent increase in numbers employed and the building industry where 0.3 per cent represented a 58 per cent increase.[16]

Female representation within Belfast's labour force was well above the UK average, a significant variation from the Irish 'norm' which tended to be lower than the UK. Between 1881 and 1901 women formed approximately 30 per cent of the United Kingdom's labour force, while in Ireland the proportion was roughly one per cent lower in the same years. In Belfast women formed 46 per cent of the labour force in 1881, falling to 41.2 per cent in 1891 and 38.0 in 1901 although actual numbers employed increased.[17] The main areas of female employment were those typical of British urban centres in these years: manufacture (especially textiles), clothing and shoes, and domestic service. These three sectors absorbed 90 per cent of Belfast's female labour in 1881 and 83.4 per cent in 1911. A peculiarity of Belfast compared with the UK as a whole was the high proportion of female labour in manufacturing compared to domestic service. Throughout this period about 50 per cent of women workers in Belfast were in manufacturing while from 1891 less than 20 per cent were in domestic service. Roughly comparable figures for Britain as a whole would be 22 and 40, and for Ireland 15 and 36 per cent.[18] However, the women themselves did not always see this as an advantage.

When you come to inspect a factory, does it ever strike you to look around and see if any of these weary women and girls have a seat to sit down on... I hope dear lady you see to this. You would never think of putting a servant to work in a kitchen without a chair in it, she would not stick it.[19]

In 1880 Belfast was growing rapidly with shipbuilding emerging as a major employment sector, but the economy of Bristol was in the doldrums. Many of the traditional industries that had formed the basis of the city's prosperity in the previous century were in decline. The once significant pottery industry was reduced to a single major producer, plus a few firms making plumbing goods or bottles for the beer and soft drink trade.[20] Bristol's soap industry dated back to the medieval period and, as late as the 1840s, had been the third largest in the country, producing about 7.5 per cent of UK output. However, increasing competition from producers such as William Lever reduced the city's share of the market to less than 3.5 per cent by 1891.[21] The glass and bottle industry, which was at its peak at the end of the eighteenth century, had declined from a dozen firms to a single producer by 1880.[22] Shipbuilding had also declined from its eighteenth century peak; by 1880 production was concentrated on small vessels, notably tugs and river craft.[23]

In addition to decline in older trades two modern and apparently prosperous industries collapsed at the start of this period. In 1881 sugar refining in Bristol almost disappeared with the closure of Konrad Finzel's large plant on the counterslip.[24] Railway locomotive construction was another major industry in Bristol from the 1830s; by the 1870s there were two firms employing over 1000 skilled workers. However, the Atlas Engine Works ceased trading in December 1878, and the Avonside company was liquidated by its creditors in July 1881. Both firms re-opened but on a much reduced scale of production, with an average of only fifteen engines a year being produced in the city in the 1890s.[25]

However, despite these problems Bristol was already displaying a quality which A.J. Pugsley the pioneering historian of Bristol industry, was to note.

> The chief feature that strikes the commercial visitor to Bristol is the complexity of its industrial activities. Practically every phase of industry is represented to a greater or lesser extent in Bristol, and no other city in the country shows such diversity of interest. Its economic life is not inseparably bound up with the prosperity of one or two trades, as is the case with other large towns.[26]

In 1883 the *Bristol Times and Mirror* published a series of articles, later published in book form, under the title 'Work in Bristol'. The twenty-four firms visited showed the diversity of the city's industries. There were three furniture factories, two wagon works, two tobacco factories and two firms makings sweets and chocolate. Other firms produced galvanised iron, boots, soap, paint & floorcloth, sugar, stationery, cotton, chemicals, leather, rope, organs, lead shot and mineral waters. In addition a firm of coal mine operators and a dairy were included in this survey. The workforce of these concerns varied from the 1600 hands at the Great Western Cotton Works to the 30 of the Gloucestershire Dairy Company Ltd.[27] As the population of Bristol grew, employment was to expand in new areas, causing fundamental shifts in employment patterns.

The growth areas of Bristol's economy were transport and communication, manufacturing (notably engineering) and food processing. Conversely, domestic service declined rapidly as new opportunities appeared for women.[28] Female employment in Bristol was concentrated in the low pay/status sectors of industry. In the boot and shoe industry, where female wages were highest, 50 per cent of female workers earned under 12 shillings a week compared to only 18 per cent receiving over 18 shillings. In the clothing industry the figures were 68.6 and 8.2 per cent, in the chocolate factories 59.1 and 0.4 per cent. However, the lowest rates were in the confectionery trade where 95.8 per cent earned under 8 shillings a week and no female worker earned over 12 shillings.[29] This was not unusual; the same can be found in Belfast or indeed any city in these years.

There was a significant local variation in Bristol with large scale female employment in the retail and food processing industries. Between 1881 and 1901 employment of female labour in this sector increased from 6.8 to 9.9 per cent of the total; in Bristol employment in this sector increased from 11.3 to 20 per cent in 1901 reaching a quarter of the total women in employment by 1911.[30] The main employers were the chocolate and tobacco industries, both of which, as the factory inspector was to note, expanded rapidly during these years.

When the sugar trade began to decline, and the refineries to close, it was naturally anticipated that the decrease of occupation would be a serious loss to the town.

These anticipations have not, however, been realised; and from such rough calculations as I have been able to make, it would appear that on the contrary, the actual number of persons at present employed in the manufacture of Confectionery, as compared with those formerly employed in the sugar trade, is as five to one. There appears to have been about 800 people employed in the sugar refineries, while there are now about 4,455 employed in Confectionery making.[31]

A striking difference between Bristol and Belfast was the absence of a dominant sector within the employment pattern. Not until 1911 did any sector of Bristol's industry employ more than 20 per cent of the total labour force.[32] Although not immediately apparent at the time, this diversification had very definite advantages for Bristol compared to Belfast.

Bristol's industries run to three hundred or more in number, and they cover a wide range of production. They are independent rather than allied, so the city is not subject to violent fluctuations of trade and employment. There is seldom deep depression, and that only when the whole of the industries of the country are at a low state at once; on the other hand, conditions never rise steeply to a very high peak of prosperity.[33]

The years between 1880 and 1925 were to see far-reaching changes in the structure of employment within the city of Bristol. Unlike Belfast the growth areas were not long established industries but rather new or previously unimportant ones. Bristol's economy can be seen as a developing one in these years with growth being led by new sectors.

Another significant area of growth in Bristol's economy was the transport and communication sector. The city had a long history as a distribution centre. In the 1720s Daniel Defoe observed,

The Bristol merchants as they have a great trade abroad, so they have always buyers at home, for their returns and such buyers that no cargo is too big for them. To this purpose, the shopkeepers in Bristol who in general are all wholesale men, have so great an inland trade among the western counties, that they maintain carriers just as the London tradesmen do.[34]

The importance of this sector is well illustrated by the employment pattern. Not only did employment rise by a factor of four, from 7467 to 29 295 in the years between 1881 and 1921 but its share of total employment more than doubled from 8.3 to 16.8 per cent of the total.[35] Mary Daly, observing the same process within the Dublin labour force in these years, saw this as a negative development indicating a weakness in the manufacturing sector.[36] However in the case of Bristol this development was a response to the changes in industrial structure.

There was a vast increase in the importation of bulk foodstuffs and raw materials through the port. In 1880 the port handled 58 tons of paper, 349 of tobacco and 288 529 of grain; the figures for 1925 were 40 216, 18 242 and 924 787 tons. In addition, in 1925, 61 604 tons of animal feed stuffs, 26 019 of wood pulp and 74 885 of bananas were imported which had not been part of the ports trade in the 1880s.[37] By 1925 imports of fourteen selected foodstuffs and raw materials increased from 446 010 tons to 1 776 743, or 57 per cent of the total goods passing through the port of Bristol.[38] Dublin was also a major port, exporting Irish agricultural produce and importing manufactured goods and raw materials. Although the city did not see the growth in this sector on the scale Bristol enjoyed, transport and communication employed a growing proportion of the city's labour force. Dock work and labouring in the warehouses and transit sheds was a vital source of employment for the vast number of unskilled labourers who formed a significant element in Dublin's population. Between 1881 and 1911 those listed by the census as employed in the transport sector increased from 9260 (11.5 per cent of total labour force) to 13 726 (14.4). In contrast the proportion of Belfast's labour force employed in transport remained at about 10 per cent throughout this period, although as the population grew rapidly actual numbers employed increased from 7156 to 11 704.[39]

The comparatively low proportion of Belfast's labour force in this sector does not mean it was unimportant; on the contrary, all Belfast's industries were dependent on imported raw materials and overseas markets. In 1902 the Belfast Harbour Commissioners reported that the city had 4.36 miles of quays compared to 5.5 at Bristol and Avonmouth and 6.2 in Dublin.[40] However Belfast's docks covered 136 acres compared to Bristol's 114 and harbour receipts were one and a half times those of Dublin.[41] Between 1800 and 1878 the port of Belfast expanded rapidly and tonnage using the port doubled every fifteen years. However, between 1880 and 1913 it was to double only once. It can be argued that by 1880 the expansion of Belfast's port was largely complete and its communication network well established. Unlike Bristol whose port and transport facilities had to expand to meet the needs of changing industrial demand, Belfast's were adequate to meet its needs.

If Belfast can be seen as a mature and expanding industrial city, and Bristol as a developing one, then Dublin, during the years of this study, can be characterised as stagnating. When the data on employment patterns are studied the main feature is continuity rather than change. Dublin in 1800 was a large and prosperous city but during the nineteenth century it underwent a prolonged and painful decline. By the early years of the twentieth century conditions in Dublin could not have been more starkly different from those in Belfast.

A priest appearing before a government inquiry in 1913 stated in evidence that he knew of a tenement house where 107 people were living. According to the 'Medical Press', 1913, the death rate in Dublin was the highest in Europe, exceeding that of Moscow, and even Calcutta where plague and cholera were rife. The conservative 'Irish Times', in a leader in Feb 1914, compared conditions in the Dublin slums to Dante's inferno.[42]

Why was there such a difference between these two cities? The main reason was that Dublin lacked, in any real sense, an industrial economy. While Belfast was a thriving centre of industry and Bristol grew rapidly to become one, Dublin remained trapped by its earlier status. The English journalist Arthur Wright noted a lack of factory chimneys in the city when he viewed it from the top of Nelson's Pillar while writing a history of the 1913 lockout.[43] The reason for the absence of factory chimneys was, of course, the absence of factories. In industrial as well as social terms the comparison with Belfast could not be more stark.

Mary Daly in her study of the city notes the low level of employment in the manufacturing sector; during the 1860s–80s only some 8000 to 9000 were employed.[44] The largest 'industrial' employer was the huge brewery of Guinness's which employed just over 2500 workers, of whom only 15 per cent were skilled workers. Those who worked for this firm were a privileged elite within the Dublin labour force. The firm was seen as a model employer providing welfare and educational benefits for their workers.[45] Next in order of importance was the biscuit factory of Jacobs which employed 2000 workers by the turn of the twentieth century and 3000 by 1911.[46] The distilling industry was also significant with a number of plants in the city although total employment was no more than a thousand.[47] In addition to these main firms there was a vast number of small concerns. In 1895, for example, the 37 general engineering plants in the city employed a total of 2654 workers, an average of only 72 per plant. Textiles and shipbuilding were present in Dublin, but on a tiny scale compared to Belfast, employing a thousand workers each in 1914. Even industries where the city gained a local dominance, such as railway vehicle construction, were only employing about 2000.[48] If Dublin's economy had a speciality it was food processing. Brewing, baking and distilling all developed as result of the city's being at the centre of communications and commercial activity in a basically agricultural economy. However, this sector, faced with heavy foreign competition, did not expand.

As Dublin had developed earlier than either Belfast or Bristol and grew less rapidly in these years, there was less opportunity for expansion in the retail trades. In 1881 Dublin's retail and food processing sector was the largest of any of the three cities in terms of total employment and percentage of labour force. However by 1911 Bristol had overtaken Dublin, following an almost 200 per cent growth in employment in this sector compared to 51.5 per cent in Belfast and 12.25 per cent in Dublin. In numerical terms employment in this sector of Dublin's economy was declining rather than expanding.[49] In Belfast these industries were by no means insignificant. The retail sector was rapidly expanding to meet the needs of a growing urban population. By 1903 there were over 830 grocers, 300 drapers, 200 butchers, 100 greengrocers and 21 fishmongers in addition to some 380 publicans.[50] Their premises varied from tiny corner shops to the huge department stores of Robinson & Cleaver and Anderson & McAuley. Food processing was also a large employer with flour milling, baking, sweets and confectionery, soft drinks, beer and whiskey all being significant local industries. The largest single employer in this sector was tobacco with two firms, Gallaher's and Murray's, proving very successful in both the Irish and the export market. By 1911 the industry employed 6000 workers, probably as many as the whole Dublin food processing industry. As in Bristol the industry employed two thirds female labour.[51]

As Bristol grew, the retail sector expanded to meet the needs of a growing and increasingly affluent population. Between 1881 and 1911 the number of bakers in the city increased by 46 per cent, butchers by 40, grocers by 29 and public houses by 16.[52] However it was food processing that was to generate the main increase in employment. The tobacco industry was to see huge growth, despite the widespread introduction of machinery. Employment rose from 515 in 1881 to 1230 in 1891, 3729 in 1901, and 5536 in 1911 and became the city's largest single employer with over 8000 workers in 1928.[53] As the factory inspector noted in 1902 the scale of the industry was immense. 'There are 100 cigarette machines in Bristol, and we have calculated that if the cigarettes they turn out in a week were placed in a straight line, end to end, they would extend for about 5156 miles.'[54]

By July 1905 W.D. & H.O. Wills had 92 Bonsack machines in Bristol each of which could produce 1 200 000 cigarettes a week.

However, it was estimated that by June 1908 the firm would need 124 machines, capable of producing 5 852 872 000 cigarettes a year, to meet demand. Of these, 93 would be producing the cheap Woodbine and Cinderella brands.[55] In addition the firm manufactured tens of thousands of hand-rolled cigars every week for the more discerning smoker.[56]

Chocolate was the other growth area with employment in the main firm of Fry's increasing from 1000 in 1883 to 5000 in 1914.[57] As was noted in the minutes of the Bristol Chamber of Commerce, cocoa consumption in Britain had risen from a quarter of an ounce per person in 1831 to fourteen ounces by 1887.[58] The industry continued to grow in the early years of the twentieth century as the Lord Mayor of Bristol observed.

> It is interesting to note that whereas twenty-five years ago imports of raw cocoa, from which chocolate is manufactured, amounted to roughly 26,000 tons, last year they amounted to nearly 65,000 tons. Exports of the manufactured article on the other hand, have risen from 1,000 to over 9,000 tons. I wonder whether the historian will take due note of the extent and importance of this silent revolution in the habits of the people?[59]

The shortage of employment opportunities was painfully evident in the city of Dublin. Yet, during the years between 1880 and 1911 Dublin displays some of the characteristics of a capital city with a significant proportion of the labour force employed in government and white collar activities. White collar employment increased in the United Kingdom between 1881 and 1901 from 8.1 to 10.8 per cent of the employed labour force. Bristol and Belfast were always one to two per cent above this figure but Dublin increased from 13.1 to 16.9 per cent during these years and reached 19.6 per cent by 1911. However, at the other extreme unskilled labour formed a higher proportion of Dublin's population than either UK or Irish averages. Manufacturing employment may have been slightly above the levels for Ireland as a whole but represented only about half the UK rate. This figure, it can be argued, shows the low level of industrialisation within the Irish economy in these years rather than any strength in Dublin.[60]

Women's employment patterns illustrate the paucity of opportunity within the city. For most of this period less than 10 per cent of female labour was in the manufacturing sector with clothing and shoes employing only about a fifth of female workers. Domestic service remained the main area of employment with well over 40 per cent for much of the period. Women formed a smaller element of the labour force than in either Bristol or Belfast: for example in 1901 they formed 29.1 per cent of the cities labour force compared to 35.3 in Bristol and 38 in Belfast.[61]

Employment in the clothing and shoes sector included vast numbers of men and women making clothing at very low piece rates in poor conditions. Charles O'Reilly of the Dublin Trades Council reported to the Royal Commission on Labour in 1892 that these were trades of fashion and 'season trades'.[62] This had serious repercussions for workers in the industry as earnings could vary greatly and there were widespread accusations of favouritism in the distribution of work. In February 1892 workers in one firm struck over this grievance, and employers in thirty-seven other firms locked out 675 other workers until the beginning of March.[63] In 1900 there was another major strike backed by the National Union of Tailors and Garment Workers demanding a new price log and the abolition of out-work, 600 workers in 34 firms were affected.[64] Although the Board of Trade stated the strike ended in an arbitration committee being appointed, the union's history claimed that the strike 'Failed impoverishing the branch and encouraging the employers to use the outwork system'.[65]

Dublin's clothing and shoe industries were organised to meet local demand rather than for mass production to supply a wider market. In the case of Bristol the clothing industry was similar to that in Dublin insofar as it mainly catered to local demand. However, as Mr Johnston the Factory Inspector noted. 'The Dressmaking is solely for local use in Bristol and neighbourhood, but in a large community it calls for special notice, so large numbers of hands are employed.'[66]

In Bristol, however, it was the boot and shoe industry that was to expand as firms moved to the area from Leeds to take advantage of lower piecework rates.[67]

> In Bristol a superior kind of boot is produced, partly in large factories and partly at home by outworkers, to who the materials are given out from the factories. The soles and heels are cut out by machinery, and the uppers stitched similarly, and are then riveted (or sewn) and finished either in factory or out of doors so that the old 'cordwainer' vis a workman who made a boot from beginning to end is nearly extinct.[68]

The clothing and boot and shoe industries were major employers in Bristol, employing 16.8 per cent of the total labour force in 1881 and 13.4 in 1911.[69] However, wages tended to be low for most workers in the industries in these years.[70] As the population increased the relative importance of these industries began to decline, but until the First World War they employed more than one in eight of Bristol's workers and were a major source of female employment.[71]

In Belfast ready made clothing and shoes were both limited to supplying the needs of the local population. However, the linen industry generated a wide range of 'making up' industries shirts, aprons but above all handkerchiefs.

> Amongst these minor industries, (of the linen trade) and now well-nigh deserving of mention in a different category, I notice that the handkerchief trade is still extending and becoming yearly a more marked feature. The consequent useful employment of females is, I need scarcely remark, satisfactory while beneficial.[72]

The industry began to create employment in other sectors as it expanded. Although later to acquire a very poor reputation it was seen as a very positive development by early observers.

> The handkerchief industry, now very extensive in Belfast, is good and advancing. The same may be said of the fancy box trade, which follows the making up of handkerchiefs etc. The operatives are doing well in all departments, there is no change in wages, no short time, and living is cheap.[73]

The scale of the trade astonished visitors to the city such as the Frenchman Paul de Rousiers in the 1890s.

> During my stay in Belfast I visited Robinson and Cleaver's great shop, a firm renowned for the fineness of its Irish linens. I was shown hand-woven linen handkerchiefs as 4s apiece which I could hardly distinguish from machine-made ones at 4d each. The manager who accompanied me, pointed out by the aid of a magnifying glass the number and fineness of the threads which could be counted in a square inch of the hand woven one. The difference was very obvious when the magnifying-glass was applied to the cheaper handkerchief. Side by side with these were cotton handkerchiefs at 2s a dozen, and children's handkerchiefs at 2d a dozen. These are what the majority of customers buy. Messrs Robinson and Cleaver say they sell 30,000 dozen handkerchiefs a week, but the costly article, hand-woven because no machine can produce the necessary fineness, forms but a small fraction of the total.[74]

Even low paid work of this kind was not available to many Dubliners. Although there existed a large class of comfortably-off professionals and 'white-collar' workers, opportunities for manual workers, and particularly women, were limited. Under-employment and lack of opportunity were serious problems for a significant proportion of Dublin's labour force in these years. The social consequences of this were catastrophic, the Dublin poor becoming trapped by poverty in conditions of increasing squalor.

> The high death-rate of Dublin is seen to be entirely due to economic causes, to rise and fall with economic classes. The rich of Dublin enjoy as long an immunity from death as do their kind elsewhere; it is the slaughter of Dublin's poor that gives the Irish metropolis its unenviable and hateful notoriety amongst civilised nations.[75]

CONCLUSION

Even this cursory analysis of the economies and employment patterns shows that the three cities in this study differ fundamentally. Belfast at the start of this period was a mature industrial town, dependent to an excessive degree, as future events were to show, upon a narrow range of industries. Between 1881 and 1911 the city's population increased by 70 per cent with the established industries absorbing the majority of the additional labour. Bristol developed into an industrial city in these years but took a different course from Belfast. Its development was characterised by a wide range of discrete industries rather than a single dominant sector. Between 1881 and 1911 population grew by 72.6 per cent with new industries absorbing the bulk of the additional labour. Dublin was not an industrial city but rather an administrative and communication centre resulting in limited employment opportunities for a significant element of the population. It was this that created the stark contrasts between rich and poor in the city and caused such social problems. The stagnation of the city's economy can be gauged from the fact that between 1881 and 1911 population increased by only 22 per cent, and if the suburbs are discounted then growth was only just over 17 per cent. What I shall examine is how these differences in economy and structure influenced the formation of the labour movement in each of these cities.

3 Trade Union Growth: a Comparison

Historically the British trade union movement is characterised by division rather than unity. Workers did not organise 'en masse' but at different times and frequently in an atmosphere of antagonism or mistrust towards other elements within the 'working-class'. There were differing, often incompatible, views of the function of trades unionism. Most skilled craftsmen saw unions as protecting their status from encroachment by employers, new processes or unskilled workers. Many such bodies saw themselves as respectable institutions seeking to preserve the status quo. For most of the unskilled trade unions had little to do with protecting status but rather preventing exploitation by employers or skilled labour. For many unskilled the status quo was not something to be preserved but overthrown.

As the trade union movement expanded, further divisions and conflicts occurred. Workers such as railway men, machine operators and miners, were not considered 'skilled labour' as they did not serve formal apprenticeships. However, such workers become increasingly powerful, forming unions which viewed themselves, and were viewed as, distinctive from skilled bodies. Likewise when women sought to organise they had to contend with employers, who saw them as a source of cheap labour, and male 'colleagues' who saw female labour as a threat. The purpose of this chapter is to see how these changes, which were a feature of the British trade union movement as a whole, affected Bristol, Belfast and Dublin.

SKILLED LABOUR

Trade unionism, in its modern form, dates from 1824 when the Combination Laws were finally repealed. From that date friendly societies were able legitimately to extend their activities into labour organisation. Although ostensibly legal, early trade unionism was not without its perils: as late as 1846 the secretary of the Belfast Ironfounders was jailed for 'combination and conspiracy'.[1] Most of these societies consisted of members of a specific trade in a single locality, either completely independent or only loosely linked to other clubs representing the same trade.[2] They were now legally able to seek to negotiate local wage rates and control the local supply of labour in the form of apprenticeships or migrant labour, as demonstrated by the rules of the Belfast Sailmakers.

> Any sailmaker coming into this town, and making application for work, shall not be allowed to work in any sail loft until he first calls with the president, who shall examine his indenture to see that he has served the full term of seven years to the sailmaking trade,[3]

As Pelling points out, such groups were able to do this because they formed an elite within the labour force whose skills set them apart from other workers.[4]

By 1861 the skilled craftsmen of Bristol, Belfast and Dublin were organised into societies of this type. The *First Annual Trade union Directory* of this year lists 28 union branches in Bristol, 25 in Belfast and 45 in Dublin.[5] Some local societies had already begun to combine into national or 'amalgamated' unions such as the Boilermakers (established 1834) and the Engineers (established 1851) who were active in all three cities. The reasons for such federations were explained by an early historian of the Boilermakers and Iron and Steel Shipbuilders Society.

> Young in years as the Friendly Boiler Makers' Societies were, it was evident they had by the foregoing resolution already realised the necessity of cohesion, the benefit that would accrue by having one strong society and not several factions or small societies, who might in future years wage war among themselves.[6]

These developments were not always accepted in a fraternal spirit by the local societies. On 3 November 1884 the Belfast Society of Operative Cabinet Makers passed a resolution condemning the actions of the Alliance Cabinet Makers Association, a national body newly established in Belfast. The new union was accused of using threats to drive out members of the older body and of damaging the position of the craft in Belfast.[7]

By 1880 the amalgamates controlled important elements of the skilled labour force in Bristol and Belfast, but had been less successful in Dublin. Joseph O'Brian demonstrates that in Dublin there survived a large number of small unions representing specialist workers.[8] Such local societies controlled significant sectors of the building, printing, food processing and transport trades. They valued their independence and were often hostile to the 'English' amalgamated unions for political reasons. Even if amalgamates were successful in establishing themselves, they could find Dublin a frustrating area. In 1895 the Shipwrights sent a delegation to Ireland to look into organisational problems. After disappointing results in Waterford and Cork they moved on the Dublin where the branch claimed to have a hundred members. The delegates found such chaos they closed the branch and transferred its books and funds to headquarters.[9] The political difficulties faced by unions trying to organise in Ireland can be seen in the experience of the United Operative Plumbers Association in 1889.

Dublin members sought the aid of the Worshipful Company of London to establish a system of technical education and registration for Irish plumbers. Certain elements in the Irish Home Rule Party immediately seized the opportunity to denounce the U.O.P.A. and urge the secession of plumbers in Ireland from the Association.[10]

EARLY NON-SKILLED TRADE UNIONISM

Non-skilled workers soon recognised the value of trade unionism in both friendly society and industrial activities. However, they were refused access to societies established by the craftsmen who saw the unskilled as a threat to their status. Consequently these groups of non-craft workers began to form their own societies. In all three cities there were small local unions of specialist dock and transport workers and builders labourers. These bodies were 'cut-price' versions of the craft societies and as they lacked leverage in industrial matters they tended to emphasise their friendly society function.

Such workers were particularly significant in Bristol due to the activities of the Bristol, West of England and South Wales Operative Trade and Provident Society. This body was established in 1872 and by July 1873 claimed a membership of almost 800 in Bristol. By January 1874 there were 46 branches containing 10 000 members spread through the South-West and South Wales.[11] There is some dispute as to whether this body was really a trade union or simply a friendly society, but the fourth objective laid down in the rules suggest it was more than a simple benefit club.

To use all legitimate means for the protection of the established rights and privileges of members in their employment, and regulate the relations between employers and employed.[12]

Although the rules provided for strike pay at a rate of 12s a week, between 1880 and 1889 only £112 was disbursed from the strike fund, less than one-seventieth of the payments made in sickness and accident benefits.[13] The cost of membership and scale of benefits offered were impressive when it is considered that most labourers earned less than a pound a week.[14] By 1892 the society had fifteen branches in Bristol, five of which were affiliated to the trades council.[15] However, it faced problems common to unions of this type. Membership was unstable, fluctuating with economic conditions. The leadership, like the craft unions, adopted a cautious and conciliatory attitude, not from any sense of 'respectability' but rather due to the inherent weakness of unskilled labour.[16]

NEW UNIONISM

The last years of the 1880s were to see unprecedented expansion in the British trade union movement as new unions of a fundamentally different type began to emerge. As well as rapid growth amongst the older established unions new bodies recruited the non-craft workers and adopted, in many cases, a far more aggressive stance on industrial matters. In Bristol 'New unionism' first emerged in the boot and shoe industry. The city had a branch of the National Union of Boot and Shoe Riveters and Finishers from that body's foundation in December 1873. In 1886 there were only 276 members although the industry employed over 4000. The union appears initially to have been fairly moderate in its dealing with the employers.

> Their action (N.U.B.S.R & F) has been marked by wise moderation and forethought, and as a result of their labours it may be said that they have been successful in protecting, in a very competitive year, their wages from reduction, and in many cases with the employers have mutually negotiated concessions of advance in wages on some classes of goods, without strikes or bad feelings.[17]

In 1889 membership reached 642, and the following year when the union joined the trades council it affiliated a membership of 1400 in Bristol and 520 in Kingswood.[18] Much of this growth was due to recruitment of Clickers and Pressmen, who had previously been 'unorganised'. The history of the union describes the Bristol Branch after 1890 as 'turbulent' and 'fast growing' with a propensity for unofficial strike action, and as a centre of opposition to arbitration.[19] This growing militancy was the result of short sightedness by local employers who delayed or obstructed the work of the arbitration boards and evaded unfavourable decisions by sending work out to outworkers and sweat-shops.[20]

However the boot and shoe workers were not the only group of semi-skilled workers organising in Bristol. In 1889 Havelock Wilson's National Amalgamated Seamen's and Firemen's Union opened a branch, which by 1891 claimed to have a thousand members.[21] In the same year the Bristol Miners Association, formed in 1887, joined the Miners Federation of Great Britain and by 1892 their membership had reached 3035.[22] The Bristol gas workers, after forming a local association in 1888, amalgamated with the National Union of Gasworkers and General Labourers in the summer of 1889 and soon affiliated 470 members to the trades council.[23] Ben Tillett's Dock, Wharf, Riverside and General Labourers Union established itself in Bristol and by 1891 claimed 2000 members.[24] Finally the General Railway Workers Union, whose inaugural conference resolved 'That the union shall remain a fighting one and not be encumbered by any sick or accident fund', affiliated 220 members to Bristol trades council in 1891.[25]

These 'new' unions were to alter the composition of the trades council, for even though the miners did not join until 1898, affiliated membership of the new bodies soon outnumbered that of the craft unions. Atkinson estimates that by 1890 10 000 Bristolians were members of unions that had not existed two years before.[26] By 1892 over 60 per cent of affiliated membership of Bristol's Trade Council belonged to such newly formed bodies.[27] In 1890 there had been 24 societies or branches affiliated; by 1898 this had increased by 160 per cent and membership was to remain at about this figure until the next great influx during the First World War.[28]

The 1890s saw a decline in the membership of many 'new' unions, and the collapse of some, due to prolonged periods of depression and high unemployment.[29] In Bristol the 'new' unions suffered a decline in numbers but survived. In 1892 the Gasworkers, Boot and Shoe Workers, Seamen and Railwaymen had affiliated 5700 members to the trades council, 66 per cent of the total. By 1904 the Seamen had temporarily disaffiliated but the miners had joined, and the combined affiliation of these unions was still 4744 or 44 per cent of the total.[30]

In Belfast the years 1891–3 saw affiliations to the trades council double to twelve thousand and average attendance at meetings increase from eleven to forty-two.[31] It appeared at first that the dominance of the old craft unions would be ended as in Bristol. By 1893 there were twenty-three delegates from the Gasworkers and the National Amalgamated Union of Labour compared with fifteen Engineers and eight Carpenters.[32] However, there were no miners in Belfast and the boot and shoe industry did not exist on a large scale. The National Union of Dock Labourers did organise in the city and had 541 members by 1891 but the branch vanished by 1895 and it was not revived until 1907.[33]

The largest employer of semi/unskilled labour was the linen industry, with only approximately 10 per cent of its labour force, mainly semi-skilled males, unionised.[34] The Gasworkers and General Labourers Union, established a separate district based on Belfast in 1890 and represented a range of unskilled occupations but it was defunct by 1896.[35] In contrast the National Amalgamated Union of Labour began to organise in Belfast in 1890 and by 1893 over half the union's 3000 members outside the North-East of England were in Belfast. By 1897 Belfast was a separate district consisting of nine branches with 2500 members in the engineering and shipbuilding industries.[36]

Although there were railwaymen, textile workers and other groups of non-craft workers represented on the trades council they were never a challenge to the skilled craft bodies as happened in Bristol. In Belfast the craft unions were able to retain their primacy because skilled labour formed a much larger proportion of the total than in Bristol. In addition both Belfast and Dublin tended to have a surplus of unskilled labour, with the proportion of workers listing themselves as 'labourers' increasing during the period rather than falling as in Bristol.[37]

If the semi/unskilled workers of Belfast were difficult to organise due to surplus labour, conditions in Dublin were even less favourable. Some groups were successfully organised. The Amalgamated Society of Railway Servants which had 190 members in the whole of Ireland in 1888, was able to increase their membership to over 4000 and form six branches in Dublin during 1890.[38] By 1897 they had 7500 members in Ireland, 53 per cent of all those eligible to join the union, nearly double the proportion for the United Kingdom as a whole.[39] The National Union of Dock Labourers branch in the city records 290 members, but like the Belfast branch it had vanished by 1895.[40] The only other unionised unskilled workers were the employees of the city's Cleansing Department who formed the Dublin Corporation Labourers Trade Union in 1883, and the city's firemen.[41] The vast majority of non-craft workers were not unionised until the emergence of the Irish Transport and General Workers Union in 1909. The craftsman in Dublin had skills employers needed, the labourer or docker had only physical strength and unlike Bristol there was a permanent surplus of muscle on the market.

Although these developments did not split the trades councils in the cities covered by this study as happened elsewhere, they created tensions in both Bristol and Belfast. In Belfast the founding president, Samuel Monro, a member of the Typographical Society, and the vice-president Joseph Mitchell of the Municipal Workers, both resigned in 1894 in protest at the over-representation of labourers' unions on the council.[42] It has been suggested that this confrontation was sectarian as the unskilled members of the 'new' unions were usually catholic and supporters of Home Rule while the craft societies were composed of protestant supporters of the Union.[43] However, it should be noted that while Munro was a Protestant Unionist, Mitchell was a Catholic Home Ruler.

The behaviour of the 'new' unions was not always conducive to good relations with the older bodies, as can be seen in Bristol. In December 1889 the trades council considered a complaint that the dockers were blacking members of the Provident Society working in the port. Although the older body had been organising dockers since the 1870s and the 'new' union had only arrived in October, the council was powerless to do anything except declare the dockers' action 'a breach of the spirit of trade unionism'. The Trade and Provident Society was progressively forced out of the docks by the new union.[44]

Relations between skilled and unskilled workers were seldom good and both sides viewed the other with distrust. This came across clearly in interviews with transport workers who had been involved in the 1907 Belfast Dock Strike:

Q — So there were sort of barriers between tradesmen and . . .
A — Yes! Oh yes, Oh a tradesman always thought you were dirt compared to them.
Q — And How did they show this?
A — They showed it, well they'd look at you very cross and they wouldn't talk to you hardly.[45]

Although trade unionism made great advances in the late 1880s and early 1890s there was slower growth and even decline over the next decade. Trade union membership broadly followed the trends in the economy, rising in the booms of 1887–91, 1894–9 and 1905–7 and declining in the slumps of 1892–3, 1900–4 and 1908–9 (see Table 3.1).[46] However, the craft unions suffered less than the 'new' unions as their members suffered lower rates of unemployment and the unions could

Table 3.1   Trade union membership 1892–1909[47]

	100 principal unions		Total trade unions	
	Membership	*% change*	*Membership*	*% change*
1892	900 636	–	1 505 238	–
1893	905 409	+ 0.5	1 482 260	– 2.8
1894	920 001	+ 1.7	1 440 146	– 2.8
1895	910 404	– 1.0	1 410 652	– 2.0
1896	958 018	+ 5.2	1 497 052	+ 6.1
1897	1 061 311	+ 10.8	1 615 893	+ 7.9
1898	1 038 686	– 2.1	1 651 993	+ 2.2
1899	1 112 576	+ 7.1	1 806 889	+ 9.4
1900	1 152 246	+ 4.2	1 915 713	+ 6.0
1901	1 169 222	+ 0.9	1 927 952	+ 0.6
1902	1 169 333	+ /– 0	1 915 506	– 0.6
1903	1 206 000	–	1 942 000	–*
1904	1 203 000	– 0.2	1 911 000	– 1.6
1905	1 220 000	+ 1.4	1 934 000	+ 1.2
1906	1 307 000	+ 7.1	2 129 000	+ 10.0
1907	1 471 000	+ 12.5	2 425 000	+ 13.9
1908	1 451 000	– 1.4	2 389 000	– 1.5
1909	1 537 000	+ 5.9	2 369 000	– 0.7

* See note.[47]

often enforce a closed shop system. Amongst the semi/unskilled workers it was the unions with a strong national organisation that tended to survive rather than the small local bodies.

WOMEN AND TRADE UNIONS

If skilled craftsmen were unsympathetic towards the unskilled, their attitude towards female labour was almost totally negative. In 1877 the Trades Union Congress recorded in the minutes that it was 'the duty of men and husbands to bring about a condition of things when their wives would be in their proper sphere instead of being dragged into competition of livelihood with the great and strong men of the world'.[48]

Attitudes changed only slowly as can be seen in the report of a conference on the position of women after the First World War. After recognising that there were 4 713 000 women engaged in industrial occupations at that time the report stated:

The underlying fact in relation to the position of women in industry is that her position as an industrial worker is, and always will be, of secondary importance to her position in the home. To provide the conditions which render a strong and healthy family life possible to all is the first interest of the state, since the family is the foundation stone of the social system.[49]

Women were paid between a third and a half of male rates for similar work and in some industries, notably textiles and sectors of the printing trade, they threatened male employment. It is thus not surprising that many trade unionists were hostile towards female workers.

A Mr Lee attends the council to get it to use its influence to form a union of the women working at the Great Western Cotton Works. He stated how they were fined and imposed upon by the management and summoned for leaving work during the strike and fined by the magistrates who were shareholders in the firm. Council adjourned the discussion of this question.[50]

Female trade unionists quickly learned to fight both employers and their male 'colleagues' as Bristol Trades Council's minutes demonstrates.

Long discussion extending over two nights regarding women's labour in the brush trade. The men had struck nominally against prison labour but really against the importation of cheap women made brushes from Birmingham. Thereupon the National Union of Working Women sent down blacklegs to take the men's places as it was a strike against women. Eventually however, on the recommendation of the trades council they withdraw their members again.[51]

By 1890 the Webbs estimated there were 100 000 female trade unionists, while the Register of Friendly Societies recorded 437 000 by 1914. Women formed 30 per cent of UK labour force, but only 10 per cent of trade union membership. Even in the professions women's work was not considered equal to that of male colleagues, head teachers in Bristol in 1914 being paid a minimum of £190 and maximum of £265 if male but only £135 to £180 if female.[52] Wrigley shows that between 1896 and 1921 the proportion of female union membership as compared to the potential membership was only 25–45 per cent of the figure for men.[53]

However in both Bristol and Belfast female participation in the labour force was well above the UK average and major industries were dependent on cheap female labour. In Belfast, the prominence of the linen industry ensured that about 50 per cent of workers in manufacturing were female, over 70 per cent in clothing or shoes and almost 40 per cent of professionals. In Bristol 65–70 per cent of workers in clothes and shoes, 55–70 per cent of food processing and 30–40 per cent of retail workers were women.[54] The trade unionists in these cities may not have felt much fraternal unity but they could not ignore women. However, like all unskilled labour, 'organising' female labour presented problems. Their wages were even lower than unskilled men and their opportunities for employment were more limited.

The need to improve the conditions for female workers led to the creation of the Women's Protective and Provident League in 1874 which later became the Women's Trade Union League.[55] This body tried to organise the Belfast mill workers, with rather grudging support from the trades council in 1890. The three unions which they established all collapsed within a year and in 1893 the council itself established the Textile Operatives Union of Ireland.[56] Some of the linen workers interviewed in the early 1970s told of the difficulties in 'organising' a dispersed and largely female labour force.

> About half them came into it (the union) the Reeling Room. Only half the Reeling Room, for there was nobody else for to try for to organize...I contacted a girl in the Spinnin' room. She was a spinner, and I contacted her to see if I could get her to start it. She was too frightened – said she was too frightened. She wouldn't take it on. I hadn't enough sense to be frightened.[57]

In Bristol the Women's Trade Union Association functioned between 1895 and 1901.[58] A branch of the National Union of Working Women's Union was in existence by 1876 and dissolved in 1898.[59] The weakness of female labour in the Bristol labour market was demonstrated in the memorandum of agreement covering the printing trade in 1918.

> Min Wage of any man, over 21, entering the trade to be 42/6; after 12 month experience 45/-
> *Women Workers* The minimum rate for qualified workers of five years experience and over to be advanced by 3/- per week from Sept 30th 1918 and a further 2/- a week from the first day of January 1919, raising the rate from 25/- to 30/- per week.[60]

In Dublin there were very limited employment opportunities for the unskilled generally and for women in particular. Domestic service remained the largest area of female employment throughout these years. Although domestic employment was to decline from 48.1 per cent of the female labour force in 1881 to 36.6 per cent in 1911 comparable figures for Bristol and Belfast in 1911 were 29.5 and 14.2 per cent.[61] Domestic workers were never successfully organised due to their isolation and extreme vulnerability to intimidation. The London and Provincial Domestic Servants Union was formed in 1891, and reached a peak membership of 562 in 1895 but dissolved in 1898. The Domestic Workers Union of Great Britain was established in 1910 reaching a membership of only 245 in 1912, and ceasing to exist in 1918. The Irish Transport and General Workers Union formed a Domestic Workers Section in 1919 which collapsed before the year ended, having attracted only 800 members.[62]

In general the female labour force lacked a skilled element, apart from those in the professions, or a well paid elite of semi-skilled workers such as miners or railwaymen who could stimulate trade union growth. The male-dominated trade union movement was often hostile and refused to accept that women workers or their labour were the equivalent of men's. As the lowest paid and most easily replaced element in the labour force women were the least likely to take action which would endanger their employment. As a result throughout the period 1880 to 1925 women tended to be seriously under-represented in the trade union movement.

WHITE COLLAR TRADE UNIONISM

Another group of workers who were slow to organise and frequently saw themselves as distinctive from the rest of the 'working class' were those described as 'white-collar'. This group included the professions, retail workers, clerical, commercial and government employees. The difference between the skilled labour in an engineering works and the office staff would perhaps have been even greater than that between skilled and unskilled on the factory floor. The wages of many 'white-collar' workers were little better than unskilled industrial labour and many were subject to petty tyranny and abuses such as the 'living in' system prevalent in the retail trade. However, those employed in shops considered themselves socially superior to those who earned their living by dirtying their hands. At the same time many industrial workers looked down upon office or shop workers simply because they produced nothing.

The retail sector was the largest 'white-collar' employer, and illustrates the problems faced in organising non-industrial workers in the 1890s.

> It was not at all unusual for the shops to be kept open, especially in industrial areas, after the pubs and music halls had shut, so that people could shop on their way home . . . Then after the pubs had closed, the shows were over, the public served – the shop had to be cleared, stock put back on the shelves, counters scrubbed, and in the case of some of the 'multiples' stock-taking had to be done.[63]

The 1901 report on early closing was to show that conditions in Bristol and Belfast were as bad as anything to be found elsewhere.

> In what I may term the middle class or better class districts of Bristol the hours would be about seventy a week, in the working class neighbourhoods from eighty to ninety.

> In the centre of the city (Belfast) amongst the better class of shops they run from eight in the morning till about seven at night – five nights a week – and eleven on Saturday, altogether about 70 hours a week. In the middle class shops they run up to 80 hours a week, and in the smaller shops still, up to 100 hours a week.[64]

The National Union of Shop Assistants was established in 1891 and was active in Bristol by 1897, affiliating to the trades council in 1898. A second union covering shop workers, the Amalgamated Union of Co-operative Employees, established in 1895, affiliated to the Bristol Trades Council in 1899.[65] By 1904 there were two branches of the Co-operative workers with a combined membership of 200, which represented almost the entire workforce of the Bristol and Bedminster Co-operative societies. However the three branches of the Shop Assistants were able to affiliate only 270 of a labour force which had numbered over 14 000 in 1901.[66]

In 1912 F.W. Mather addressed a talk to the shop workers conference on the topic of 'Why I was dismissed' in which he quoted cases he had known.[67]

> Woman (27 years of age) engaged as assistant, afterwards ordered to do house work in addition, hours 7 a.m. to 11 p.m., gave notice.

> Dismissed for bringing a sandwich

Ate a plum

Caught serving a customer

Temporary 'Birth'

Held responsible for shortage of stock while I was on holiday

Alleged defiance, singing in bathroom

For eating a scone at tea time – the preference for this rather than bread and butter was regarded as a personal insult

Dismissed, employer doesn't quite know why.

Despite these conditions most trade unionists felt little in common with the 'counter-skippers' but rather contempt for the shop workers who in turn did not regard themselves as belonging to the 'working class'. The nature of employment combined with the fear of intimidation or the refusal of a reference and sharp divisions within the retail trade made effective 'organisation' difficult.[68]

Conditions were also poor for female office and commercial workers, who formed a growing element in the workforce in all three cities between 1880 and 1914.

Girls earning five shillings a week were fined a penny for every five minutes lost time. This represents a wage of a penny an hour and a fine of a shilling an hour... That girls in offices were working 60 hours a week passed without remark. But that was in 1904.[69]

The National Union of Clerks was established in London in 1890 with the aid of a £20 grant from Amalgamated Society of Engineers.[70] In 1905 there were only 200 members, increasing to 2500 in 100 branches by 1910 when a full time general secretary was appointed.[71] The poor success of this union can be judged by the fact that in 1911 there were 11 500 commercial workers in both Bristol and Belfast, plus over 9000 in Dublin.[72]

White-collar organisation was weak compared to craft or semiskilled manual occupations in the years before the First World War. Shop and office workers had no tradition of trade unionism and were easily subject to victimisation by employers. There were exceptions where an employer encouraged union membership, such as the Cooperative workers, or where the workers had specialist skills, such as teachers, but in 1914 white-collar workers as a group were weakly organised.

REVIVAL AND EXPANSION 1909–14

The years after 1910 saw a change in the British trade union movement which expanded at a rate not seen since the boom of the late 1880s and early 1890s. By the outbreak of the First World War almost one worker in four was a member of a trade union, a proportion double that of 1905. These years were also marked by increasing union militancy and industrial unrest.[73] This development has been presented by some writers, notably Dangerfield, as part of a potential social revolution threatening British society before the First World War.[74] Is this view of trade union activity in the years before the First World War exaggerated? How relevant were these developments within the English trade unions to Ireland? How important was Syndicalism, the *enfant terrible* of the trade union movement, in these years? All three cities, to different degrees, saw these changes and can provide some answers.

The boom in the British economy in the last few years before the First World War greatly benefited the city of Bristol. The demand for labour was at a peak as Evelyn Tivy was able to report in 1914 under the heading of 'Girl Labour in Bristol'.

> Taking the general question of girl labour in Bristol the demand far exceeds the supply. It is therefore quite easy for a normal child to enter almost any factory she wishes to select when she leaves school.[75]

She noted that women were replacing men in some areas of employment and while conditions in factories were not always good they were tending to improve. Some parents were unwilling to send their daughters into factories or domestic service and as a result there were too many girls seeking clerical work. The dressmaking and millinery trades were finding it difficult to attract apprentices due to poor pay even for trained workers. However as recently as 1908–9 Bristol had seen the worst unemployment since the mid-1880s, particularly among dockers and transport workers and it was from these groups that the new militancy emerged.

By 1900 the Bristol branch of the Dockers Union had shrunk to 800 members, mainly amongst corn-porters. In 1910 under the leadership of the young Ernest Bevin the branch went on unofficial strike in defiance of local union leaders who supported an arbitration agreement of 1900. The strike involved 3000 dockers and other transport workers and although they failed to achieve all their objectives the men regarded the settlement as a victory.[76] The strike was the largest in Bristol since 1892, the initiative being taken by the rank and file in defiance of local and national union leaders. This militancy was beyond the control of the trades council as well as union leaders. Such 'bottom up' militancy, a feature of many disputes in these years, was particularly marked in Bristol.[77]

The 1910 dock dispute radicalised union members, giving them a sense of their own power and bringing the simmering discontent with moderate union officials to a head. The following year saw carters, dockers, railwaymen and miners taking strike action.[78] Although troops were called out and shots were fired over the heads of strikers in Bedminster, there was little violence when compared to Hull, Liverpool or South Wales. The railwaymen went back as part of a national settlement and the dockers a week later after a locally arranged compromise. As soon as this dispute ended the miners struck from 4th September to 15th November. The initiative was taken by non-union members and the moderation of Whitefield the local miners' leader was widely condemned.[79]

1911 was the critical year in Bristol. Although there were to be strikes and lock-outs in the city in the succeeding years they were not on the same scale. The main beneficiary of this upsurge in militancy was the Dockers Union, which by 1914 had 5000–6000 members and enjoyed an almost total monopoly of waterfront labour and carters and had even organised the brickyard workers in Mangotsfield and Almonsbury. The newly formed National Union of Railwaymen had 1853 members at the start of 1913 and 3419 by the end of 1914, while the Bristol miners increased their membership to 2000.[80]

In Belfast it was again the dockers who were to lead the upsurge in trade union activity after 1907. In January James Larkin was sent to Belfast as the organiser of the National Union of Dock Labourers and within three months he had recruited 2900 dockers and all the carters.[81] That summer saw a prolonged, and ultimately unsuccessful, dock strike, which attracted widespread support within the city. Although the dispute never involved more than 3500 strikers directly the attendance at the daily strike meetings was five to ten thousand with about 100 000 taking part in a Trades Council demonstration at one point.[82] However, the weakness of the unskilled in Belfast was demonstrated with painful clarity during the strike. An attempt was made by the unskilled labourers at the Sirocco engineering works to form a union, and the response of 'friend' and 'foe' alike illustrates the hostility faced by non-craft trade unionists in the city. Robert Greig of the NAUL, the union which might have been expected to recruit them, refused to extend aid to the strikers. The trades council's secretary went further and wrote to the employer criticising the labourers for striking prematurely.[83]

There appeared to have been a massive mobilising of the unskilled labour force, but this did not last. The Workers Union, which by 1908 had five branches in Belfast, had declined so much by 1913 that it withdrew its organiser and effectively suspended activities. The organiser, Joe Harris, blamed the Home Rule Crisis which, he said, employers were using to divide the workers.[84] By 1913 the situation was summed up thus by Thomas Johnson, the Belfast born labour leader,

> Such were the conditions as I remember them in Belfast in the first few years of the century. The skilled tradesmen had their trade unions and were reasonably protected by them, but the big mass of unskilled labour (and this includes dockworkers, vandrivers, navvies, shopworkers and the like) were unorganised and at the mercy of their employers. Women workers, including the mill hands, were in a similar defenceless state.[85]

The Dockers were weakened in Belfast by schism and fratricidal conflict, when Jim Larkin broke away to establish his own union in 1909. Larkin's Irish Transport and General Workers Union had a branch in Belfast by the end of 1911 whose membership was mainly Catholics working in the deep sea wharfs. The National Union of Dock labour continued to represent the mainly protestant labour force in the cross channel trade.[86]

Belfast's trade unionists saw that politics were damaging the trade union movement in the city.

> Before the ordinary business was proceeded with the chairman (W.R. Campbell) referred to the recent shipyard troubles, and expressed his regret at the unfortunate occurrences connected therewith, which affected a considerable number of organised workers. It was a deplorable thing that many persons had allowed their political feelings to run away with their better judgement and resorted to violence. He hoped that before long a better feeling would prevail among the workers, in spite of their religious and political opinions.[87]

In September the Flax-dressers presented a resolution to the trades council condemning the outrages in the shipyards and calling on other trade unions to do the same. Two weeks later in response to a question from the floor the chairman had to admit that 'very few unions had taken any action regarding the assaults on the shipyard workers'.[88]

Dublin saw the most explosive expansion of unskilled trade unionism before the First World War. In 1909–10 Larkin formed the Irish Transport and General Workers Union which soon had over 2000 members, most of whom had previously belonged to the NUDL.[89] The fact that the two unions recruited the same groups of workers, combined with the animosity which existed between the leaders, led to very poor relations from the start. Sexton was to accuse the ITGWU of poaching his membership, which was technically true, and went so far as to challenge the new union's right to attend the 1909 Irish Trades Union Congress.[90]

The early years of the new union would not have been easy but Larkin's character made matters worse. He was rejected by the Unionist workers of Belfast as a nationalist, while Arthur Griffith dismissed him as a professional agitator.[91] Growth was sporadic. By the end of 1911 there were branches in Belfast, Cork, Wexford, New Ross, and Kilkenny although some of these had only a paper existence.[92] It was in Dublin where by the end of 1911 there were three branches, that the union really established its strength. After winning a bitter struggle with the NUDL and the Workers Union the ITGWU finally represented all 'organised' unskilled labour in the city other than the corporation labourers who retained their own union.[93] According to the Registrar of Friendly Societies the ITGWU increased from 18 098 members in January 1912 to 24 135 in December although only 14 000 members were affiliated by the union to the ILPTUC in 1913.[94]

The growth of trade union power was a feature of Bristol and Dublin in the years before the First World War. In Belfast the same process began but was swamped by the political crisis of Home Rule. In all three cities the transport sector was central although other groups were swept up in the agitation. In Bristol the main unions which expanded were the Dock, Wharf, Riverside and General Labours and the National Union of Railwaymen. In Belfast the National Union of Dock Labourers was the initial beneficiary with the Workers Union later benefiting from the divisions within that body. Railway workers were not a feature of the Irish expansion, as they were already highly organised in Ireland. In Dublin the development was perhaps most explosive because unskilled labour was, unlike the other two cities, almost totally unorganised in 1909 and the Irish Transport and General Workers adopted highly aggressive tactics.

One final question is what was the role of syndicalism in this wave of union expansion? Clegg suggests that of the fourteen major disputes in these years at least four saw a significant syndicalist involvement or were led by men sympathetic to their aims and methods.[95] Contemporary newspapers and observers often blamed syndicalist agitators for the labour militancy in these years. In the case of both the Cambrian and Liverpool strikes the syndicalists appear to have enjoyed considerable influence.[96] However in both cases only a tiny number of committed members were involved in both areas and the bulk of the strikers were less radical in their politics or aspirations. Holton points out that there were only about fifty committed syndicalists operating in either Liverpool or South Wales and that maintaining militancy was extremely difficult without overt social or industrial conflict.[97]

The *Industrial Syndicalist* regularly printed lists of those 'Willing to speak as advocates of industrial syndicalism in their respective districts'.[98] There were no speakers advertised for either Belfast or Dublin despite strong support in Liverpool and northern England. The syndicalists were clearly active in Bristol, being one of the groups who attempted to disrupt a meeting of the ILP addressed by Philip Snowden.[99] However, there is no indication that they acquired any influence on the trades council or among other socialist bodies in the city. It was not until March 1911 that Herbert E. Eady of the Clerks Union advertised his willingness to lecture on syndicalism, giving his address as the prestigious Clifton district of the city.[100]

In Ireland syndicalism is usually connected to James Larkin, James Connolly and the Irish Transport and General Workers Union. However Emmett O'Connor suggests that the real success of Irish syndicalism was to be after these years.[101] In fact Irish workers tended to be nationalists or unionists rather than socialists or syndicalists. Those who followed Larkin did so because of his charisma and ability rather than any socialist ideology he espoused. It is debatable how far the rank and file revolt against conservative trade union leaders was provoked by the propaganda and leadership of revolutionary groups. In fairly general terms it can be said that while syndicalist ideas and propaganda may have fuelled the discontent in these years, they did not create the situation. The bottom-up nature of events in Bristol, Larkin's methods in Belfast and many of the ideas of the Irish Transport and General Workers Union may appear syndicalist, but the syndicalists were not responsible for these developments.

CONCLUSION

On the eve of the First World War trade unionism had developed to a similar point in all three cities. The skilled workers were well organised, the semi/un-skilled, notably the transport workers, were partly unionised. However women, casual labour and most white-collar workers were still unorganised. Beyond this there was considerable variation due to the extent and nature of industrial development in each city. This dictated the relative strength of the skilled and unskilled elements of the labour forces. Although the skilled saw themselves as intrinsically superior to other groups of workers there were also considerable divisions between various trades. This was not a purely financial division: a white-collar draughtsman could earn less than a riveter in the shipyards but his status as an office worker was far higher.

From the point of view of trade union development these differences were critical. When combined with the printing and building trades Belfast's main industries, shipbuilding and engineering created an elite of craft unions which dominated the labour movement. The largest employer of non-craft labour, the linen industry, was weakly unionised with only the 'aristocrats' tending to be organised. In Bristol engineering, printing and building craft unions faced competition from semi and unskilled unionised labour in the boot and shoe, tobacco, food processing, clothing and transport sectors from the 1890s and quickly lost their dominance. In Dublin the small body of 'aristocrats' in the craft societies faced no challenge until the emergence of the Irish Transport and General Workers Union after 1910, although that union rapidly came to dominate the labour movement in the city. The unskilled formed a differing, and changing, proportion of the total labour force in each city over these years. In Bristol the demand for unskilled workers in the expanding industrial sectors was so great that the proportion of general labourers declined throughout this period. Conversely, in Dublin the proportion of unskilled general labourers increased, due to the absence of an expanding industrial employment sector.

By 1914 there were three very distinctive trade union movements in the cities covered by this study. Belfast had seen a revival in non-craft trade unionism but this had already faltered, leaving the powerful skilled unions in control of the labour movement. In Dublin the old craft societies had been totally eclipsed by the new Transport and General Workers Union, which despite the defeat of 1913, still dominated the labour movement in the city. In Bristol the uneasy balance between skilled and non-craft unions that had emerged in the 1890s continued, although the non-craft bodies were becoming increasingly powerful.

4 The Labour Movement: a Wider View

Trade unions did not exist in isolation. They formed part of a wider 'labour' movement, coexisting with a range of organisations sharing common objectives. Between 1880 and 1925 some of these bodies, such as the Independent Labour Party, were purely political, seeking to promote the election of 'working class' representatives. Socialist groups sought to spread their belief in a new social order in an evangelical manner rather than simply gaining political representation. Others sought to redress specific problems within society, for example, pacifists, suffragettes and temperance campaigners. Finally there was the vast Co-operative movement which formed such a feature of contemporary 'working class' identity.

It is important not to overstate the links between these bodies. Many trade unionists in this period would have been horrified if accused of being socialists. Co-operators were not necessarily supporters of either trade unionism or radical reform and were sometimes poor employers. Many pacifists and supporters of female suffrage had no sympathy with the 'labour movement'. However, links did exist between these groups both in terms of personnel and ideas. Thus it is possible to discuss these groups within the terms of a 'wider labour movement' although many contemporary observers would have rejected such a concept. In this chapter I will look at a range of organisations to try and assess the degree of similarity and difference within the cities.

THE CO-OPERATIVE MOVEMENT

It is appropriate to begin with the largest element of the 'labour movement', the Co-operative societies. In some histories of labour in Ireland and the Co-operative movement the role of such bodies is presented as minor or even negative.

> It was apparent almost from the start that due to the extreme poverty of the Irish people, the conditions there were absolutely minimal for the success of the co-operative store; the situation was in fact almost the exact opposite of that which existed in England: to

be successful, the Consumers Movement demanded a well fed and self conscious aristocracy of labour, the product of a mature, industrial economy, whereas predominantly agricultural Ireland constituted what one might today call an 'underdeveloped country', its labour force consisting of a horde of religiously divided and economically indigent peasants.[1]

This appears to be confirmed by the absence of a large scale co-operative movement in Dublin. Although a number of societies were established in the city, including a store set up in 1913 by students at University College Dublin there was very limited support.[2] However, Backstrom's view of conditions in Ireland ignores the fact that by the 1880s Belfast had 'a well-fed and self-conscious aristocracy of labour, the product of a mature, industrial economy'. It is notable that when the Belfast Co-op was established in 1889 it was by skilled industrial workers of the Shankill area, a class that Dublin largely lacked.[3]

The Co-operative movement in Bristol had a longer if more mixed history than Belfast's. Two societies were established in about 1860 but both went out of business in the early 1870s due, according to John Wall, to mismanagement.[4] In 1882 a new co-op was formed in the Bedminster district of south Bristol. The size and success of this society was such that when the Bristol co-op was established in 1884 the committee were not even aware of the older body's existence. A comparison of these three societies shows the considerable differences that characterised these early co-operative groups. The Bedminster Co-operative was established in 1882 by 30 members with an initial capital of £13. 13s. 6d.; two years later the 48 initial members in Bristol brought a capital of £40 to the project. The Belfast co-operative was not established until 1889, when an initial membership of 199 produced a capital of £200; in its first year Belfast's turnover was £3747 compared to £1067 in Bedminster and £774 in Bristol.[5]

By 1903 Belfast had 1200 members and the society was establishing its own bakery with the assistance of the Glasgow Co-Operative Society.[6] In 1905 when the Bristol Societies finally amalgamated the result was a combined membership of 11 485 and annual sales of £205 409.[7]

The success of co-operation in Belfast and Bristol is in stark contrast to Dublin. As an institution the co-op catered for the 'aristocracy of labour' who could invest capital in such ventures. 'By far the largest proportion of shareholders in a Co-operative Society are of the working class, whose income, including interest and dividend, do not reach £160 per year.'[8]

Table 4.1   Comparative development of the co-operative movement[9]

	1911	1916	1921	1926	1931
Bristol					
Membership	15 836	18 484	24 347	32 064	51 202
Employees	409	538	707	1022	1791
Sales	279 983	366 634	992 684	1 006 425	1 682 122
Belfast					
Membership	7000	14 200	24 800	29 500	43 200
Employees	208	524	782	885	1396
Sales	177 515	423 096	1 331 744	1 114 897	1 529 804
*Dublin**					
Membership	845	1685	2300	1965	2080
Employees	29	34	41	27	22
Sales	20 725	26 206	84 331	26 734	19 283

* The figures for Dublin include the Industrial, Consumers, and University co-operative societies.

It was not the unskilled labourers or the mill workers earning a pound a week but the well paid skilled and semi-skilled who formed the membership of co-operative societies. Relations with the trade unions were not always cordial as commercial considerations could replace idealism in co-operative stores.[10]

THE INDEPENDENT LABOUR PARTY

The Independent Labour Party sought to further 'working class' representation using the democratic process. The party was active in all three cities but success varied according to social and political conditions. In Dublin where politics were dominated by the Irish National Party the position of labour as a political force was weakest. Although Labour under the banner of the Labour Electoral Association won six seats in the local elections of 1889, the long-term results were far from encouraging.[11] Although there were branches of the ILP and various other socialist bodies in the city in the early years of this century their impact was minimal.[12] It was the rise of Larkinism which resulted in the formation of an Irish Labour Party in 1912, linked to the Irish Trade Union Congress and quite distinct from the British Labour Party.[13] The new party enjoyed considerable success in the 1912 election but this provoked a backlash from Nationalists and their supporters in the Catholic clergy. In the aftermath of the 1913 Lock Out the 1914 municipal elections in Dublin saw attacks upon Larkin and Labour candidates.

> Labour agitators canvassing the Mountjoy Ward, for example, were fair game for the curates at the pro-cathedral who supported Lord Mayor Sherlock in the 1914 election by damning his Larkinite opponent as a member of 'the motley crew of dangerous lunatics ...socialists, syndicalists, Orangemen, Suffragettes, decadent poets and armchair philanthropists'.[14]

Socialism was linked to Orangism to discredit the labour candidates in the manner of the dominant local political tradition.

In 1885 the first labour parliamentary candidate in Belfast, Alex Bowman, stood against the mill owner Sir William Ewart in the North Belfast consistency. He lost, but from that point on labour candidates were to feature in almost every election. As a result of the TUC meeting in Belfast in 1893 the Independent Labour Party was established in the city. In 1898 the trades council and the ILP were successful in getting six candidates elected to the city council, and they formed the first 'Labour Group' on any local authority in Ireland.

However, Belfast politics were dominated by Unionists and Labour was unable to win a parliamentary seat in the 'working class' city of Belfast.

> Great propaganda was put in, and the contests demonstrated the right of any section of the community to come forward and take part in the Civic and National life of the country – a right not always recognised in a city where every effort has been made to keep the workers in two camps, respectively labelled 'Orange' and 'Green'.[15]

If the Nationalists were willing to equate socialists with Unionism then the Unionists were happy to class them with the Nationalists. Protestant clergy were as quick to condemn the 'atheistic' ideas of labour as their Catholic colleagues had been, and the results were as damaging.[16] As Robert McElborough, a member of the Liberal Party noted, 'To be anything but a Unionist or a Nationalist in those days required courage'.[17] The Independent Labour Party organised open air meetings on the Custom House Steps in Belfast, the local equivalent to Hyde Park Corner. This antagonised the extreme protestant/unionist clergy who already preached there and sparked violent confrontations. Although a number of leading labour speakers from Britain attended these meetings, police presence was often required for the protection of their audiences.[18]

Despite widespread and often violent opposition the ILP survived and even prospered: by 1907 there were five active branches in the city and many progressive trade unionists were active members.[19] As in Dublin 'labour' remained a secondary issue compared to Home Rule. It is notable that prominent individuals such as William Walker and Harry Midgley had no difficulty in combining 'labour' ideas with opposition to Home Rule. The depth of distrust of labour felt by unionist leaders and their supporters was shown in 1920 when socialists were expelled from the shipyards along with Nationalists.[20]

By way of contrast Bristol's ILP, although not liked by the establishment, did not face such an entrenched political culture as encountered by their comrades in Dublin or Belfast. The first 'labour' victories were in 1886 when John Fox was elected to the School Board and 1887 when R.G. Tovey was returned as the councillor for the St Pauls ward of the city.[21] The ILP was established at a meeting of twenty people in a house in the St Philips area in 1894, and began to contest municipal elections from that time.[22] Opposition to the South African War resulted in violent attacks on meetings and members and as a result the party was forced to suspend its public activities.[23] However, recovery was rapid and by 1911 a new party headquarters was opened and they employed a full time secretary.[24] By the end of 1913 it numbered 615 members in 14 ward organisations, and Walter Ayles, was able to report considerable activity.

> The St Paul's Ward is again at work organising street by street. Horfield has formed two committees, one for visiting members and sympathisers, one for Bazaar work. We have formed a Women's group in Bedminster, and hope that the next month or two will find it as flourishing as those in Brislington and Easton.[25]

The Independent Labour Party in Bristol developed into a highly organised political machine with a full time official and permanent premises. In Belfast the party was able to organise in all the city's constituencies, under the energetic leadership of William Walker, but did not achieve the level of membership or organisation seen in Bristol. In Dublin the supporters of 'labour' proved unable to challenge the dominance of the National Party and its clerical allies and gain the support of the 'working class' as a group during these years.

OTHER SOCIALIST GROUPS

In general the fortunes of other groups favouring socialist ideas were similar to those of the ILP in the cities of Bristol, Belfast and Dublin. The same factors which limited the growth of the Labour Party also affected more specifically Socialist and Marxist bodies.

The Fabians were active in all three cities. They were not revolutionaries but saw socialism as so inherently logical that it would inevitably emerge. Their role was simply to speed the process by education and propaganda. Although never a mass movement the Fabians had enormous influence in the development of British Labour thought. In 1891 they established their first Irish branch in Belfast but this ceased to function during 1892. The Dublin branch established in 1892 struggled on until it too closed in 1899.[26] The short life span of these branches may not be due simply to Irish conditions but also to the attitude of the society towards Ireland.

> This has been the life-work of the Fabian society, the working out of the application of the broad principles of socialism to the industrial and political environment of England. I say England advisedly, because the industrial and political conditions of Scotland are in some degree different, and the application of the principles of socialism to Ireland has not yet been seriously attempted.[27]

In Bristol the Fabians were to work with other groups including the Socialist Society, ILP and Workers Education Association. They were clearly active by 1891 when they published a tract on political and social conditions in the city.[28] However, as in Ireland this group also appears to have ceased to function during the later 1890s when many local Fabian groups were effectively converted into ILP branches.[29] In an interview in 1913 Stephen Smith claimed that the Fabians had only been active in Bristol for four years. However, during the previous year the society had arranged a hundred lectures in the city on topics such as 'The Curse of Charity', 'Trade Unions Past and Present', and 'Religion and Business'.[30]

As educators the Fabians were seen as eccentrics rather than a challenge to the established political parties. Their desire was to 'permeate' existing parties and institutions with socialist ideas. They remained middle class, reasonable and pragmatic seeing themselves as, and to a degree acting as, shapers of the labour movement's political thought.

Revolutionary phraseology, the language of violence, survived and still survives, just as in ordinary politics we use the metaphors of warfare and pretend that the peaceful polling booth is a battlefield and that our political opponents are hostile armies. But we now wave the red flag in our songs, and we recognise nowadays that the real battles of socialism are fought in committee rooms in Westminster and in the Council Chambers of town halls.

The forty or fifty thousand members of the I.L.P. and B.S.P. are roughly no larger a proportion of the working class than the three thousand Fabians are of the middle class.[31]

Other more radical socialist groups hardly developed beyond a few dedicated individuals in Belfast and Dublin.[32] However, in Bristol there was a tradition of radical activity which in the 1880s became centred on the Bristol Socialist Society. This body dated from 1884 when the Radical Reform Association became an affiliate to the Social Democratic Federation.[33] In 1885 following a dispute over the London SDF's decision to nominate separate candidates in elections, which Bristolians felt favoured the Tories, the branch withdrew.[34] They then established themselves as a branch of the Socialist League, later joining the Socialist Democratic Party, and adopted the title Bristol Socialist Society.[35]

This body was more socialist than 'labour' in its politics although most members defined socialism in Christian rather than Marxist terms. John Wall, the 'Bristol Socialist Poet', was an active member and divided his writing between social issues, history and religious topics.[36] From today's perspective the activities of the Bristol Socialists appear almost quaint. Their booklet 'Labour Songs', for example, is very tame for modern tastes; the 'Red Flag' is included but most songs are socialist words to popular tunes.

(To the tune 'Heart of Oak')
Come Gather, O People, For soon is the Hour,
When Princes must fall with their pomp and their power:
For the power of the future, we know it to be,
A People united and sworn to be free.

Chorus — Firm and fast we will stand,
         Heart to heart, hand in hand.
         In fair or foul weather,
         Brothers together
         A people united and sworn to be free.[37]

It is difficult to imagine a modern left wing group in need of funds to further their activities organising an event such as 'Liberty Faire' held at Easter 1911.

> The Castle Green Council Schools have been taken, and will be transformed into an old English village called Liberty Faire, comprising old houses, gardens, village inn, post office, stocks, village well etc; village folk in costume, and numerous side shows including menagerie, dramatic entertainments and visits to the Castle dungeons to name a few.[38]

The programme which described Liberty Faire as 'something akin to the village William Morris pictures' lists amongst other activities, the 'Sweet Corner' offering Easter Eggs, Red Flag Toffee, Marseillaise Chocolate and 'other toothsome dainties'.[39]

Although the socialists were distinctive from other 'labour' groups in the city in terms of ideology the attitude of the opposition made alliance inevitable.[40] By the mid-1890s the Independent Labour Party, Labour Electoral Association, Fabians and Socialist Society were putting up mutually agreed candidates.[41] However, relations were not always cordial as the ILP noted after one of its public meetings in December 1913:

> There were interruptions by Suffragettes and members of the Daily Herald League and the Syndicalists. I was informed that two members of the B.S.P. also interrupted. This is denied by the officials of the Bristol North Branch, and I am happy to publish their denial. In other quarters I am informed that these interrupters had been members of other branches, but have now left. This I am glad to hear as it would be a thousand pities if any misunderstanding was put in the way of our welcoming any proposals tending towards Socialist unity.[42]

PARLIAMENTS OF LABOUR

One critical element of the 'labour movement' which can be found in all three cities was the trades councils. These bodies were established to co-ordinate the activities of trade unions within a specific district and later began campaigning on social and political issues. The first trades council was established in Liverpool in 1848 and although it was another decade before the next was established in Glasgow, after 1860 expansion was rapid.[43]

The three cities were all comparatively late in forming trades councils, Bristol in 1873, Belfast in 1881 (the first in Ireland) and Dublin in 1886.[44] Their evolution was similar. Initially all were bodies representing skilled craft unions and increasingly saw a shift to semi-skilled and non-skilled unions.[45] In theory such bodies were non-political, seeking only to advance the cause of labour by whatever means were practical. Almost all trades councils had rules prohibiting the discussion of party political issues which were seen as divisive. However, inevitably most councils tended to adopt the political opinions of the bulk of their membership. Thus Dublin was sympathetic to Home Rule, Belfast basically supported the union with Britain, while in Bristol there was pro-Liberal feeling until the later 1880s.

The trades councils were the institutions where organised labour and working class politics combined and 'labour politics' finally emerged. In all three cases this was marked by internal conflict between the politically neutral and more explicitly socialist or Labour elements in each council. In Bristol other bodies such as the ILP and the Labour representation committee increasingly took over the earlier political activities of the trades council.[46] In Dublin and Belfast the development of alternative bodies was less pronounced and in both cities the emergence of independent labour representation was marked by the control of the trades councils by ILP and other socialist elements. In consequence in Ireland Trades Councils retained far more influence within the Trade Union Congress and Labour Party than similar bodies in Britain.

FEMINISTS, PACIFISTS AND ABSTAINERS

There is nothing uniquely 'labour' about the demand for female suffrage, opposition to war, or concerns about the social effects of drunkenness. These were all issues which in the late nineteenth and early twentieth centuries were the subject of widespread debate. They can however be considered as part of the 'wider labour movement' simply because many trade unionists and socialists were deeply concerned about these issues and they influenced contemporary 'labour' thinking.

The Suffragettes, as opposed to suffragists who advocated constitutional change, were profoundly shocking to contemporary society, not just due to their political demands but also because of the methods adopted. All three cities saw widespread campaigns in support of the extension of women's political and social rights. In Dublin the

Women's Suffrage Federation and other bodies combined the demand for women's rights with a basically nationalist political outlook. Belfast and Bristol were to see the activities of the Women's Social and Political Union, the presence of this 'British' body being bitterly resented by Dublin.[47] The methods used, disruption of political meetings, arson attacks and deliberate damaging of public and private property alienated many within contemporary society. The WSPU seems to have frequently used members from other areas to carry out attacks. In her memoirs Elizabeth Hutchinson recounts how her mother helped 'visitors' from England make up incendiary bombs disguised in expensive cake boxes. In old age the same lady visited London and went to the West End to look at the shop windows she had once smashed with a hammer.[48]

Many members of the socialist and trade union movements supported the demand for improvement in women's social and political status, although critical of the violent methods used by some elements. However, others were less sympathetic to what they saw as the campaign for 'votes for ladies'.

In the following remarks on the above subject. I shall premise that my intention is only to appeal to those persons whose minds are warped in favour of feminism by certain plausible sounding arguments, which they have been in all sincerity accepting because their fallacy has never been pointed out to them. The ruck of hysterical molluscs, who are imposed upon by hollow sentimental whines about their "mothers and their sisters" (why not their grandmothers, their aunts, their female cousins and their mothers-in-law?) may be fairly left to stew in their own rather thin juice.[49]

Although often seen as a consequence of the First World War, opposition to war, conscription and militarism were a feature of 'labour' thinking from a much earlier date. In November 1913 *Co-operative News* published an attack on plans to introduce universal military training in New Zealand under the headline 'The Campaign against Militarism'.[50] In Bristol pacifism, due in part to the long association of Quakers with the 'labour' movement, influenced early labour thinking. The ILP publicly criticised the war in South Africa in 1899 and was to continue, along with the Fabians and the Socialist Society, to oppose war and militarism.[51] Some socialists however, such as Bristol's John Wall, were not so much opposed to war as to the reasons for which some wars were waged.

The chief crime of the French revolutionists was not so much *blood*-spilling as spilling the blood of kings and aristocrats: not so much *war* – as war against potentates: not so much the changing of laws – as changing them to benefit the workers. If the revolutionists had let out thick dirty plebeian blood instead of translucent blue blood; if they had warred against ignorant mobs instead of old-established thrones; and had made laws to strangle the workers; much could have been forgiven them; At least by the section of society which shudders apprehensively the very moment the workers cries become articulate.[52]

The question of pacifism in Ireland was more complex, since like so much else it was linked to the question of Nationalism and Unionism. There was wide spread opposition to the South African war, although perhaps inspired by opposition to British policy rather than moral objections to war as such.[53] However, there exists evidence for pacifist sentiments among 'labour' supporters in Ireland. In February 1911 the Belfast Trades Council was read a pamphlet on compulsory military training, and referred the matter to the executive committee for action. In April 1912 the Council agreed to support the 'World Petition to Prevent War Between Nations' and in June unanimously agreed to support the objectives of the 'National Peace Congress'.[54] In Dublin there were similar pacifist sentiments. James Connolly was certainly an exponent of class war, urging the formation of an armed militia in defence of the working class. But he was deeply opposed to militarism.

The Cabinets who rule the destinies of nations from the various capitals of Europe are but the tools of the moneyed interest. Their quarrels are not dictated by sentiments of national pride or honour, but by avarice and lust of power on the part of the class to which they belong.[55]

Temperance was another great moral issue which was of interest to the 'labour' movement from an early stage. There was a widely held belief that alcohol was a fundamental evil which destroyed the lives of workers and their families. It is notable that although many of the early trade unions met in public houses, later bodies displayed a strong preference for coffee taverns or unlicensed halls. Many early trade union leaders tried to set an example, some even adopting teetotalism, and were violent critics of practices such as paying off labourers in pubs which they felt encouraged men to drink. However once again there were those who were critical of the temperance campaign and the ideas behind it.

The teetotal movement, which also started in Lancashire, at Preston (in 1832), mainly holds forth the material advantages to be gained from a sober life, instead of advocating the righteousness and morality of temperance. Its lecturers and disciples are always pointing out the thrifty side of teetotalism; what an advantage it gives a man over his intemperate fellows, and so forth. The result is that most teetotallers are very narrow and bigoted persons, who are teetotal simply from a scraping, saving point of view, and who, consequently, come not only to regard drinking, but even all innocent pleasures as waste of time and money. I have found most teetotallers mean and grasping, devoid of all love of humanity, caring nothing for their fellow-man, so long as they were securely housed and fed themselves, and the teetotallers who have 'got on' and become employers of labour, are generally the hardest and most skinflint of masters. These things I write not because I am against temperance, for I never take alcoholic drinks myself, but because they are facts.[56]

Temperance was by no means confined to the 'labour' movement; they adopted a belief which had widespread public support during this period. The sensitivity of the issue in the labour movement can be seen in the rage which was created in Bristol when a liberal accused them of being 'pot house politicians'.[57] The indignation felt at such a slight was all the greater because it affected not only their political beliefs but also their personal morals. Temperance bodies, notably those with a religious connection, had considerable political influence in this period, and in 1906 in Bristol there were no fewer than fourteen organisations, whose membership numbered tens of thousands.[58] Thus the pragmatic desire to gain votes reinforced a desire for respectability among 'labour' supporters.

WORKERS' EDUCATION

In 1889, as the outgoing president, G.W. Wolff addressed the annual meeting of the Belfast Chamber of Commerce on the question of strikes and offered a solution to the problem.

> We can only trust that the work people themselves with better education will learn that even if a strike is successful in obtaining larger wages or reducing the hours of labour, the consequent increase in the cost of the article produced will make its sale in competition

with similar articles by others more difficult and ultimately react upon themselves.[59]

Many trade unionists shared his ideas on the value of education, although they might not have accepted his logic on wages and hours. Trade unionists and socialists saw education as a way of changing society through the young. The Independent Labour Party and other 'Labour' political groups organised public lectures and debates on matters of interest as did the co-operative movement and the Fabians. However, the most impressive body was the Workers' Educational Association, a national and theoretically non-political body, which enjoyed widespread support.

Consisting at present of 2,555 organisations, including 953 trade unions, trades councils and branches, 388 co-operative committees, 341 adult schools and classes, 15 university bodies, 16 local education authorities, 175 working men's clubs and institutions, 65 teachers associations, 151 educational and literary societies and 451 various societies mainly of workpeople...[60]

The WEA was established in 1903 in Reading, and branches were established in Bristol in 1907 and Belfast in 1910.[61] These were part of a huge national growth in this body in the years before and during the First World War.[62] However, the WEA was never able to establish itself in Dublin, due to religious opposition and the simple poverty of the workers of that city.

The Association was rather bourgeois in terms of membership and activities and it can be seen as the 'middle' classes trying to improve the 'lower orders'. However the sheer scale of the organisation was such that it was to have an effect far beyond what was originally intended. The Association's activities are well illustrated by the Bristol branch which in 1914 offered, among other courses:

A course of four lectures on 'The life of St Paul' by the Rev John Gamble, B.D. at the St Nicholas Schoolroom, Queen Charlotte Street.

Special courses for Adult School Workers on 'Making the map of modern Europe' by Miss Hilda Cashmore, B.A.: and 'A study in the Fourth Gospel' by Mr E.H.C. Wethered, at the University Settlement.

A series of Four Chamber Concerts by Mrs Fitzherbert and friends, at the University Settlement New Hall.[63]

Despite this apparent elitism the WEA represented an element of the extension movement which at this time was seeking to broaden education to include the mass of the population. Even though such bodies sought to present themselves as non-political they created a demand for improvements in education which the 'labour movement' supported.

SUNDAY SCHOOLS AND CYCLISTS

An important aspect of the early 'labour movement', which many would now say has been lost, was its social function. As the history of the Bristol Trades Council points out such bodies saw their role as going far beyond industrial and political matters. The council not only had its own brass band but organised concerts, sporting events and social functions, frequently in co-operation with other labour and socialist groups.[64] The WEA staged a monthly social event on a Saturday night organised by the 'Song and Sketch Party' for the amusement of members.[65] On the eve of the First World War the Independent Labour Party was able to inform its members of another successful event.

Garden Fete — This was held on July 11th at Fishponds Vicarage, when 140 sat down to tea. The thanks of the branch are due to the comrades of Easton and Fishponds, and to the Rev. C.P. and Mrs Wilson and their staff.[66]

Even during the war social activity continued as members met in each other's homes for a 'Potato Pie Supper', 'Cornish Pasty Supper' or 'Shepherds Pie Supper'.[67]

A wide range of 'labour' and socialist groups appear in these years organising social activities with a political flavour. In Bristol and Belfast supporters of Robert Blatchford's newspaper *The Clarion* formed sections of the Clarion Cycling Club and Scouts, combining a desire to sell the paper with healthy exercise.[68] Edward Pease of the Fabian Society saw value in the activities of such groups.

Perhaps its most valuable contribution to the movement was 'high spirits'. The Clarion found much to enjoy in life, notwithstanding the poverty and oppression of the workers; its boisterous good humour was helpful because social reconstruction can only be wisely planned by those who see things from all sides, and the fanatical

socialist who looks only at the gloomy aspects of society is misled
into exaggerating the discontent of the workers.[69]

A similar body, the Bristol Socialist Rambling and Propaganda Society, engaged in activities which were marked by enthusiasm rather
than success.

> The actual propaganda was in practice less than anticipated but
> always a quantity of socialist literature was distributed among the
> villages and there was never a jaunt without paste pot and brush
> handy with which to affix socialist mottoes and texts to gateposts,
> stiles and the like.[70]

Work among young people was always considered of the greatest
importance. As early as 1894, a socialist boys' club was established at
Baptist Mills Coffee House, and in 1898 a Socialist Sunday School was
established by the Socialist Society.[71] This later group was not seen as
challenging the existing Christian basis of society but rather offering a
fresh interpretation.

> Socialism is a religion teaching morality and brotherhood of men, as
> taught by Christ and others. Its central principle (its god) is love –
> love of humanity – It strives to abolish unjust laws and customs
> which enable the idle rich to rob the industrious poor. It demands
> honesty, truthfulness, frankness of charter and purity of life.[72]

The Co-operative movement began holding 'children's classes' in
Bristol in 1899, although such activities had to compete for funds as
general propaganda work was controlled by the same committee.[73] At
the start of the First World War the ILP in Bristol established its own
youth wing called the 'Band of Young Socialists' (BOYS) which by
early 1915 had over thirty members. This appears to have been a successful extension of the party's activities.[74]

In Dublin this form of political/social activity was not a strong feature of the labour movement, although social activities were organised
by various bodies and formed an important aspect of the Irish Transport and General Workers Union. In general it was the church or nationalist groups who were successful in appealing to the Dubliner
rather than socialist or labour organisations. Compared with the Hi-
bernians, Gaelic League or Gaelic Athletic Association the efforts of
trade unions and other bodies met with a limited success. As A.J.
O'Rahilly informed the WEA the nationalists were already performing
their function.

It may surprise English readers to be told that in no country is adult education so flourishing as in Ireland. The Gaelic League and related activities are really the Irish equivalent of the Workers Education Association. The greatest educational achievement of Ireland, is to be found in the Gaelic Movement.[75]

The nationalists saw labour as at best a distraction and at worst an English 'import' and sought to create social organisations which emphasised the 'Irishness' of their activities. The Catholic Church disapproved of many aspects of 'labour' and sought to ensure that it did not challenge the role of the church as the centre of its members' religious and social lives.

In Belfast the community formed social structures mirroring the religious/political divisions of the city. Although the nationalist population might have accepted that 'the Gaelic League and related activities are really the Irish equivalent of the Workers' Educational Association', Unionists quite clearly would not. In part they substituted bodies such as the Orange Order and Freemasons which excluded the Catholic community. However, there existed other groups which can be seen as 'working class' rather than sectarian in nature. A good example of this would be the WEA whose activities also had the desirable effect, from a Unionist point of view, of showing links with a wider British labour movement. On another level, activities of the Socialist Sunday School, as in Belfast and Bristol would have been unacceptable in Catholic Dublin.

CONCLUSION

In the cities of Bristol, Belfast and Dublin in the years 1880 to 1925 quite distinctive 'working class' cultures emerged. This is not to say that there was no underlying ideology common to all three cities, rather that local conditions created local adaptations. In Belfast and Dublin 'Labour' was very much a secondary issue to nationalism and unionism. In these cities labour had to adapt to local political conditions rather than developing as an independent force. Bristol had a powerful radical/liberal tradition which actually assisted the emergence of 'labour' as a force in the city's politics.

However, beyond this the basic wealth of the 'working class' was a critical factor in the emergence of 'labour' institutions. The well paid industrial and transport workers of Belfast and Bristol could afford to invest in co-operation, the impoverished casual labourer in Dublin could not. In Bristol, and to a lesser degree Belfast, the 'middle class' began to support 'labour' institutions such as the Fabians or the WEA In Dublin the professional and white collar classes were involved in the National Party and its cultural and language activities. Without the support of an aristocracy of Labour or a sympathetic middle class the Dublin 'labour' movement was short of money and organisers.

Bristol had the most diverse and developed 'labour movement', Dublin the least advanced. Belfast shared qualities with both cities but can hardly be considered a truly intermediate example. As with Dublin the politics of Belfast were dominated by the issue of Unionism and Nationalism and labour was forced to develop within this context. Like Bristol a wide range of 'labour' organisations were established in Belfast, notably the Co-operative Society and the Workers' Educational Association neither of which enjoyed success in Dublin. The ILP in both Belfast and Bristol was able to establish a city-wide organisation and successfully contest local government elections from an early date. In Dublin the ILP and other bodies such as the Irish Socialist Republican Party were little more than pressure groups within the trades council, and did not establish an extensive ward organisation.

If a labour supporter from Bristol had gone to Belfast in 1914 he or she would have found the city somewhat strange, notably the idea of 'Unionist Labour' which was so dominant. However, there would also have been many familiar groups and organisations reminiscent of home. Conversely the same individual would have found in Dublin a very different political structure and labour movement which was comparatively weak and poorly organised. Clearly Ireland was a source of irritation and worry to contemporary British 'labour' leaders and organisations.

It is very difficult to estimate the prospects of the whole movement in Ireland. It does seem clear that the conditions, except for a slight exception in Belfast, differ altogether from those in England; so that the analogy of English experience is not particularly helpful. Even in Belfast, which is in some respects similar to the north of England and in others to Glasgow, public opinion on social questions in general is in much the same state as it was in England 40 or 50 years ago. In the ordinary English sense there is hardly any labour movement in Ireland. There is a certain amount of trade union activity and a revolutionary labour section more or less closely connected with the Sinn Fein body. Even there, however, strongly political or national sentiments play as vigorous a part as those more distinctive of working class movements.[76]

British trade unionists and labour politicians, like Irish nationalists, seriously underestimated the 'Britishness' of Belfast working-class culture, assuming that Dublin was typical of Ireland as a whole.

5 Belfast's Shipyard Workers: a Study in Organised Labour

How did the growth of trade unionism affect industrial relations within specific industries? I have selected as my basic case study the workers employed in the Belfast shipyards. This group were certainly highly unionised, containing a high proportion of skilled workers, and are often presented as an 'aristocracy of labour'. Were all those employed in the shipyards members of the privileged elite or were there divisions within the labour force? What problems faced the unions in 'organising' these workers? Were industrial relations within the industry improved or harmed by the unionisation of the labour force? My intention is to use this group as a sample against which, in a later chapter I will compare other groups within the labour force.

As a result of the industry's success the labour force within the shipyards of Belfast increased rapidly, and in common with the rest of the industry there was increased dependency upon skilled labour. Although the precise proportions varied, Pollard and Robertson suggest that in the years before the First World War, 60–65 per cent of the labour force in the industry was 'skilled', 12–15 per cent 'unskilled', and much of the remainder apprentices.[1] Within the firm of Harland & Wolff the exact composition of the work force varied, but unskilled labour formed a higher proportion of the labour force than Pollard and Robertson suggest in the years after the First World War, skilled labour forming 49 and 59 per cent of the workforce and unskilled 34 to 45 per cent.[2] This could represent a degree of 'dilution' during the war years, or large scale employment of 'Labourers' in the foundries and engine works. These 'specialist' labourers could be considered as semi-skilled but were counted as unskilled by the firm.[3]

As a result of this concentration of skilled labour, by 1888 thirty-six per cent of the labour force in British shipyards was unionised increasing to 60 per cent by 1901. Comparable figures for transport workers were five and twelve per cent.[4] Within the labour force as a whole union density was only 10.4 per cent in 1892 and 12.6 in 1901.[5] This did not, however, signify unity; between 1892 and 1896 there were seven unions of riggers and 17 of sailmakers, most of them confined to one port. In addition there were 130 'general' shipbuilding unions plus 'amphibians' such as carpenters, joiners and plumbers. Although there was consolidation in later years, fragmentation remained a serious problem. Between 1906 and 1910 there were still 18 general ship-building unions and 5 societies of sailmakers and riggers.[6]

Long established shipyard trades, such as shipwrights, found their skills redundant and their status and position further threatened by competition from other workers such as Boilermakers or Joiners.[7] The shipwrights, who had refused initially to work in iron, were marginalised. Whereas in 1850 over 90 per cent of new tonnage was built in wood, by 1880 this had fallen to only 4 per cent.[8] Within a generation these workers who had been the primary trade within the shipbuilding industry, declined to mere supporters of iron workers. Shipwrights drew the lines of hulls in the mould lofts, performed the small amount of heavy timber work required on iron or steel vessels and supervised launching.[9]

Friction between shipwrights and carpenters was a major problem in the Belfast yards, as John McIlwaine told the Royal Commission on Labour.[10] Demarcation disputes between the two trades led to strikes in Belfast in 1890, 1891, 1911 and 1913 which in each case resulted in the joiners gaining the work.[11] Many other traditional shipbuilding crafts were increasingly redundant as a result of changes in the type of ships being built. Makers of masts, sails and blocks were all vital skilled workers when ships were propelled by sail, but superfluous in the era of the steam engine. In a changing world old crafts had to adapt, and as Hirsch points out in the case of the sailmakers who quickly adopted new methods and products sometimes with great success.[12]

However, if the decline of the old trades presented problems so, too, did the emergence of new skills and trades. As ships became more sophisticated employers had to employ increasing numbers of highly skilled specialists. The long term costs to the employers were inflexibility in allocation of work, disruptive demarcation disputes and restrictions on their freedom to deploy labour across craft boundaries or introduce new methods.[13] On the other hand Pollard and Robertson argue that in fact the industry itself had to create new groups of skilled workers such as shell riveters as no comparable trades existed elsewhere. These new trades organised into powerful unions to protect their 'traditional' skilled work from unskilled labour or new methods.[14] New technology, such as acetylene welding created new demarcation disputes involving trades such as blacksmiths and plumbers.

Flange connections which have been carried out by engine black-smiths for years is now being done in the plumbers' shop by the process of acetylene welding. Where this machine is used on work previously done by members of our society it is to be carried on by our members, as the acetylene welding machine does not belong to any one trade.[15]

During these years a major concern of unions was to prevent the erosion of working conditions by changing employment practices. The Operative Plumbers represented an important group of 'amphibious' craftsmen, who, while involved in the shipbuilding industry, found greater employment in the construction sector. However, the less seasonal work in the shipyards was more attractive to many plumbers. By 1892 the union's executive was facing internal pressure, notably from the Birkenhead branch which pointed out that plumbing work was being done by gas-fitters in the yard of Laird Brothers. The Union replied that if plumbers took work in the yard not only would they have to work for less than union rates but they would also be scheduled as gas-fitters and lose their union protection.[16]

The Plumbers black-listed the firm of Harland & Wolff during these years. Although the reason was not recorded, it was in all probability the question of wage rates. The dispute throws an interesting light on contemporary attitudes among a local group of skilled workers. They appeared to be more concerned that the 'blacking' of the yard had been broken than that two members had been fraudulently claiming sick pay from the branch.[17] The dispute continued for some time and there are a number of references to members being fined for working in the yard or attending meetings to admit their fault and 'make their peace' with the union.[18] Finally, in October 1891, the General Secretary used his influence to start negotiations. These were successful, and at the end of the month the branch agreed to pay the delegates' expenses of £5.2s.0d. and admit new members from Queens Island.[19] That the problem at the yard concerned pay appears to be confirmed by the minutes of 13 November 1891, when one of the new members there raised the question of being paid under the union's rate.[20]

Such 'Amphibians' were always to present problems when it came to trade unity within the shipyards. The complexity of their relationships with other unions in the industry is well illustrated by the Amalgamated Society of Carpenters and Joiners. Although this trade formed up to 20 per cent of the skilled labour force of Harland & Wolff the building and furnishing trades employed more joiners.[21] Their relationship with the Engineering and Shipbuilding Trades Federation was influenced by the need to satisfy the demands of members in different industries. Although a founder member of the Federation in 1891, the ASC&J withdrew in 1904 on the grounds that greater solidarity in industrial disputes was not being achieved. They reaffiliated in 1915 when they found that exclusion from the joint negotiations was adversely affecting their members in the yards. In 1923 the question of membership was again raised by shipyard joiners because, amongst other reasons, the union's prohibition on piecework was creating problems over wages. By this time relations with other Federation members were not good as a result of the 1920–1 strike in which the joiners had been critical of other trades for their 'unhelpful attitude'. In 1924 the union voted by 18 490 votes to 1686 to disaffiliate again.[22]

Some unions made efforts to adapt to new working conditions only to be frustrated by developments within the labour movement. The General Union of Tin Plate Workers represented, amongst others, those involved in light metal work and fabrication in the shipbuilding industry. By the late 1890s the Boilermakers had begun admitting sheet iron workers, ultimately planning to claim all such work in shipyards. The 1898 Delegate Meeting passed a resolution to try and prevent encroachment by the more powerful body, by agreeing only to work plate less than one-eighth of an inch.[23] However, having agreed a demarcation line with the Boilermakers, a group of their members in Glasgow seceded and formed a rival union in 1900. Although consisting of only sixty-eight members, the Sheet Iron and Light Platers Society, began an aggressive policy of membership poaching in the shipyards.[24] Relations rapidly deteriorated until a crisis on the Tyne forced the local committee of the General Federation of Engineering and Shipbuilding Trades to hold a public inquiry into the dispute. The Light Platers were criticised for 'being wanting in the spirit of fair play and recognised trade union principles'.[25] Despite this rebuke, the Light Platers continued their activities and the two unions were to remain bitter rivals for years to come. In 1919, by which time they had 1428 members in the shipyards, the light platers merged with the Boilermakers Society. In 1921 they split away again and remained an independent union until 1950 when they finally amalgamated with the Sheet Metal Workers.

Not all unions were to indulge in such internecine conflict: a good example of such a local co-operation can be found in Harland & Wolff. In July 1914 the firm arrived at an agreement with the unions for settlement of demarcation disputes. One of the eighteen bodies that signed was the Amalgamated and General Union Society of Carpenters.[26] This is something of a mystery as a union with this name never existed. There appears to have been a joint committee within the firm representing the General Union of Carpenters and Joiners and the Amalgamated Society of Carpenters and Joiners. Both bodies were independent; indeed the General Union rejected amalgamation with the newer, and larger, body in 1902, 1904 and 1907. The two societies did not combine until 1921 when they formed the Amalgamated Society of Woodworkers.[27] The committee was clearly more than a temporary negotiating body, as they had written to Harland & Wolff in April 1911, concerning the employment of non-union members.[28] Whatever the ill feeling at national level, the carpenters at Harland & Wolff were capable of working together to further their interests.

Within a shipyard the question of demarcation was a critical one. Although these disputes may seem trivial and wasteful, they were serious confrontations in which unions sought to protect the employment of their members in a changing industry. The agreements that resolved such disputes may appear over-precise and rather ludicrous but they sought to safeguard the employment of craftsmen.

> *1. Netting Eyes (Jackstay Eyes)* These are lined and marked off in all cases by Shipwrights, and fastened by them when they are on wood, but when they come on iron, the hole-borer drills the hole; if tapped, the Caulker taps and finishes fitting; if riveted, the riveter finishes fixing, but if plain hole, the shipwright finishes fixing.[29]

The problem of competing unions was to bedevil labour organisation throughout this period. The Boilermakers and Iron and Steel Ship Builders Society was perhaps the most powerful union in the industry and was viewed with open hostility by some employers, the Chairman of the Shipbuilding Employers Federation in 1907 going as far as to state that no alteration in working practices could be made without their consent.[30] The Amalgamated Society of Engineers was also of great importance particularly in the engine and machine shops where the fitters and turners who formed 90 per cent of their membership were concentrated.[31] However, despite the size and power of these bodies, smaller groups were often in a position of local dominance. Jeffreys, in his history of the ASE, dismissed the other specialist unions within engineering as 'pygmies'. However, he had to accept that 'Their attraction for many engineers came from their compactness and specialisation on the problems of particular trades'.[32] By 1914 a smith in

Harland & Wolff could belong to any of four rival trade unions depending on the exact nature of his work or his personal choice. A foundry or light plate worker in the same yard could belong to any of three bodies, and wood workers could belong to any of no less than five competing bodies.[33]

The unskilled shipyard workers were a very diverse group. In March 1911 Lord Pirrie was informed by the Belfast office that Workman Clark planned 'If we have no objection' to give their shipyard labourers an increase of 1/- or 6d. a week. The reply was scribbled on the bottom of the original memo: 'If Messrs Workman Clark and Co. grant an advance of 6d. per week I am disposed to advocate our doing the same rather than that there should be any feeling of discontent on the part of our men.'[34]

In the pay office Samuel Bartlett calculated that a large number of unskilled workers would benefit from such an increase.[35]

We have at the present time, 589 Labourers, watchmen, sweepers and storemen, leading rate 18/6 per week. If they got an advance the following would also be looking for the same.

Shipyard	*Engine Works*
363 Scrapers	636 Boilermakers' helpers
202 Fitters' assts	739 Fitters' assts
238 Plumbers' assts	76 Coppersmiths' assts
206 Wood labourers	116 Labourers
15 Carters' assts	29 Wood labourers
4 Sailmakers' assts	
111 Elect Dept labours	
1139	1596

The most important union among unskilled shipyard workers was the National Amalgamated Union of Labour (NAUL) formed on Tyneside in 1889 to protect platers' helpers directly employed by skilled craftsmen of the Boilermakers Society.[36] In Belfast there were similar problems. In March 1889 there was a strike by over 200 platers' helpers and rivet heaters in the shipyards, against, it was noted, the platers rather than the employers.[37] There were to be a number of similar disputes where helpers or assistants struck against the craftsman who acted as their gang leaders.[38] In view of such antagonism it is perhaps not surprising the NAUL found the Belfast yards a fruitful recruiting ground.

In addition to such direct opposition there were other problems involved in organising unskilled workers at this time.[39] Relations between skilled and unskilled labour, even when working side by side, were shaped by ideas of status. In an unstable employment situation the unskilled worker could not afford to offend the skilled by displaying union activity. This did not represent a contradiction as far as skilled labour were concerned, because to them unions were about protection of status, and most would have felt the unskilled had no status to protect. The result was frequent ill feeling and resentment.

> There was no association. The labourers herded together went off together. But an odd one would have curried favour with a foreman but much more likely to be currying favour with the skilled employee than his fellow employee. He was anxious to be on good terms with him because his job was more secure. He felt that if he could be on good terms with the craftsman then his value to the craftsman was seen and if a choice had to be made he was likely to be retained in preference to the fellow who was probably the better man but harder to work with.[40]

Despite these problems the union was able to establish itself within the yard, and management had to treat the NAUL with respect. In October 1911 the union wrote to Harland & Wolff enclosing a copy of a resolution passed by their members in the foundry Department demanding the removal of non-union labour.[41] The reply of the company to this uncompromising demand for the imposition of a closed shop was surprisingly conciliatory.

> As you are aware, the firm have always fully recognised the various trade and labour unions, and have endeavoured to work amicably with them, and we are somewhat surprised that your members should take this step. We hope, however, that on further consideration they will see some other way out of the difficulty.[42]

The relationship was not entirely negative; co-operation seems to have been considerable. In June 1913 the company wrote to the NAUL requesting help with the problem of bad timekeeping.

> We regret having to complain of the bad timekeeping of the platers helpers and angle iron smiths helpers. From one fourth to one third of the platers helpers are absent every morning and quite a number

absent every day. The angle smith's helpers are even worse. We should be glad if you can do anything to effect an improvement in their timekeeping.[43]

The union's reply, while expressing relief that members of another union had a worse record than theirs, enclosed a copy of a notice sent to every plater's helper.

For some time past the firm has strongly complained about bad time keeping on the part of a large section of our helper members. So bad has this become lately that they have decided on taking drastic action to deal with this evil unless there is a marked change in the immediate future. No union can defend bad time keeping and we therefore hope this warning will have the desired effect.[44]

Although the unskilled labourers in the shipyards were the best paid workers of their class in the city, their conditions and security bore no comparison with the skilled workers. In common with all non-craft labour the shipyard labourers shared a serious disadvantage in terms of negotiation with their employers.

It might be expected that the white collar workers in the shipyards would have followed the example of skilled workers in unionising to safeguard their status. However, in the years before the First World War there was very limited progress. The first national body in this sector was The National Union of Clerks (NUC) founded in 1890 and affiliating to the TUC in 1903. The union made its first systematic effort to organise engineering office staff in 1913, meeting with only limited success.[45] Routh suggests that the different relationship between worker and employer and their sense of separation from manual workers makes white-collar staff difficult to unionise.[46] By 1910 when union density was approx 22.5 per cent of the employed labour force, the figure for white collar workers was only 10 per cent.[47] In 1914 the total national membership of the National Union of Clerks, the largest clerical union, was 12 680.[48] Significantly from the point of view of organisation, the shipbuilding employers refused to recognise white collar trade unions until the 1960s.

In the case of Harland & Wolff, however, there appear to have been earlier contacts with clerical trade unions. By late 1918 the union was discussing war bonus for timekeeping staff in Harland and Wolff.[49] In 1920 the union appointed a full time organiser in Belfast 'where there was a substantial membership in the ship building industry'.[50] Of 44 interviews granted to the unions in January–October 1921 one was

A Tale of Three Cities

with the Clerks Union.[51] It is not clear what proportion of the 'office' staff joined the union but if the timekeepers, pay office staff, drawing office and foremen are included the 'office' at Harland & Wolff represented almost 9 per cent of the labour force.[52]

If the clerical staff were difficult to organise what about supervisory staff? This group was of great importance within the shipbuilding industry and enjoyed considerable status. Their conditions of employment were superior to other shipyard workers. A study of the salary books of William Denny & Bros, by Pollard and Robertson illustrates the highly privileged position of these workers.[53] The seventy-five time keepers employed by the Harland & Wolff in 1914 earned between 22s. 6d. and 55s., with most earning over 30s.[54] Many of the supervisory staff had worked their way up from the shop floor and had invaluable experience, while the drawing office staff were a highly trained body of specialists. The importance of these workers is reflected in their favourable pay and conditions. It is notable that even female tracers in the drawing office enjoyed reasonable earnings and comparative security although not perhaps equal to those of male colleagues.[55]

None of these workers, like the clerical workers, formed trade bodies until comparatively late in the period. The Draughtsmen and Allied Technicians Association was formed in 1913 and affiliated to the TUC in 1918, being recognised by the Shipbuilders Employers Federation in 1941.[56] There was a branch in Belfast by late 1916, and by August 1917 it was strong enough to merit two, rather than a single, representative at the delegate meeting.[57] The foremen and other supervisory staff were not to unionise until 1917 when bodies such as the Amalgamated Managers and Foremen's Society, the National Foremen's Association and the Association of Supervisory Staffs, Executives and Technicians were established.[58] The National Foremen's Association was the main body in the shipbuilding industry and affiliated to the TUC in 1920, but it was never recognised by the Shipbuilding Employers Federation. A foremen's union seems to have existed in Harland & Wolff in the form of the Foreman's Mutual Aid and Social Society before this date, although a letter to the management during the 1919 strike would indicate it was not a very militant body.

I am instructed by a number of foremen and assistants in your employ to inform you that they were turned by pickets on the Queen's Road this morning and informed that this was the only warning they would receive and if they persisted on going, it would be at their own risk. Hoping this will be a satisfactory explanation of our absence from work.[59]

Generally speaking, the white-collar employees within the shipyards were slow to unionise and felt little in common with the manual labour force. This was due to their perception of themselves as being superior to other workers, intimidation from the employers, and their comparatively generous pay and conditions. As a group they were highly valued as their special training or extensive experience made them difficult to replace. In these circumstances there was little motivation for these groups to organise until their status was threatened by the general improvements occurring during the war years.

INDUSTRIAL RELATIONS WITHIN HARLAND & WOLFF 1880–1914

One of the major claims made by Hume and Moss in *Shipbuilders to the World* concerns industrial relations within the firm of Harland and Wolff in the two decades before the First World War.

So as to maximise production, Pirrie resolved to improve the machinery for dealing with demarcation disputes. The Company's industrial relations had been remarkably good since the 1895 strike. There had only been a handful of trivial disputes since the formation of the committee of managing directors in 1907. Pirrie had gone out of his way to win the confidence of the representatives of the numerous trades employed at Queen's Island and at the new works on the mainland. He insisted that, wherever possible, demarcation disputes should be settled amicably between the unions involved, with the management acting as referee. He made a rule that his managers, and more recently his managing directors, should always be prepared to negotiate with union delegates.[60]

This certainly makes the firm sound very advanced and liberal when compared with certain other companies in the shipbuilding industry. However, a couple of points undermine this cosy picture of paternalistic harmony. Firstly, this mainly applied, before the First World War, to those unions representing skilled labour. Harland & Wolff did not include unions representing unskilled workers in the Memorandum of Agreement of July 1914.[61] The main object of this agreement was settling demarcation disputes between tradesmen, a problem not found among the unskilled although they frequently suffered as a consequence.

Moss and Hume mention only two serious labour disruptions prior to 1895: in 1884 on the question of wage reductions, and in 1886 due to the political issue of Home Rule.[62] This appears a very creditable record, but is it complete? There was certainly a one-month stoppage which affected the shipyards in 1887 in protest at the introduction of fortnightly payment of wages among Engineers and Boilermakers.[63] The history of the Boilermakers Society mentions a dispute in Belfast involving over 5000 workers in 1888, which is confirmed by the Board of Trade report on strikes and lockouts.[64] The Board of Trade's Annual Reports of Strikes and Lockouts record at least seventeen industrial disputes which affected the Belfast shipbuilding industry between 1888 and 1894 although not all of these would have affected Harland & Wolff.[65] Further in 1892, although there is no reference to a major shipbuilding strike in the Board of Trade Reports, the factory inspector reported 'The large shipbuilding yards, with the exception of a three months strike, have been very busy.'[66] It would appear Moss and Hume's statement that the dispute of 1895 '.. *seems to have been the first major industrial dispute in the firm's history*' is questionable.[67]

The 1895 dispute itself suggests that relations were not as harmonious as the official history of Harland & Wolff implies. This was a carefully planned attempt by the employers in both Belfast and on the Clyde to introduce joint bargaining procedures covering both areas.[68] When the strike began in Belfast the Scottish employers began to lay off their workers at a rate of 25 per cent a week.[69] Although Moss and Hume suggest that the strike collapsed in the face of determined management action, the union's version suggests that the Belfast workers were not very conciliatory. Although the workers on the Clyde voted to return to work those in Belfast wanted to continue the strike. In the end they were forced to return by their union's executive cutting off strike pay, an action greatly resented by the Belfast members.[70] Such bitterness and determination would not indicate a high degree of harmony existed between the Belfast shipbuilders and their labour force.

In fact there were a large number of disputes affecting the engineering and shipbuilding sectors. An example of this would be the Patternmakers, a small, but important union representing highly skilled craftsmen. Their history shows that the union was in dispute, usually over pay rates, on no fewer that eighteen occasions between 1881 and 1916.[71] Not all of these ended in strike action but some, notably in 1887, 1892 and 1907, were bitter conflicts often involving confrontation with the Society of Engineers as well as the Employers. Some of the disputes which occurred after 1907 were hardly 'trivial', as despite only details of 'major' disputes being reported after 1901, there were still eight worthy of mention.[72]

But while Hume and Moss often present an over-optimistic view of labour relations, it would be equally inaccurate to go to the other extreme. Due to local shortages of skilled labour and the difficulty of recruiting and retaining these workers, local employers were inclined to be paternalistic. The Lord Mayor of Belfast was no doubt exaggerating slightly when in 1898 he told the TUC that the city was '*an elysium for working men*'. However it has generally been accepted that Belfast was a good place for organised labour.[73] Belfast trade unionists were able to tell the Royal Commission on Labour in 1893 that, although they had a number of complaints, disputes were rare and relations good.[74] However, if conditions were good for the unionised skilled labour force whose leaders gave evidence to the Royal Commission, what about the great mass of unskilled and women workers? Perhaps it is necessary to recognise that there existed within the city of Belfast a number of highly distinctive and frequently hostile 'Working Classes'.

CONCLUSION

By 1914 the average shipyard employed a vast range of skills and no fewer than 90 trades were to be found within the industry.[75] Belfast did not have a large reservoir of skilled labour and thus the expansion of the shipbuilding sector was dependent upon attracting and retaining craftsmen from Scotland and England. As a consequence the unions and their shopfloor representatives acquired a great deal of power within some sectors of the labour force, as Robert McElborough found when he visited the yard of Harland & Wolff to fit a gas meter. After watching a shop-steward of the AEU dictate to his manager that only a fitter could connect the meter he noted 'It shows the power of the worker when organised'.[76] It must however, be recognised that not all the workers or unions within the shipyards enjoyed such power.

The shipyards could not afford prolonged and costly disputes, not least because of the heavy penalty clauses which were a feature of contracts. As Moss and Hume state, the underlying reason for good industrial relations within Harland & Wolff was the desire to maximise production.[77] Although not motivated by high idealism, this pragmatic acceptance of the need for co-operation is an early feature of industrial relations within Harland & Wolff. A vital component of the labour force were skilled and hard-to-replace workers; thus wage rates and conditions of employment had to be good compared to other sectors. Even the labourers in the shipyards enjoyed some of the highest rates paid to unskilled workers in the city. In many ways the labour force in Belfast's shipyards, and notably Harland and Wolff, was not typical of the city's workforce. This large group of privileged, unionised workers was to influence profoundly the development of the labour movement in Belfast. Were the employer–labour relations in the yard exceptional, or did the city of Belfast enjoy an unusual degree of industrial harmony? Were the shipyard workers an isolated elite within the labour force or were other groups in a comparable position?

6 Industrial Relations

Relations between Harland & Wolff and the trade unions that represented their labour force were generally good. But how typical was this? How far did economic conditions in each city shape employer–labour relations? Was Harland & Wolff unique or can they be fitted into a wider pattern of industrial relations in these years? To try and assess these factors it is necessary to look an industrial relations in other sectors of Belfast's economy and compare these with the other cities in this study. Employers throughout Britain faced with the emergence of organised labour did not always seek co-operation. Some simply ignored the unions in the hope that they would go away, others drove them out using lockouts and free labour.

In the aftermath of the Dublin lockout of 1913–14 a Government Commission investigated the causes of the dispute. During the hearings the employers produced reports of a speech by Jim Larkin which they claimed was irresponsible and provocative.

> He wanted to draw their attention to the fact that they had in their midst an organised clique of exploiters and robbers, thieves by Act of Parliament. William Martin Murphy was a renegade politician and a renegade to his church, of which he was a standing disgrace... If William Martin Murphy got into heaven, by hook or by crook, then he wanted to go to hell. Murphy had sold his soul for gold.[1]

Such extreme language was not unique to Ireland, the most famous example being Ben Tillett's prayer during the London Dock Strike of 1912, 'O God, strike Lord Devonport dead'.[2] Such outbursts are often presented as typical of industrial relations in this era.

Some contemporaries saw industrial relations as conflict between 'Grasping Capital' who 'knows no more what is its own interest than what is due to its working partners' and 'Grudging Labour' who 'attempt to do as little as they can in the time'.[3] Frank Shepherd, the Bristol labour leader, was to complain that those who simply blamed industrial unrest on 'agitators' showed 'an ignorance of the problem so dense as to make one feel impatient'.[4] Others, such as the Frenchman de Rousiers, present the employers as suffering as a result of the unreasonable behaviour of their workers.[5] Conversely some saw the need for powerful unions to engage in the apocalyptic struggle for economic survival between capitalism and labour.

Both labour and capital have long ceased to be local in their interests; they are national and international in their outlook. All great businesses are centralised in funds and management, and none but a union that has centralised funds, that is national in its scope, and international in its influence can give its members the backing they need or deal efficiently with the ramifications of modern capitalism.[6]

In such a struggle deep feelings and strong language was inevitable. To justify their positions both sides were willing to state their cases in a manner that at times lacked subtlety.

The life blood of women, that should be given to the race, is being stitched into our ready-made clothes; is washed and ironed into our linen; wrought into the laces and embroideries, the feathers and flowers, the sham furs with which we other women be-deck ourselves.[7]

The efforts that are being put forward by the so-called 'Labour Party' in the House of Commons, to gain special favours for the 2,000,000 Trade Union workers, by oppressing the 12,000,000 Free Labour and Independent wage earners of the country, and to perpetuate industrial war and intimidation on the old fallacious lines.[8]

However, despite these apparently irreconcilable positions, as the situation in Harland & Wolff demonstrates, options were not as limited as these authors would suggest.

Under existing circumstances, in view of the hostile position assumed by many organisations of labour, it frequently becomes a serious question to employers what attitude to adopt towards those organisations. Three courses are open to them (1) to ignore their existence as far as possible, but treat them courteously when approached by them; (2) to encourage their men to organise, and meet them on the footing they desire; (3) to refuse to employ union labour, or deal with any organisation whatsoever.[9]

The years 1889–90 saw huge increases in union membership and industrial unrest on an unprecedented scale in Bristol.[10] The 1890 Annual Report of the Bristol Chamber of Commerce commented upon these events.

It has been felt that in the past this matter has been regarded too much as one between masters and men only, too much as though the settlement of labour disputes was properly left to the disputants;

and that the existence of a third and, in many cases, a predomin-
ant interest was simply ignored, that interest is the interest of the
public.[11]

Ignoring the unions and hoping that they would go away, was never
really practical. The most heavily unionised elements in the labour
force were those skilled workers upon which many industries were totally dependent. In some cases a double standard was employed.

It (the Shipping Federation) refused to treat with Mr Havelock
Wilson or to have anything to do with the sailor's union, although it
was prepared to talk to 'respectable unionists' like the Boilermakers
Society.[12]

It was recognised by many observers that the relationship between
labour and capital was symbiotic.

That the great disaster to all interests involved in strikes may be
averted by timely concessions made by employers whenever trade
conditions will admit of them, and by the recognition on the part of
the workers that steady and continuous employment at moderate
wages in a place where the cost of living is exceptionally low is of far
more substantial benefit to them than a high scale of pay with the
danger of frequent periods of difficulty in finding work.[13]

In Belfast, and to a degree Bristol, this inclination towards moderation
was reinforced by a shortage of skilled labour which made good industrial relations a necessity. However in Dublin where there was a
surplus even of skilled labour, a less paternalistic relationship developed. Of seventy-three strikes reported by the Board of Trade in Dublin, between 1889 and 1899 twenty-three (36.5 per cent) were settled by
the replacement of the strikers by other workers. In Belfast this tactic
was used (often replacing only some of the strikers) in 17.8 per cent of
disputes compared to only 12 per cent in Bristol.[14]

The inter-dependence of employer and worker was not always the
basis of industrial relations. The atmosphere of mutual antagonism and
distrust could prove frustrating for those seeking industrial harmony.

If one can say without offence, class hatred has been helped by the
stupidity of the majority of employers, ... labour leaders, who have
preached war and discontent, and theoretical changes, when the
advocacy of unity, better understanding, better chances for their
flock would have gained more for themselves and for others than
anything they have been able to obtain.[15]

Although some employers were conscious of the need for co-operation and adopted a paternalistic approach, others were aggressively exploitative. Harland & Wolff may have needed to act with a degree of moderation towards their skilled shipyard workers, but the Dublin shop owner had less reason to do so.

> I have witnessed myself upon Saturday nights up to the hour of midnight, and past 12 o'clock, these young men standing outside the doors of these establishments and inviting in customers, absolutely with the rain falling on their bare heads.[16]

The Dublin sackmaking firm of Keogh's employed female workers, on an average wage of 6s. a week, and the proprietors felt they should show gratitude for this rather than seek an increase.[17] As always in Dublin the problem was one of surplus labour, which meant there was little pressure to improve either wages or conditions. A further example of this pattern is the Dublin Laundry Company, a significant employer of unskilled labour, whose wage structure changed little between 1888 and 1913.[18]

Dublin may have had exceptional problems but in all three cities the unskilled, and particularly women, were subject to harsh conditions. In 1905 the Factory Inspector was critical of the methods used in the Bristol tailoring trade for paying outworkers, claiming it left the worker 'wholly at the mercy of the master'.[19] The previous year there were details of a prosecution taken against a Kingswood boot-making firm after they had deducted 4s. 9d. from a woman's wages of 14s. 6d. The magistrates held that such stoppages were fair and dismissed the case.[20] Even in the prosperous printing and packaging industry female workers were poorly paid averaging, for a 53.5 hour week, 11s. a week on time and 12s. 1d. on piece rates.[21] In Belfast the workers in the making up trades were perhaps the most exploited element of the labour force. A Report on this sector carried out by Margaret Erwin for the Scottish Council of Women's Trades was to cause embarrassment even to its supporters by its blunt denunciation of conditions.[22] Amongst unskilled male workers wages were higher, but conditions were often equally poor.

> There didn't seem to be any basis on which you could improve your wages. There was no approach whatsoever such as we have today by means of a trade union. If you didn't like the job there were two things you could do – you could remain on it and complain or you could leave and if you left you had finished your work in that district because nobody else would take you on.[23]

Compromise and moderation in industrial relations found supporters amongst both workers and employers. In April 1891 J.H. Howell
proposed the toast 'Capital and Labour' to the Bristol Chamber of
Commerce, in which he suggested that antagonism had no place in
industrial relations.[24] In reply the Chairman of the Arbitration Board
was happy to continue the theme of unity and interdependence.

> In Bristol there was a good feeling existing between employers and
> employed and a sincere desire on the part of many on both sides to
> meet these difficulties whenever they arose in a conciliatory and
> satisfactory spirit. Many strikes began with ignorance, and were
> carried on with prejudice and bitterness, light was wanted on both
> sides.[25]

The annual reports of the Belfast Chamber of Commerce contain
many examples of similar sentiments.[26] In February 1925 J.M. An-
drews, the Minister of Labour in the first Northern Ireland government, explained that mutual understanding between capital and
labour was vital to the economic well-being of the new 'country'.[27]

Was this mere rhetoric? Idealism can be overshadowed by cynicism
at times, but it would be wrong to assume that there was not a desire
for understanding. However, such hopes did not blind trade unionists
to the need to be ready to deal with less reasonable employers.

> The old policy of the trade unions was to build up strong reserves; to
> refrain from exasperating the public and the employers by never-
> ceasing threats of strikes; to exhaust every possible means of con-
> ciliation before calling out the men, and then not to do so unless
> there was a reasonable chance of victory. By this policy the unions
> entered upon the strike with the most useful of all assets – namely, a
> public sympathy which had been won over by the willingness of the
> men to adopt every possible means to avert a strike.[28]

The reasons for adopting such policies were as varied as the employers
themselves. Some non-conformist employers, notably Quakers, sought
to improve conditions for their employees out of a sense of social and
Christian responsibility.[29] In Bristol the non-conformist *Bristol
Christian Leader* published an article on the Christian duty of employers not to oppress workers for profit.[30] In Belfast the General
Assembly of the Presbyterian Church in June 1908 passed a resolution
condemning the unlawful employment of children.[31] The Papal en-
cyclical *Rerum Novarum*, often seen as a response to the rise of socialism, also emphasised the duty of the employer towards the worker.[32]

In other cases it was recognised that a happy and contented worker was more productive and less likely to strike.

> There will always remain in prosperous concerns a margin wholly controlled by the management, with which it can never be forced to part, but which it ablest representatives can be induced to share with the workers, not as philanthropy, but as a business investment.[33]

B. Meakin, who wrote *Model Factories and Villages* to try and convince employers of the advantages of such paternalism, used Fry's as one of his examples of good employment practice. He recorded that facilities included a staff restaurant and recreation rooms and that by 1905 up to two thousand attended the morning religious services which were led by one of the Fry family.[34] Another large Bristol employer, the tobacco firm of W.D. & H.O. Wills, were paternalistic in their attitudes. From 1880 to 1890 the firm organised an annual staff outing for ever increasing numbers.[35] After that the workforce had expanded to such an extent that a week's holiday with pay was substituted.[36] The firm also granted pensions to long serving members of staff and factory workers from an early date.[37] All staff also received an annual bonus based on the company's profits.[38] As early as 1889 the Bristol printing and packaging firm of Robinson's allowed its staff a week's holiday with pay.[39] In 1912 this firm instigated a profit sharing scheme for workers earning under £3 p.w. which it was hoped would give each worker the equivalent of two weeks' wages a year.[40]

In Dublin Meakin observed that both Guinness's brewery and Jacob's biscuit factory were good employers, although the latter were not paying high wages.[41] In Belfast Davidson & Co. (Sirocco) was considered a 'model' employer by Meakin, who could not know that within a couple of years, they were to crush an attempt by their labour force to unionise.[42] However, in 1905 conditions at Sirocco compared very favourably with other employers in the city.

> Messrs Davidson and Co., Makers of the Sirocco Tea drying apparatus, have established a comfortable dining-room for their 250 to 300 employees, where each customer has a numbered square at table, on which he finds at meal times the dishes ordered beforehand.[43]

There was a powerful element of paternalism even in the case of an allegedly harsh employer such as Richard Nance of the Belfast Tram Company.

There were points in Nance's favour, you were rewarded at Christmas with 2 sovereigns if your receipts were correct for 12 months, I received this on a number of Xmas and another one was a sovereign to the driver who was free from any accident during the year and he also rewarded any driver who saved a life or averted an accident.[44]

Employers such as Fry, Guinness and Jacob's were very much the exception; other commentators pointed out that conditions were less harmonious in most firms.

The socialist, who trumpets the native equality of all men, finds the masters in the wrong because they hold the capital in grasping hands; the individualist, who claims that society has its foundations in competition and the triumph of the mighty, finds the proletariat in the wrong, presumably because those to who he once cried *vae victis!* are now threatening him with the terror of united numbers. Between these extremes certain authorities have the wit to see that the fault lies not primarily with the masters, many perhaps most, of whom are merciful and just, nor yet with the employees, who, we must, after reading this book and notwithstanding their harsh judgements of their masters, admit are denied many of their rights as men. Such authorities, looking at the question with less prejudice, see that what is wrong is the system itself; that if either socialist or individualist had their own way, the result would be only the further strengthening of that system which is destroying the humanity of capitalists and employees alike.[45]

Although Meakin was very impressed by the facilities offered by Davidson & Co. at the Sirocco Works the Factory Inspectorate was less happy. The problem was the firm supplied tea and butter for consumption off the premises on credit and this constituted a breach of the Truck Acts.[46] This legislation made it unlawful to pay a worker in goods rather than coin and further sought to control such practices as giving credit in company shops or selling materials to outworkers on a deduction basis. There had been a long history of trying to control such abuses, but the main legislation in 1900 were the Acts of 1887 and 1896.[47] The factory inspectorate took this responsibility very seriously and acted with great vigour on what might appear minor infringements, as in the case of a halfpenny reduction in boot-making supplies in Bristol.

This halfpenny reduction means a saving of 6d to 8d per week or 30s a year, to each of these 40 workmen. In other words, the firm had been depriving them of about £60 per year. I could enumerate more flagrant cases than this, for as much as $1\frac{1}{2}$d per lb on an article has been obtained.[48]

The Belfast linen trade was notorious for abuses of the Truck Acts among both factory and home workers. Many of the agents who supplied and received outwork were shopkeepers or publicans who expected at least part of the worker's earnings to be spent on goods.[49] In the factories there were complex and frequently unfair systems of fines and charges in addition to direct credit dealing or cash loans.[50]

In Bristol the worst abuses of Truck tended to be found in the boot industry where a complex system of charges were levied by employers many of which contravened the Act.

> The boot industry at Kingswood has also given much trouble in the administration of the Truck Act. Many factory owners charge for standing room, light, use of tools and sell materials to the men, in fact, it seems to be the usual custom for the workers to spend several shillings per week of their wages in buying materials from their employer to make into boots in the factory.[51]

The extent of the problem became clear in 1912 when the inspectors checked sixty boot factories in Bristol and Kingswood and discovered considerable abuse.[52] Due to the enforcement of these regulations the practice of boot workers in Bristol purchasing boots on credit from their employers was stopped, as was the custom of paying part of bakers' wages in bread.[53]

An important responsibility of the factory inspectors was to ensure that premises conformed to the minimum standards of safety and comfort laid down by the various Factory Acts. Regulations regarding fire escapes, for example, were improved in 1891, although the inspectors often found them difficult to enforce.

> When it is my duty to inform an occupier that the means of escape, in case of fire, were inadequate and that additional doors should be erected, I have invariably been met with the remark 'You should see the workers clear out at the meal times: I can have this place empty in two minutes: they can go through this door, and that door, in fact there are any amount of doors'. After receiving such a statement I have proceeded to examine the doors, and, in almost every case, I have found the doors referred to fastened in such a manner that in case of fire or panic they were unavailable.[54]

Belfast City Council were unsympathetic and were criticised by the local inspector for failing to use their planning consent powers to ensure safety standards in mills.[55] The provision of heating and ventilation in working spaces was another constant source of friction between inspector and factory owner.

It is difficult to understand how employers, apparently kind hearted men, can go into their workrooms and bear to see poor girls, blue with cold, striving with benumbed fingers to do their work. Even from the point of view of their own interests, it would be the best policy for employers, who want to get all they can out of their hands to make the conditions under which the work is done as favourable as possible.[56]

At the other extreme in premises where high temperatures or atmospheric pollution was a problem, forced ventilation was sometimes insisted upon by visiting inspectors.[57]

On the more general question of safety the inspectors sought to enforce a wide range of regulations which tended to make workplaces safer.

I consider that of recent years, and owing no doubt to recent legislation, the whole subject of secure fencing has attained increased importance in the eyes of occupiers. Much I am happy to recognise, is done, and readily done, for the sake of humanity; and where the higher motive may, perhaps, halt a little, a possibility of legal contingencies renders some assistance.[58]

New industrial processes which reduced the number of accidents were frequently drawn to the attention of the public by the annual reports. At times these appeared trivial, such as the introduction of the 'Penny Monster' aerated drinks bottle by the Bristol producers. Its advantage was that it did not explode in the hands of the worker filling it as often as older types.[59] Amongst Bristol's boot workers the prevalence of mercury poisoning was noted, due to the use of machinery using warmed mercury as a lubricant, rather than oil which might have stained the leather.[60] Careful monitoring of such avoidable industrial illness was part of the inspector's work, as well as checking into cases of more serious problems such as outbreaks of anthrax.[61]

As might be expected with such a huge range of responsibilities and very limited resources there were serious problems for the inspectors, as Mr Johnston of Bristol stated in the report of 1892. 'The new provisions requiring notices to and from the sanitary authorities, whilst they are useful, help to swell the office work and *pro tanto* to diminish the time available for inspection.'[62]

Their job was made no easier by the attitude of local magistrates when prosecutions were brought against persistent offenders. The Belfast inspector, Mr Snape, told of a case against a scutch mill owner who refused to install a fan to remove dust. Despite medical evidence as to the harmful effects of such dust the magistrates imposed only the minimum fine. This was however increased, at the request of the defendant, to 21s. to allow an appeal to be lodged.[63] In Bristol Mr Owner had a similar complaint following a prosecution against a jam factory which operated excessive overtime in the peak season. The firm had received warnings in 1902 and 1903 and after ignoring a further warning in 1904 the case was taken to court. The firm pleaded guilty on all charges and was fined 1s.[64] Such conditions would try the patience of anyone and Miss Martindale, the 'lady' inspector in Belfast, was never afraid to speak her mind.

> The standard of cleanliness in Ireland cannot be considered a high one, and when one finds a Medical Officer of Health refusing to require the walls and ceiling of a workshop to be limewashed (although it was admitted that no cleansing of this kind had been done for nearly seven years) and stating that the workshop in question was no dirtier than his own consulting room, it is difficult to see how improvement will be effected.[65]

It was invariably the worst cases which reached the press. What were normal relations like? In the 1900 report Mr Pendock of Bristol offered a broader view of relations between inspector and factory owner.

> In this Connection, however, it is only fair to say that nine employers out of ten will cheerfully comply with the bare suggestion of an inspector (especially when backed up by a circular in which the suggestions are outlined) without the application of any greater pressure being resorted to.
>
> In a word, H.M. Inspectors have in this respect the complete confidence of the vast majority of occupiers, and advice is commonly extended by the one and accepted by the other in a perfectly friendly and cheerful spirit.[66]

This relationship occasionally got too close and the inspectors could be seen as being in collusion with the employers rather than policing them. In May 1911 at a meeting of Bristol dockers 'A question arose asking how the employers got to know when the government inspectors were coming'.[67] Despite these doubts the Factory Inspectors were the main attempt by the state to control or improve factory conditions and their success was limited by what they could achieve with the employers' co-operation.

How did employers respond to trade unionism amongst their workers? There is no simple answer to this question, since attitudes varied considerably. Paternalism could be used as a weapon against the trade unions, as Mr Wright told the Bristol Master Printers in 1910.

> He urged upon employers the wisdom of looking after their non-union men, in regard to unemployment assistance and superannuation, for a lesser rate than the trade unions charged. They could help non-unionists in the same way as the Typographical Association did the unionists.[68]

The idea of 'looking after their non-union men' led to the formation of various 'free labour' bodies dedicated to preserving the right of the worker not to belong to a union,[69] a 'right' which many employers were only too happy to support.

The largest of the 'free labour' bodies was the National Free-Labour Association, founded in 1893 by William Collison, a renegade trade unionist.[70] By 1905 the Association was presenting itself to potential members as a form of insurance against strikes, which it claimed cost the country £3 million a year compared to £2.5 million in fires. Employers were invited to subscribe two guineas a year which would place the Association's staff of fifty at their disposal.[71] In the event of industrial action there subscribers were told they could call upon the organisation to supply workers at no additional cost beyond train fares.[72] The Association was careful to point out that while it opposed trade unionism, it also saw the employer as possessing responsibilities towards the worker.[73] Their methods were simple: in the event of industrial action workers were recruited, if possible from outside the district, and the strikers replaced.[74] The employer was then under a moral obligation to retain the workers supplied after the strike had ended.[75] Thus, for example, in April 1900 a strike among Bristol dockers was broken by men recruited in Manchester, while the 1901 tram strike was defeated following a nationwide recruitment campaign.[76] By 1909 the Association was claiming half a million workers on its books and to have 'defeated' 592 strikes.[77]

The most infamous exponent of 'free labour' was the Shipping Federation. This body, formed in 1890, maintained not only a system of regional officials but also a permanent force of workers and depot ships to accommodate and support them, which were employed as far afield as Antwerp and Hamburg.[78] Perhaps more than any other employers' organisation the Federation saw itself as being in open conflict with organised labour. The body's own history says it was formed 'To counter the strike weapon, and made no secret of the fact'.[79] Shipping Federation labour, or the threat of it was used to break dock strikes in all three ports between 1890 and the First World War.[80] By 1911 there was a 'Belfast Labour Bureau' with offices on Donegal and Queen's quays. Its operations were heavily subsidised by the shipowners and merchants of the city, allowing it to offer a cut-price benefit club to non-union labour.[81] However, they saw their role in industrial relations as going far beyond the provision of friendly society benefits, to the active encouragement of non-union labour.[82]

In addition to such bodies there were what can only be considered 'entrepreneurial' strike breakers. These individuals did not bother putting a moral or ideological rationale on their activities but simply offered to break strikes and unions for a cash price. During the 1892 strike among Bristol timber porters a free labour agent named Graham Hunter wrote to the employers, offering his services. He claimed to have 'tackled' eighteen strikes, including an Irish dock strike and one among Scottish railway workers, twelve of which he had 'won' and assured the employers that he could supply up to 1500 men.[83] When Hunter came to Bristol by train on November 24 the strikers were waiting for him and 'men swarmed the platforms over-ruling the railway officials and Hunter was kicked and beaten'.[84] However, Hunter and the employers continued in their plans to import labour, resulting in considerable violence and bitterness. Strikers intimidated and attacked the imported labourers at every opportunity, even checking strangers in pubs for the 'splinters and grooves' which proved they had been carrying timber.[85] The police, caught between the two sides, found their resources insufficient and requested assistance. On 12 December the Lord Mayor reported to the Home Office that of 324 policemen available 80 were permanently engaged in guarding the imported men.[86] About 200 cavalrymen arrived on the 22 December and the next day attempted to disperse a demonstration resulting in violent clashes between troops and strikers.[87]

It was not uncommon for the introduction of 'free-labour' to lead to such violence. The National Free-Labour Association's 'humble non union worker, standing alone and seeking to live by his labour' was invariably going to be a 'blackleg' to a trade unionist. There was no ground for compromise; the introduction of 'free-labour' was a challenge that even the most moderate trade unionist had to resist. Although the press, employers and 'free-labour' were quick to accuse the unions of violence and intimidation, the NFLA often deployed 'emergency men' (thugs) to protect the 'rights' of their workers. Free labour was particularly resented amongst dock workers, and its introduction by the Shipping Federation in Bristol in 1910 triggered a strike which could only be settled when they were withdrawn.[88] In 1913 the Shipping Federation requested a plot of land at Avonmouth docks to erect an office, and the recommendation of the General Traffic Manager on this matter is very informative.

> In view of the resolution of the committee on the 30th of Oct 1911, on an application from the Dockers Union to be allowed to erect an office inside the fence. That the committee did not see their way to let any portion of their land for the erection thereon of offices connected with industrial organisations, and also the probable friction which would be caused with the labour organisations, it is recommended that the application not be acceded to.[89]

As a tactic the introduction of free labour represented a gamble. Were the gains which came from breaking union power sufficient to compensate for the disruption and ill feeling such action created?

Other employers adopted the opposite view and argued that the unions were a positive, even necessary development, and that strong unions were better for everyone than weak ones.

> I think that a highly organised industry is more likely to be led by men of ability and experience than an industry which has no such organisation (applause). I think that such men will have sufficient ability to advise their fellow workmen to keep clear of those wild social theories which do more harm to themselves than to anybody else.[90]

In the same way as it is impossible to talk of a 'working class' it is too general to discuss an 'employing class' in Britain at this time. Many trade unionists, particularly among the skilled workers, would have accepted the views of Bristol's Chamber of Commerce: 'The working classes demanded, and naturally and rightly demanded, a living wage. But a living wage could not be permanently paid if the employer had not a living profit.'[91]

This desire for co-operation between employer and trade unions can be seen in the formation of local arbitration boards in the 1890s. In both Bristol and Belfast such bodies were established in hopes of avoiding mutually destructive industrial disputes. The Bristol Board was formed in 1890–1 in an atmosphere of mutual good will and optimism.

> It affords your council great pleasure to recognise here the manly intelligent, fair, though rightfully independent, way in which the labour representatives bore their part in the discussions and negotiations . . . and manifest good will on both sides the document was signed by the representatives of your council and the accredited delegates of over thirty trades societies.[92]

The Ulster Board which covered Belfast was established in 1895 with equally high hopes and mutual praise from both sides.[93] The history of the Bristol board in the following years is typical of such bodies. On its establishment it consisted of twelve members equally drawn from employers and workers, with one side holding the chair and the other supplying the vice-chair.[94] The reports of this body in the next few years presented a very positive picture of industrial relations in the area.[95] However, the Board of Trade reports show that between January 1892 and December 1894 there were no fewer than 35 strikes and lockouts in the Bristol area.[96] These strikes included at least six where over 7000 man-days were lost. Why, despite the creation of the Arbitration Board, is it possible for Atkinson to describe 1892 and 1893 as 'among the most troubled in the history of industrial relations in Bristol'?[97] The reality of industrial relations in the city clearly had little to do with the idealism of those who established the Conciliation Board.

There were serious limitations on the Board's activities. According to the rules the Board could only intervene if both the chair and vice-chair agreed it should. Even then action could only be taken if a quorate meeting of the full board agreed. As the quorum was seven it was possible for either side to block action by simply refusing to attend.[98] The official history of the National Union of Boot and Shoe Operatives, noted that the Arbitration Board in fact made industrial relations more bitter.[99] Short-sighted behaviour on the part of the employers, who sought to evade the Board's decisions, led many workers to reject conciliation.[100] The Board continued in existence until 1919, but failed to improve labour relations in the city.[101]

The idealism of those who sought conciliation was undermined by the realities of industrial life. It seems to be the case that the history of labour relations in the late nineteenth and early twentieth centuries was one of confrontation rather that compromise. As with so much else within the labour movement this varied greatly depending on which groups of workers and employers were in conflict. The nature of contemporary skilled trade unionism greatly impressed a French visitor who came to Britain to look at the 'labour question' in the 1890s.

It is the aristocracy of the trade which is at the head of the movement, out of 3000 plumbers in London only about a third belong to the union, but they are the cream of the trade. This must necessarily be so in the first place it is generally the best workmen who are the readiest to combine for an advantage which is not immediate, for such a course pre-supposes a certain degree of foresight and of judgement of which not everyone is capable. Secondly, the best workmen are precisely those who cling most to their specialism, who are the most eager to defend it, who lose most by being confronted with unskilled labourers and who feel the greatest pride in their position and think other work beneath them.[102]

These were men with whom the employers could feel much in common even during a strike, as was noted by a member of the vice-regal staff in his memories of his time in Ireland.

Lord Mayor Pirrie, of Belfast, and the corporation presented an address, which deserves notice. Belfast at that time, and for some months or so previously, had been the scene of a serious strike in the ship-building trade. The strike was in full swing, and no settlement was in sight. Lord Pirrie, as one of the principals of the great firm of Harland and Wolff, was of course, up to his eyes in it; yet, mark the calmness and generosity of the reference to the strikers in the address of the corporation: – "We have pleasure in bearing testimony to the exemplary character and conduct of those affected by the strike, not a single case of lawlessness having arisen once through it, though there has been much suffering".[103]

However trade unionism was changing rapidly, many unions were no longer the respectable institutions with whom the employers felt they could co-operate in mutual respect. Some unions representing the unskilled differed so much in terms of organisation and social outlook, that they created a sense of challenge amongst employers.

We are out, therefore, to take our rights as human beings, and with this end in view, to organise the entire working class of Ireland into one big union. The only effective instrument of working-class emancipation, in this great object we count with confidence on the help of those who have heart and conscience enough to turn with loathing from the horrors that spring naturally from the present scheme of things as fruit from the tree.[104]

This alienation was reinforced by the tactics used by the new bodies, since men like Larkin were not inclined to avoid lawlessness in the face of 'much suffering'.

> The first dispute after the passing of the new Trades Disputes Act was at Belfast in 1908, and the picketing quickly became a matter of the gravest concern. A contemporary report says: – "The mob rushed the police and severely maltreated the imported men, some of whom were captured and marched through the town to the union office" again "hundreds of an infuriated mob attacked us with such 'peaceful' weapons as lumps of ore, stones, bricks, iron bolts, screws and catapults filled with bullets and small stones etc".[105]

Relations between the old skilled bodies and the new unions were strained by the tactics employed in industrial disputes. As Philip Snowden noted, men like Larkin did not follow the old established policy of appearing reasonable and trying to win public support.

> The new policy is to enter upon a strike without any effort to obtain a settlement of the grievances by negotiation; to exasperate the employers by every possible means; to indulge in wild and sanguinary language, which makes it impossible for a self-respecting employer to meet such leaders of the men; to never pay any attention to the rather important matter of preparing some means of support during the strike; and to endeavour to cause as much public inconvenience as possible, by involving the services upon which the public needs and convenience depend.[106]

If even a fellow trade unionist such as Snowden found it hard to sympathize with the new methods, we should not be surprised if employers found it impossible. The relationship between employers and 'responsible' trade unionists was going to differ from that with 'agitators' stirring up social discontent amongst the unskilled. As the trade union movement began to organise new industries and groups of workers there was increasingly a tendency to see unions as a threat to the status-quo rather than a partner in industrial harmony. If this was combined with a leader such as Jim Larkin who inspired the unconditional loyalty of his followers and the uncompromising loathing of opponents the results could be explosive.

Personality was of great importance in industrial relations, some employers and union leaders being seen as 'good' while others were presented as 'bad'. In Bristol for example Fry's were always seen as a model employer, while the employees of Sanders & Co. were nicknamed the 'white slaves'.[107] Lord Pirrie of Harland & Wolff never thought to provide a canteen for his workers yet was seen as a generous and liberal employer, while Davidson of Sirocco, despite his efforts to improve conditions, was seen as harsh and anti-union.[108] The story of Jim Larkin's rise to leadership of the ITGWU shows how important the personality of an individual could be.

Although the influence of Larkinism on the Irish trade union movement may have been exaggerated, it was still a major formative influence.[109] He began his career in Ireland as the representative of Sexton's National Union of Dock Labour and he successfully re-established the union in Belfast, Cork and Dublin.[110] During the 1907 strike in Belfast, he roused great passions, as George Askwith found when travelling to Belfast to try and settle the dispute.

We arrived at Belfast on the morning of August 13, not encouraged by meeting a distinguished Irishman on the boat, who I thought might be a possible arbitrator, if one became necessary. This hope of impartiality was stopped by his remark at breakfast that he knew his countrymen; I had no chance of settling the dispute, even if I was not shot, as I probably should be, and Larkin ought to be hanged.[111]

Even such a potentially hostile witness appears to have warmed to Larkin.

He was an interesting man. "I don't know how you can talk to that fellow Larkin" said a Dublin employer at a later date. "You can't argue with the prophet Isaiah." It was not an inapt description of a man who came to believe he had a mission upon earth; and when one reflects, Isaiah must have been rather a difficult person and liable to go off at a tangent. It is not wise to argue with such men, but it is possible to suggest to their minds a different facet of thought.[112]

However, it was amongst the workers he led that Larkin gained the greatest respect, becoming what is known in Belfast as a 'Big Man'.

I knew Larkin for many years and I would say that although Larkin was a tough guy and there was much said about him that was true – Larkin had no regard for law and order – just saw one thing – a social injustice and he went for everything and everybody that stood between social justice and that person or body of people and that to the average man or woman Larkin was an idol. (A)[113]

The arrival of Larkin was a godsend to the dockers and carters he was a man that gave them a lead. (B)

It was all the same to him no matter what you were, Roman Catholic or Protestant you got the same as the rest, you got your ten shillings a week of strike pay. (C)

He was a lovely man, he was a big man and he wore no waistcoat and he always wore a big white shirt and a big rimmed hat ... he was a powerful well made man and he always wore black clothes and always wore a purty big coat. (D)

The Belfast strike caused a rift between Larkin and the NUDL which resulted in the establishment of the Irish Transport and General Workers Union and a damaging internal conflict amongst Irish transport workers.[114]

Larkin was seen as a particular threat by some employers but he was by no means the only union leader of the 'new school'. In the Bristol Channel there was 'Captain' Tupper of the National Union of Seamen, a strange, larger than life individual who challenged employers to boxing matches and organised racist attacks on Chinese immigrants.[115] Like Larkin he won a grudging respect even from those against whom he organised strikes. Even the Shipping Federation had to admit that 'he exercised power over the seamen in that area (the Bristol Channel) during 1911'.[116] Tupper was soon to be surpassed by another leader who was to prove even more dangerous in the eyes of the Bristol transport employers, a young man named Ernest Bevin. In 1910 as chairman of the Avonmouth Carters Branch of the Dockers Union, he led an unofficial strike and began a career that would lead him to the Cabinet.[117]

One response to the power of organised labour was to form employers' bodies and trade associations. This was not always seen by the trade unions as a negative development: it was better, in the case of skilled workers such as printers, to deal with one body rather than individual employers.[118] There was also a feeling among the unions that dealing with federations of employers made the two sides equals, as in the case of the Bristol stonemasons in 1876.[119] In a strange reversal of the normal roles, the Amalgamated Engineers tried to ignore the formation of Employers' Federation of Engineering Associations but were forced to grant recognition following a lockout in 1894.[120]

Unions began to recognise that the employers often enjoyed the advantage of greater unity than labour. In 1925 at a delegate meeting of the Draughtsmen, one speaker pointed out that there were almost fifty unions in the engineering and shipbuilding sectors but only one employers' federation.[121] Even the Shipping Federation, a body formed for the expressed purpose of 'union-busting' was not seen as wholly negative by a union leader such as Havelock Wilson. His argument was 'by having a strong combination on each side, we would have more respect for each other'.[122]

The position of the Belfast shipyards on the question of employer organisations is rather confusing. In the official history of Harland & Wolff it is stated that the company, and Workman Clarke, had remained aloof from the Shipbuilding Employers Federation.[123] They may never have paid an affiliation fee, but in the Harland & Wolff papers are several files of correspondence with employers' organisations. The Belfast yards were clearly in continuous contact with employers' groups and a couple of examples illustrate that the relationship went beyond exchange of information:

William Gallocher: Riveter
Messrs Napier and Miller Ltd, one of the members of this association, advise that the above named riveter started a berth on the shell of a vessel at present being built in their yard, and left the same without completing his job. He is understood to have found employment in Belfast.
I shall be obliged by your kindly giving the usual co-operation.[124]

Strike of Shipwrights: Belfast
Messrs Harland and Wolff Ltd, Belfast, advise that their shipwrights struck on Wednesday last on a question of demarcation of work as between themselves and the joiners. They went out without giving notice, and the firm ask that the members of the Federation might be advised of the stoppage. In some cases the Belfast firms have been asked by the Federation for co-operation in similar circumstances.
Please advice your members of the foregoing, and invite their co-operation when setting on shipwrights during the currency of the strike in Belfast.[125]

The Belfast employers may not have been members, but given this sort of co-operation they cannot be said to have opposed the ideals of the employers' federation.

However, to return to the original suggestion that there were three ways in which an employer could deal with the unions trying to represent the workers. This account would seem to suggest that industrial relations were dominated by conflict in the years covered by this study.

> They resented the idea of you coming in to tell them how they should run their business, and the attitude usually of employers was one of gross offensiveness – vulgarity...is a modest word. To open a door ask what the hell you want and bang the door in your face after telling you to get away to hell as quick as you could go. That was an experience I had year after year.[126]

Certainly there was animosity and confrontation but was the desire for peaceful coexistence totally lost? Was there still room for day-to-day courtesy as suggested by Meakin in the dealings of Capital and Labour? The problem is that our view of industrial relations tends to be shaped by the records of strikes and disputes rather than day-to-day relationships. In addition to conflict there was clearly some degree of mutual respect and co-operation in these years.

In the records of the Flax Spinners Association there are a few routine letters, such as the one from J.H. Stirling to Harry Midgley of the Linenlappers Union dated 2 February 1920: 'I was very pleased to have such a full and frank talk with you on Saturday last, and I think that as one result each of us understands the other's point of view better than before.'[127]

On 2 May 1919 Sam Kyle the District Organiser for the Workers Union wrote to the Linen Merchants Association to request their help. An employer seems to have had problems concerning the payment of a 5s. increase, but, Kyle's letter was anything but antagonistic.

> I have written the Firm about this matter and they have paid from the 7th April 1919, but it is perfectly clear that they are entitled to pay from 1st October '18, and I am quite sure from my previous dealings with Mr Webb that he is always willing and desirous of keeping to arrangements, so that if you send him a letter assuring him that the above statement is a fact, I have no doubt he will pay the arrears.[128]

In a rather bizarre exchange of letter in May 1920 Harry Midgley tried to convince the firm of John A. Lowery and Co. that they should persuade one of their employees to join the union. Although when the letter was passed on to the Household Linen & Piece Goods Association, they said it was 'absurd' that they should be asked to act as the union's agents, the reply to the union was hardly uncivil.

In reply we desire to say we consider your request somewhat unusual and although we recognise any trade societies which are approved of by the Household Linen & Piece Goods Association, of which we are members, we do not think that we should interfere for the purpose of compelling any of our employees to join a particular Trade Union. We are, however, submitting your letter to the Council of our association and will communicate with you as soon as we receive their advice on the subject.[129]

How typical of the industry as a whole are these few surviving letters? The far more complete Harland and Wolff trade union correspondence contains literally thousands of communications, invariably polite and businesslike.[130] I would suggest that in many firms reasonable working relations between employers and unions were the norm.

CONCLUSION

Labour relations in the late nineteenth and early twentieth centuries were highly complex. The temptation is to try and create a 'typical' situation, which at least one contemporary warned against.

These remarks may be upsetting to the complacency of historians or writers who wish to make labour movements fit in with their theories or follow what they have mapped out as desirable.[131]

There were good, bad and indifferent employers just as there were virtuous and villainous trade unionists. As the whole range of human nature was represented from principled paternalism to uncaring exploitation, it would be unrealistic to try and create some sort of Frankenstein 'typical' employer.

The major differences in industrial relations in the three cities reflect, primarily, their differing economic structures. There was no pressure on the Dublin employer to be generous in a saturated labour market, while in labour-hungry Belfast paternalism would be motivated by self-interest. What is clear is that labour relations were more likely to be based on co-operation in expanding employment areas than in those where the supply of labour exceeded demand. The demand for labour in Bristol's tobacco, chocolate and transport sectors tended to create an environment that had much in common with Belfast. The need to recruit and retain workers in cities where there were plentiful alternative sources of employment inevitably created a more moderate atmosphere of employer–labour relations.

The shipyards of Belfast may have been exceptional in so far as the employer was at the mercy of his skilled workers, but most industries were dependent on skilled or semi-skilled labour to some degree. Even in Dublin firms such as Guinness and Jacobs adopted a paternalistic attitude to ensure the retention of trained workers even if they were theoretically unskilled. However, compared to the other two cities in this study there was little alternative employment in Dublin and thus employers were not so constrained in their treatment of labour.

In the period of expansion before the First World War the industrial relations in both Bristol and Belfast were shaped by ever growing demand for labour. In Belfast a large element of this demand was for skilled shipyard workers, but like Bristol other industries created demands for semi-skilled and unskilled labour. In such an atmosphere of growth and prosperity there were reasons for both employers and labour to be reasonable in their dealings with each other.

7 Working Class or Classes?

The Belfast shipyard worker was well paid and organised compared to many other groups in the city's labour force in the years before the First World War. Did their privileged position give them the status of a 'labour aristocracy' distinct from the rest of the 'working class' in these years? How did their experience compare with other groups of workers in Belfast and perhaps more importantly were there similar 'elites' in the other cities?[1] The debate about the existence and importance of the 'Labour Aristocracy' has been a feature of labour history.[2] I shall examine the wide variation of experience within the 'working class' in the years 1880–1925. Such divisions were, as Gray suggests in his study of skilled workers in Edinburgh, reinforced by contemporary racial and social values among the 'working class'.[3]

The desire for respectability amongst members of the 'working class' was frequently noted by contemporary writers. This sense of status created powerful divisions within the 'working class'.

As soon as a girl takes any thought for herself at all, her desire is to 'keep herself respectable' and when one realised the environment in which many of these girls live, their familiarity from their earliest years with the surroundings of vice and crime, one can understand how this desire, once awakened, becomes a ruling power in a girl's life, and also why rigid class distinctions permeate the rank and file of manual workers. These distinctions are familiar to most social workers, but those who speak generally of the 'working classes' or 'the poor' can have no conception of their influence or their extent. For instance, a warehouse girl often knows very little or nothing about the work-girls in the factory, and many similar examples will be found in the work-rooms themselves.[4]

Loss of respectability was so generally feared that it was considered a suitable subject for 'improving stories' for the middle and working classes.

It is a sad and pathetic thing to see in Bristol the large ever-increasing army of 'might have beens' men who have 'come down in the world' as it is commonly termed ... men of good education, who have held responsible positions in the past, but who have sunk step by step, until they are forced to join the ranks and help swell the

93

growing army of house-to-house interviewers, struggling on day-to-day some in the arduous endeavour to scrape together a little money for their half starved wives and children; other alas! to provide the wherewithal to commit suicide by swallowing 'old' beer, brewed about a fortnight.[5]

The Belfast shipyard worker was seldom affected by seasonal unemployment and wages were frequently above the average. The dependence of the employers upon skilled labour gave their unions considerable negotiation power. But even this group faced problems.

Our shipyards offer up a daily sacrifice of life and limb on the altar of capitalism. The clang of the ambulance bell is one of the most familiar daily sounds on the streets between our shipyards and our hospitals.

It has been computed that some seventeen lives were lost on the *Titanic* before she left the Lagan; a list of maimed and hurt and of those suffering from minor injuries, as a result of the accidents at any one of these big ships would read like a roster of the wounded after a battle upon the Indian frontier.[6]

In 1907, 48 foundry workers in every thousand were subject to industrial injury and their average life expectancy was about 59 years.[7] The average life expectancy of engineers was under 38 years in the 1860s and only 48 years by the end of the 1880s.[8] In such trades physical injury and disablement was a common, and accepted, feature of working life.

It may be taken as a fact based upon experience, that artisans who are exposed to such loud noises as are made in hammering rivets suffer from deafness. Boilermakers and riveters become deaf at an early age, while their comrades engaged in other kinds of work in the shipyard do not suffer.[9]

In 1912 in the shipyards of Belfast, the Clyde and the Tyne 1448 workers were injured and 62 killed in falls while 1400 were injured and 15 killed by articles falling on them.[10]

Did the experience of the shipyard worker differ from skilled workers in other industries? They certainly tended to share social origins; as Anderson argues 'it was the sons of skilled workers who received apprenticeships'.[11] In Belfast the apprentice system appeared almost designed to maintain the elite status of the skilled working class. In August 1912 Govan shipyard wrote to Harland & Wolff enclosing details of their apprentice pay rates and requesting similar information. Belfast apprentices were paid less than those on the Clyde, by two to three shillings a week and had to place a deposit of between two and five pounds, a practice abolished in centres such as Govan.[12] In addition to earning low wages for many years an apprentice would have to supply his tools, a considerable financial outlay.[13] Only a family with a comparatively high level of income, usually skilled workers themselves, could put a boy through an apprenticeship in Belfast.

Charles More suggests that many, though not all, shipyard tradesmen were trained by a system of 'regular service' as apprentices.[14] However, even in the shipyards, important groups such as platers could 'pick up' their knowledge doing the job.[15] This less formal training method was of great importance in industries such as boot and shoe making, where technological innovation was rapidly undermining the old apprentice system.[16] In Bristol the decline of the 'craft' training of boot makers was accelerated by the huge expansion in the industry.

the work is carried on partly in factories and partly in workshops; for the uppers are cut out and sewn, and the soles and heels cut out by machinery in the factories. Of the materials thus prepared a part is made up into the finished articles in the factories and part is given to out-workers to be done in their homes.[17]

If some trades were beginning to decline in status due to technical advances, others, as in the shipyards, were losing their value completely.

Mr Sharland also mentions the dying out in Bristol of wicker basket workers and comments on their conditions of labour. The work is described as 'The most depressing and worst paid', the system is piece work, and a hard working man earns only from 13 to 15 shillings a week ... Machinery has yet to be brought into use in this trade at Bristol.[18]

Such problems were a notable feature of Dublin where the city's craft based industries largely failed to adapt to changing conditions and were increasingly unable to compete with better equipped British and continental producers. In 1885 the Dublin Coachmakers informed the Royal Commission on the Depression that the decline in their trade was due to 'foreign' competition. The coach-builders saw the abolition of an Irish parliament rather than economic or technical developments as the reason for the decline of their industry.[19]

However, even in Dublin some groups of skilled workers were able to maintain their privileged status whereby they were able to control access to a trade. The Dublin Typographical Provident Society maintained many traditional privileges, including a seven-year apprenticeship until the 1940s.[20] Their rivals in Ireland, and the main union in Belfast and Bristol, was the Provincial Typographical Association. This body, although forced to accept a five-year apprenticeship in 1911, was able to improve the wages and conditions of its membership during the years 1849–1914.[21] The success of these unions is even more surprising considering the rapid technological advances within the industry.[22] These 'traditional' print unions refused to accept workers who had not served an apprenticeship, and thus there emerged bodies representing machine minders and other ancillary workers. In the City of Bristol between 1880 and 1925 there existed, at various times, eleven unions in the printing and packaging industries.[23] Although a number of these unions were short lived or local bodies, in January 1914 there were at least four societies in Bristol and Dublin and three in Belfast.[24]

In all three cities the building industry was a major employer of tradesmen and semi-skilled assistants. Robert Tressell's novel about Mugsborough shows these tradesmen faced very different conditions from the printers and shipyard workers.[25] Employment in the industry was seasonal. For example, building tradesmen formed 17.7 per cent (63.5 per cent of 'skilled') of those registered with the Bristol Distress Committee during the winter months of 1905–6.[26] In Dublin between 1910 and 1914, 54 per cent of the 11 584 who were employed on distress works had listed themselves as building workers.[27] Even those who were able to find work could find the winter a harsh period as the working week was reduced during the shorter daylight hours. In Bristol the summer working week of 50 hours was reduced to 47 in November and February, and only $41\frac{1}{2}$ in December and January.[28] For the tradesman who was paid $9\frac{1}{2}$d. an hour this meant a reduction in earnings from 39s. 7d. to 37s. 3d. and finally 32s. 10d. with little or no overtime in the winter months. Building workers were difficult to unionise, being mainly employed on a casual basis by small firms. The operative stone masons had 26 330 members in 1876 but by 1911 only 8065.[29] The census for the later year shows there were 47 077 masons and 3691 monumental masons in the country.[30] Although the building industry was as dependent as shipbuilding on skilled tradesmen, the workers enjoyed nothing like the security or negotiating power of the shipbuilding trades.

The number of 'skilled' jobs available to women was more limited, although women were important in trades such as bookbinding (58.7 per cent) upholstering (34.8) and french polishing (21).[31] However, the largest area of female employment, after domestic service, was that group of trades categorised by the census as 'Dress'. This included wig, umbrella and artificial flower makers as well as more conventional clothing and footwear workers. The workforce was a mixture of 'skilled' and semi-skilled, a small minority of whom served a formal apprenticeship, and in general wages for females in the tailoring trades were low.[32] In Bristol even the appeal of a 'skill' was not enough to compensate for low earnings and by 1914, in the face of increasing factory and clerical opportunities, the tailoring and millinery trades were finding it hard to attract apprentices.[33] As early as 1910 the tobacco firm of W.D. & H.O. Wills found they were experiencing problems recruiting cigar makers, who served a formal apprenticeship, because wage rates were too low.[34] Even in industries such as printing and packaging where female labour was increasingly important, skilled or semi-skilled female wages seldom equalled those of unskilled men.

The 'semi-skilled' worker differed fundamentally from most tradesmen in not undergoing an apprenticeship. In their case a lesser task was performed before passing on to a more demanding one. Thus a linen worker would enter the mill as a 'learner', a miner began as a 'boy' and an engine driver as a cleaner in the sheds. Once these skills were gained these workers formed an indispensable element in the labour force of their industries. The employers frequently refused to recognise unions which tried to organise these new groups of workers, thus confrontation was frequent. George White of the Bristol Tramway Company went to great lengths to prevent his labour force being organised by Will Thorne's Gasworkers Union. In 1901 a strike demanding union recognition was crushed as part of a campaign against 'interference by outside interests'.[35] The Board of Trade report of this dispute notes that the company replaced those workers who had struck, whilst the National Free-Labour Association reported that it had supplied not just tram workers but also 'emergency men' (thugs) to break this strike.[36] It would appear that the employees of the tram companies were often subjected to petty tyranny, the 1913 Dublin Lockout being sparked by an attempt by Jim Larkin's ITGWU to unionise these workers; this was resisted by the Company owner William Martin Murphy. This appears to have been a personality clash rather than an objection to unions as such, Murphy had opposed neither previous attempts to establish a local union nor to bring in the

Tramway and Vehicle Workers.[37] Conditions on the Belfast trams were little better,

> You were given a special duty board on Easter Monday and Tuesday and on the 12th and 13th of July, painted on the top of this in red ink **NO RELIEF** that meant from 7am till 11.30pm without food still no one would protest against this treatment. During my time we had no covered trams, there was half a roof over you and the drivers were issued with sou'westers, the drivers had to face all weather, and the conductors when not collecting fares stood beneath the stairs to keep the rain off, when you had completed 12 hours under those conditions you were ready for a rest.[38]

There began to emerge an increasing sense of identity among the semi-skilled, which tended to create divisions rather than unity. On the railways those who worked on the footplate of engines looked down upon other railwaymen and broke away to form their own union.[39] However, as they became increasingly aware of both their potential power and their grievances, even engine drivers became increasingly militant.

> The senior drivers in my depot – men whom I respected one by one mounted the platform and gravely explained to us who were ignorant, the facts of the case. They weren't accomplished orators – far from it – but their sincerity couldn't be doubted, or their facts disputed. The harsh discipline to which most of us were subject needed no stressing. The unjust punishments, the total lack of consideration given to our very modest claims for the decencies of life, the long hours the low wages – all these were part and parcel of our calling. But we learned much also that we did not know. We learned that we were now an organised craft.[40]

In Belfast semi-skilled female labour was critical to the linen industry. In the spinning sector females outnumbered men by approximately three to one although certain departments such as roughing, hackling and bundling were male dominated.[41] In the weaving sector the domination of female labour was even greater and if a man possessed the skills it was not really considered suitable employment.

> It was not man's work... It was really women's work, a weaver's work... In the first place, there was no money. On the other hand, it was a nimble job for the fingers; it didn't let a man express himself or use his energy. It was frustration all the time, and a woman has more

patience than a man . . . It was just against a man's nature to be stuck between two looms while he was getting no physical exercise.[42]

However in Bristol and Dublin it was the clothing and boot and shoe trades that were the largest employers of semi-skilled women. Although high class tailoring and shoe making remained male dominated the mass produced sector relied increasingly on women's labour. Dressmakers, machinists, seamstresses and others formed a labour force whose skills were considerable but whose wages were low. Although it was considered 'respectable' for a woman to earn a living by her needle, it was recognised there were problems.

> Though the occupation is a light and 'Genteel' one it is not really healthy, and now that men are agitating for a working day of eight hours I think that some consideration ought to be shown for a class of workpeople who being 'genteel' and in superabundant supply cannot afford to lose their situations by complaining and who are consequently very helpless.[43]

The 1906 wage census was to show that the lowest rates in the ready-made tailoring trade were paid in Bristol and Norwich.[44] In the boot and shoe trade Bristol again comes almost bottom with only Norwich and Leicester county, both of which specialised in cheap or light-weight women's shoes, paying a lower male wage.[45] The rates paid to female workers in the industry were particularly poor.[46]

The vast majority of domestic servants gained their skills by 'on the job training' the situation in Ireland being no different to the rest of Britain.[47] The weakness of this system and the absence of 'professional training' was recognised in a government report on the 'industry' in 1898.[48] The attitudes of young women towards domestic service could vary enormously as researchers in Birmingham found in the early years of the twentieth century.

> When a girl goes into service at a gentlemen's house she is more able to get into better company than factory girls. To be a servant it is much healthier and comfortable, girls who are in service are generally much more quiet and more ladylike than those which work in a factory.
>
> Why I prefer to work in a factory – because there is a fixed time for meals and you know when you are done. You are not all hours of the day and you have only one to serve and you can go to as many classes as you like in a week and you have Saturday and Sunday to yourself.[49]

The life of the domestic servant depended to a great degree on the character of the employer, as did the lives of shopworkers. Both gained skills through their work rather than by formal training, and were seen as 'respectable' despite suffering poor conditions of employment.[50] The frustration of such workers could result in strike action.

The strikers numbered seven men, three girls, and four boys. Their grievances, which the firm refused to redress or arbitrate upon, were that the men worked 79 hours a week, the women 74, inclusive of mealtimes, which hours extended to as many as 100 during busy seasons ... The assistants used to get three nights off at 6.30 p.m. fortnightly, but this had been discontinued the previous summer.[51]

Legislation was passed to try and regulate the hours worked by young people in shops. However, as the report of Bristol's solitary inspector indicates legislation was one thing, enforcement was another.

I have explained the Acts to four thousand one hundred and seventy three employers, cautioned one thousand six hundred and ninety-one who were contravening clause 4 of the Act of 1892, and succeeded in bringing about the shortening of the hours of sixty-two young persons.[52]

Although the wages and conditions of female textile workers, shop assistants and domestic servants were poor when compared to the skilled workers they were better off than many in the labour force. If their work was poorly paid it was regular, and as a group they possessed experience or skills which could ensure a degree of demand for their labour. In the case of totally unskilled workers or those possessing skills or experience in abundant supply the situation tended to be one of poor wages and irregular employment. It was those workers classified by the census as 'general labourers' who suffered the worst effects of poor housing and low incomes in terms of health and life expectancy.

Perhaps the most obvious example of this group, in all three cities, was the dock workers, a diverse group with considerable skills but who suffered from an over-abundance of their labour at most times.[53] The system of piecework under which bulk cargo was unloaded meant that vast quantities had to be off-loaded to earn a reasonable wage.

Well the Dockers in their days was very poorly you know – very poorly paid. There were men working for – well I suppose about – they were getting an average of about tuppence or thruppence a ton for unloading stuff down the quays taking stuff off the boats too –

down the planks so much a time – they'd earn about five or six shillings – mightn't have earned that much.

Well now the docks, the dockers in that day was nothing else but [slaves]. They practically were all casual workers and there was nobody to organise.

Well I'll tell you what it was like, A man wouldn't load a donkey or a pony as hard as they put on the truck for you, and it was all up planks you know, see there was no cranes down there then. It was planks and there were three men at a truck, and a fellow giving you a pull at the stage, like, called him a stager, do you see? and you never went up the stage with less than half a ton on the truck, it was just slavery.[54]

In 1909 only a small minority of dockers in Bristol were permanent men employed by the week; most were employed by the day or hour. Details of the number of men employed on a busy and a slack day were submitted as evidence to the Royal Commission on the Poor Law in 1909. On the busy day 1132 men were employed but only 84 were permanent staff compared to 451 employed by the day and 597 'casuals' employed by the hour. On the slack day 204 men were employed 85 were permanent, 115 day workers and only 4 hourly paid casuals.[55]

The constant fear of the unskilled worker was unemployment regardless of which industry they worked in. During the year ended 31 March 1906 the unskilled formed 72 per cent of the 2900 workers who requested assistance from the Bristol Distress Committee.[56] The irregular employment pattern of unskilled male workers was to prove particularly damaging in Dublin where the workforce contained a larger proportion of such workers. However, in all three cities the unskilled labour force faced serious problems of low pay and seasonal unemployment.

Unskilled female labour was even more disadvantaged than male; low status domestic work was as washerwomen, chars or scullery maids but this was very limited. In some industries it was possible to obtain low paid unskilled factory work as in the Bristol confectionery trade. In the 'liquorice room' of one factory the average weekly wage of five female workers over a six-week period varied from 7s. 6d. to 12s. This was for a 52-hour week, the lowest weekly payment being 6s. and the highest 15s. 6d.[57] Others were employed in tasks such as rag sorting or match works which were considered so unpleasant that nobody else wanted them.

There are 19 rag-sorting workshops [Dublin] in which dirty rags are dealt with, the sorting is done on the floor, and except in two workshops no screens are provided. The rags are never washed before being sorted, as the occupiers have no facilities for doing so.

Lucifer match works – I am informed that there is a marked improvement in the class of workers engaged in this trade. In former times the industry was somewhat looked down on, and there was considerable difficulty in securing respectable hands.[58]

Female unskilled workers received the lowest rates of pay and had to compete for employment in a very limited market. But even this group were perhaps better off than the outworkers who in this period produced a vast range of goods on piece rates.

In 1888 W. Johnston, the Factory Inspector for Bristol, in written evidence to a House of Lords Select Committee described conditions in the Bristol tailoring trades.

It is among these Jewish tailors, who employ from 12 to 20 hands each, that one would expect to find sweating, if anywhere; but on enquiry it appeared that good wages are paid to their workpeople; in fact rather more than the current rate... A very large proportion, however, of the work in this trade is taken by females residing at home, either in Bristol or the surrounding villages.[59]

A decade later a report on women's employment in Bristol was presented by Clara Collie to the Royal Commission on Labour. She found that the clothing industry was heavily dependent upon the outwork system with 2000 outworkers on the books of six factories compared to 769 who worked on the premises. She went on to say that this was probably an under-estimate as from her experience for every worker on the register there were two actually working.[60] A major employer of outworkers in Bristol was corset making, which employed a highly skilled but poorly paid labour force.[61] The 'outdoor' system was a feature of the Kingswood boot and shoe industry.

In the Bristol district which is an important centre of the boot and shoe trade, the indoor system has lately been established with the general concurrence of both parties, while a few miles off, at Kingswood the industry is almost entirely carried on the 'outdoor' principle, in small workshops built at the back of the operatives houses, and at present there is no very strong movement in the direction of indoor work; the habits of many of the operatives in this somewhat isolated district being opposed to the regularity and constraint of factory hours.[62]

However, the outworkers were soon to find their living increasingly precarious as new technology began to erode their markets and force down prices. In 1909 it was reported that competition from machine-made boots had forced Kingswood payments to outworkers as low as 9d. a pair.[63]

In 1908 the Anti-Sweating League organised an Exhibition in Bristol to shame certain local employers and increase public awareness of conditions. In tailoring rates of 5–8s. a week were reported, with one worker receiving only 1s. 10d. for making three tram-drivers' over-coats. Workers making blouses and underwear received 7s. 6d. to 8s. a week despite working a nine-hour day. Bootmakers were earning as little as 9–13s. a week, working a ten-hour day. Stay and corset ma-kers, despite the skill involved in their work, received 7–8s a week for low class work, 10s. for average and 12–15s. for top quality work.[64] The exhibition provoked a negative response from Miss Vynne of the National Home Workers League, who informed a parliamentary committee that the exhibition had displayed only the cheapest work.[65]

In 1888 James C. Laird the President of Newcastle upon Tyne Trades Council described the extent of outwork in Ireland to a House of Lords Committee: 'In a large number of places it is practically un-known; I mean in some of the large towns. It has increased in Belfast, for instance, this last three years, but not to any great extent.'[66]

There was little demand for such workers in most parts of Ireland. Even in Dublin there was no large scale boot and shoe, ready-made clothing or corset industry that would require home workers, although it was suggested that this method of production was becoming more prevalent in the Dublin tailoring trade following the unsuccessful strike in 1900.[67] In this at least Belfast was different to the rest of Ireland.

The linen industry in Belfast stimulated a range of 'making-up' trades which generated large scale employment, as the factory in-spectors noted as early as 1887.[68] The products varied: shirts and collars, blouses, pinafores and above all handkerchiefs. Originally welcomed as a suitable source of employment for the labouring poor, increasing competition and the introduction of new technology soon undermined the position of the outwork.

This appears to be particularly the case in stitching factories, where owing to the high speed of the power driven machines, the output has materially increased, while the rates of pay have been lowered to meet the altered conditions. One worker told me she had stitched 32 dozen handkerchiefs in a day, whereas about eight years ago 16 dozen was considered a hard days work. These conditions also materially affect the position of outworkers who do machining in their own homes; work that is fairly paid in the factory becomes terribly sweated as outwork if it takes twice or even three times as long to do it on a treadle machine, and for this reason some employers are now having all the machining done in the factories, and only giving out handwork.[69]

In 1910 the Scottish Council for Women's Trades published a report on the wages and conditions of outworkers in the north of Ireland, claiming it represented 'the most barefaced sweating of the industrious poor'.[70] In September J.J. Mallon, secretary of the National Anti-Sweating League, visited Belfast and addressed the trades council.

Since he arrived in the city he had seen on hoardings an announcement that 'the wages of sin is death' but when he took up the papers he saw that the wages of virtue was three farthings per hour. He thought there was hardly sufficient distinction.[71]

The employers were quick to respond to allegations which they claimed were 'entirely baseless' and likely to 'do a great deal of harm to an important Ulster industry'.

In the County Down, where the bulk of the linen work is done, it is not unusual for the sewers to earn as much as 17s in the course of four days, and it surely cannot be said that their remuneration does not compare very favourably with that received by skilled workers in the best paid trades of the United Kingdom.[72]

However, other contemporary witnesses support the findings of the Scottish investigation, and James Connolly who knew the city well claimed the normal rate was only a penny an hour and was often below this.[73]

Some outworkers, such as the Bristol stay makers, although low paid could acquire considerable status due to the skills they possessed.[74] For making a dozen poor quality corsets the worker might receive as little as 1s. 7d. while much more labour intensive, good quality work did not pay more than 5s. a dozen. However, even these rates were deceptive as the worker had to supply much of the material used so that low quality work in reality only paid about 11d. per dozen.[75]

Perhaps the most exploited groups in the labour force of all three cities were those classified as 'youths and young persons'. Although there were increasingly strict regulations governing the employment of juveniles local conditions often made them difficult to enforce effectively. For example in Bristol a child could not start work until the age of fourteen, while in the neighbouring district of St George the age limit was thirteen.[76] Two decades later the state of affairs in Ireland was still confused. Although Belfast imposed strict regulations the factory inspector covering the Dublin district reported 'the master in many cases is quite ignorant of what is required of him, or his duties as regards the certificate'.[77] In one of her blistering attacks on child employment practices in northern Ireland[78] the formidable Miss Martindale accused the local teachers of worse than ignorance of their responsibilities.

> On visiting a flax-scutching mill one morning I found a little girl, aged 12 years, striking flax with a rapidity and dexterity which showed considerable practice. My enquiries were met with what is far too common in Ireland – the most bare-faced untruths. I was told that the child was at the mill for no other purpose than bringing tea to the workers. On visiting the school in the neighbourhood, I was immediately told that this little girl and her sister, aged $10\frac{1}{2}$ years, worked for alternate weeks at the scutching mill, and were employed there from 8 a.m. to 8 p.m. on every weekday including Saturday. I could not, however, hear of any steps having been taken by the teacher or managers to stop this obviously illegal employment.[79]

Young persons' labour was an embarrassment and by 1890 the factory inspectors were reduced to publishing details of other countries' restrictions to try and prove Britain's were effective.[80]

The system of 'half-time' employment was declining throughout the 1890s in industrial areas such as Bradford and its passing was not considered a bad thing by social reformers.[81] By 1903 Mr Bellhouse was able to report that there was only one mill in the Dublin district, which covered all of southern Ireland, employing half-timers, and three years later there were none in the Bristol district.[82] However, in Belfast far from declining, half-time employment seemed to have been increasing as was the employment of juveniles generally. The Factory Inspector noted that during the year 1905–6 the number of half-timers under 14 years had increased by 223 to a total of 3488, while full time workers under 14 had increased by over 50 per cent to 500. In addition to this the number of full time workers aged between 14 and 16 years had increased by 1180 to 7672.[83] Miss Martindale was highly critical of this aspect of Belfast life, as was James Connolly who lived in Belfast in these years.

> In these industrial parts of the North of Ireland the yoke of capitalism lies heavy upon the lives of the people. The squalor and listless wretchedness of some parts is, indeed, absent, but instead there exists toil for the old and young – toil to which the child is given up whilst its limbs and brains are still immature and underdeveloped, and toil continued until, a broken and enfeebled wreck, the toiler sinks into an early grave.[84]

Half-timers were to remain a feature of Belfast's mills until it was finally abolished by Fisher's Act of 1918.[85] However, the employment of 'young persons' remained very much a feature of all three cities, and for most people working life began at fourteen. In the linen industry it was common practice only to employ boys until they reached the age where adult wages were payable; it was only in times of labour shortage that male weavers were employed.[86] In evidence to a Parliamentary Committee J. McFarlane, the biscuit maker, said that van boys worked an average of 56 hours a week in Belfast.[87] The Board of Trade informed the same committee that 32 van-boys in Ireland had earned 3s. 6d. to 8s. a week (average 5s.) while 125 boys in Bristol received from 4s. to 12s. (average 6s.).[88] Many 'boys' were made redundant between eighteen and twenty, as employers were unwilling to pay adult wages.[89] The Bristol Charity Organisation Society encouraged young workers to think in longer terms and take apprenticeships rather than better paid jobs which would be lost in a few years.[90]

At the other extreme it was difficult for workers to find employment as they got older. Amongst domestic servants this was a particular problem: Hearn suggests that after forty-five servants found it increasingly difficult to get another position.[91] This problem was not confined to domestic servants and John Wall writing of conditions in Bristol felt it was a case of 'too old at forty'. Writing in response to a notice which appeared in the city asking 'Can a man live an X-tian life on £1 a week?' he felt the local unemployed might answer,

> We wish there was a chance for us to show what could be done on such a sum; but Ah! we are become unpopular with the people who employ labour. When we answer an advertisement they look du-

biously at the "tokens of honour" appearing on our heads, the "lines of experience" crossing our faces, the "mellowed way" we walk into the office and straightway they shake their heads in the peculiarly decisive way we are getting used to. "How old did you say?" "forty-five?" "My dear fellow you won't do" "What we require is a young man strong, alert and bustling!" "Send your son along and we'll see."[92]

If Bristol did not share Belfast's tradition of half-time workers it was notorious for the casual employment of school children.

I remember well a case in point where the schoolmaster said that in a class of 36 boys, of from 10 to 12 years, more than half of them had been to work, of some kind or other, before coming to school that morning, and he said they would go again after they had left school in the evening. But I should add that these lads are chiefly employed in running errands and generally making themselves useful in retail shops.[93]

Dr T.J. McNamara MP who sat on the committee investigating the employment of school children told his colleagues 'I was a teacher in Bristol, where this employment of school children was very serious'.[94] The evidence given by H. Coward, headmaster of Anglesea Place Board School, on behalf of the National Union of Teachers clearly detailed the extent of the problem. In his own school there were 210 boys aged from 8 to 13 years, drawn from the well-to-do suburbs of Clifton and Redland. Of these 53 were employed (25.5 per cent) for between 3.5 and 31 hours a week and earned from a few pence to four shillings a week.[95] In the 67 schools in Bristol 1392 of the 17 864 pupils were said to be employed, 85.3 per cent of these young workers being boys.[96]

School teachers are a good example of the 'professional' working class. Teaching offered employment to a large number of educated men and women from fairly modest social origins at comparatively high salaries.[97] Although female wages in the profession were good compared to other areas of employment they were still lower than men's, although over 70 per cent of teachers in all three cities throughout this period were women.[98] The female teacher was expected to dress to a 'ladylike' standard and the daughter of a prosperous Birmingham tool maker had to spend £10 a year on clothes to maintain appearances.[99]

As some contemporary commentators pointed out it was difficult for a female teacher to live even on comparatively high salaries.

> We ask her to arrange to be housed, fed and carried to and from work for about 30s a week, to dress well on about £15 per year and if we leave her about £7 per annum for to keep herself up to date, books, longer journeys, doctors fees and savings, we consider she is well paid.[100]

Male teachers earned more and were more likely to be promoted, hence the pay scales allowed for a longer teaching career structure for women in the Irish National Schools.[101] However, female teachers were expected to resign on marriage. Although they enjoyed reasonable salaries and considerable status school teachers did not enjoy security of employment. In Belfast there were frequent references to dismissals by managers in the minutes of the executive of the Irish Protestant National Teachers Union. In 1912 their general meeting passed a resolution demanding the protection of 'efficient teachers of good character' from arbitrary dismissal.[102]

Government employees were a significant element in all three cities, and it might be expected that they would be paid on common rates. However, this was not the case. Not only were wages for female workers lower than those of males, but there were considerable variations over short distance. An example of this was postmen in Bristol who were paid on three different scales.[103] Anderson looked at pay amongst male clerical workers and fixed a division point of £160 per year (£3 a week) as a method of assessing the comparative prosperity of each group. Those employed by insurance companies were the best paid, with 46 per cent of them earning over the £3 threshold; this compared with Banking (44 per cent) Civil Servants (37) Local government (28) industry and commerce (23) and lowest of all the railway companies (10). Amongst those clerks earning less than £160 per year the best paid were the civil servants (£95 per year) followed by banking and local government (£90) with the railways and industry paying least (£80).[104] Thus there were divisions even amongst clerical workers created by levels of income and perceived status. The clerical sector, both government and commercial, expanded rapidly in these years creating vast numbers of new comparatively well paid jobs for the educated children of the middle and upper-working classes.[105] However, clerical workers felt very little in common with their 'blue collar' fellow workers, and in fact saw themselves as closer to the employers in most cases.[106]

CONCLUSION

Although the teacher and the handkerchief stitcher can both be seen as 'workers', and both groups were increasingly unionised, they clearly had little in common. Distinctions created by concepts of 'respectability' were far more powerful than any sense of 'class'.

Asked whether the slum dwellers resented their poor conditions, A.C. Telfer, president of the (Edinburgh) trades council, a joiner by trade, told the Royal Commission on Housing: 'properly speaking it is generally the Irish element, labourers and what not, who live in that locality, and I must confess that I do not come into communication with them as a rule, so to feel as it were the touch of their inner feelings in that respect'.[107]

The Belfast shipyard worker formed with groups such as printers a powerful self-perpetuating elite within the city's labour-force. Other tradesmen and certain groups of semi-skilled workers could enjoy good wages but had a distinctly lower status. Below these groups were others whose economic position was progressively weaker. Such a structure was clearly not unique to Belfast – similar hierarchical social structures can be found in all three cities. However, the structure of each varied according to the economic developments in each city; the number of workers at each level of status was not constant. Status cannot be defined in simple economic terms, a 'respectable' occupation could be badly paid. However, in simple terms the quality of life enjoyed by the 'aristocrats' was superior to that of other groups in the labour force. Housing, food and education were the symbols, or rewards, of attained status in these years.

How far did Belfast's large skilled elite created by the shipbuilding industry affect the social conditions in the city? How did housing and other indicators of quality of life compare with Bristol, which lacked such a concentrated 'elite' or Dublin where employment opportunities were so limited that even skilled labour could not always protect its status?

8 Living Conditions and Problems

This chapter will focus on living conditions in the cities of Belfast, Bristol and Dublin between 1880 and 1925. Were they totally dissimilar or were there discernible 'urban conditions' common to all three?

Rapid growth was a feature of both Belfast and Bristol during this period. In 1881 Belfast had a population of 208 000 and Bristol 207 000, which represented a growth rate of 197 and 66 per cent respectively over the previous forty years. By 1911 both cities had expanded their boundaries and Belfast now contained 387 000 and Bristol 357 000, increases of 86 and 72 per cent over the period.[1] In both cities the growing 'working class' population was increasingly living in newly built suburbs.[2] A government commission in 1884 received evidence on conditions in Belfast from the Borough Surveyor. He told of strict local bye-laws which had ensured that Belfast's growing population was already comparatively well housed.[3] The same body heard about conditions in Bristol from the Rev. E. Girdlestone.

> The improvements in some of the worst districts of Bristol are banishing, if I may use the expression, the working classes just outside into the suburbs. If you approach Bristol, for instance, from London by the Great Western Railway, or if you go out towards the Severn passage, you see thousands of new dwellings which have been put up in the last two or three years.[4]

A development of critical importance in the creation of these suburbs was cheap and effective public transport. 'Owing to the enterprise of the Bristol Tramway Company, in extending their electric system of lines into the suburbs, a revolution is being rapidly effected in the domestic life of work people.'[5]

Such innovations were not seen as positive by everyone, one member of the Bristol Chamber of Commerce going so far as to blame trams for reduced demand in the boot industry.[6] In some minds the mobility offered by the tram threatened the collapse of social distinctions.

> Sir – Is it not something terrible and most wicked that the disgusting tramway is to bring the nasty, low inhabitants of Bristol up into our

sacred region? We have nothing common or unclean amongst us at present. Poor people do not walk about on Clifton Streets . . . And now here are those money-making plebeians of Bristol talking of running tramcars through our beautiful and lovely Clifton![7]

Such considerations aside, Bristol Tramway Company was of great importance in the development of outlying areas of the city such as Horfield, Fishponds and St George.[8] However, the company was frequently criticised on grounds of inefficient management, excessive fares and poor service, becoming the subject of a long running dispute over 'municipalisation'.[9]

While Bristol's tramway were to remain a private concern until 1938, that of Belfast was owned and operated by the city council from 1904, when the private company was purchased and the whole system electrified.[10] In 1881 the system had carried a million people, a decade later the figure was ten million and when 'municipalised' it was carrying 28 million passengers a year.[11] By 1906 the tramway systems of Belfast and Bristol were fully developed. Bristol had a higher ratio of population per mile of track which perhaps created overcrowding when compared to Belfast.[12] Despite being a 'public' concern the manager, Richard Nance, treated his workforce no less dictatorially than George White in Bristol.[13] The development of an effective public transport system was critical to the growth of Bristol and Belfast in the form of new 'working class' suburbs.

Although housing in Bristol had improved by the 1880s to a point where the Rev. Girdlestone could state that there were no longer any cellar dwellings.[14] In 1891 the older portions of the city still contained courts and tenements where conditions were very poor.

Thousands of Bristol Families are huddled together in the 600 courts, and the very large number of houses without any backlet which are mostly unfit for human habitation. The houses in the courts are densely crowded, there being an average of four persons to each room.[15]

Two years earlier a report by Bristol Council's Sanitary Committee shows that there was little exaggeration. Although there were no areas sufficiently bad to be condemned as 'unhealthy' they warned that many houses were 'unsuitable for human habitation' and 600 houses were without backlets in the city.[16] Bristol's Medical Officer of Health regularly inspected and even closed houses considered as substandard under the Housing of the Working Classes Act of 1890.[17] However, in

1906 the Bristol Housing Reform Committee could still find plentiful evidence of poor housing in the older areas of the city.

In district No. 4 , In 3 3-roomed cottages, 27 persons were found to be living; 12 children in one of these cases. 1 case of consumption and 1 of diphtheria reported. In a 2-roomed house there were 5 adults and 7 children; w.cs in a very bad condition; wash-house only two feet from w.c.[18]

The standard of the new accommodation in the suburbs was incomparably superior. In his study of housing in British cities Burnett quotes examples from the Easton district of Bristol. Here a four-roomed house had a floor area of 670 sq. feet and a five-roomed house 850 sq. feet, these being fairly typical of the new housing built in the city in these years.[19]

Belfast also had poor housing in the older districts: as late as 1898 29 per cent of the city's houses lacked a separate rear entry. However in that year a record 4500 new houses were built and it was reported that 10 000 working class houses were standing empty in the city.[20] The 1870s and 1880s saw Belfast's housing stock quadruple, providing a range of styles at rents which different groups of workers could afford.[21] In such circumstances rents were low and there was pressure on landlords to demolish sub-standard housing and build new to a degree perhaps not seen in Bristol.

By 1914 the effects of new house building in Bristol and Belfast was clearly evident in terms of quality of accommodation and rents paid in both cities. In 1901 only 0.4 per cent of Belfast's population were living in a single room, the figure for Bristol being 1.6 per cent. At the other extreme 29.1 per cent of Belfast families lived in four-roomed houses and 59.4 per cent in dwellings of five rooms or more, comparative figures for Bristol being 10.5 and 74.3 per cent.[22] Rents were slightly higher in Bristol, with a four roomed house costing between 4s. and 5s. in 1905 compared to 3s. to 5s. in Belfast.[23] However, despite the fact that slightly more families were living in one room, the standard of housing in Bristol tended to be slightly better. In general terms, while accepting that many were living in poor conditions, accommodation in Bristol and Belfast was good, and fairly similar in quality.

The new suburbs of Bristol and Belfast were built by private individuals for rent, at a profit and there was persistent criticism of Bristol City Council for failing to provide working class housing.[24] The authorities argued that there was no need for them to do so as private enterprise was easily meeting demand.[25] The objection to building housing at public expense could be taken to extremes. In December 1899 the Health Committee adopted a proposal to purchase 33 houses in three courts off Pile Street, demolish them and build 22 dwellings for rent.[26] The officers reported that the cost of this would be £7575 but that a significant element of this could be obtained as an interest-free loan from the Local Government Board. On 1 January 1900 the full council rejected the project by 53 votes to 13.[27] A second proposal was then put forward for purchase and demolition only, which would cost £3625 plus £100 expenses.[28] This was accepted in February 1900 and the site was cleared. Some of the land was used for road improvements and the rest sold at public auction in July 1902.[29]

Belfast, like Bristol, built very little corporation housing in the years before the First World War as private enterprise met demand. The housing of the Belfast 'working class' was frequently commented upon favourably. Hilda Martindale, critical of so much in Belfast, told a government inquiry 'I think the housing is good in Belfast, in nearly every case a family has a separate house'.[30] Even James Connolly was forced to admit that although he disliked the politics of the city, 'The homes of the poor are better, house rent is lower, and the city is cleaner and healthier than Dublin'.[31]

A good indicator of the general standard of living in a city would be the health of its inhabitants, if the populations of Bristol and Belfast were similarly housed were they equally healthy? Although the worst of the historic plagues had vanished, late nineteenth and early twentieth century cities were not particularly healthy places to live. If the crude death rate per thousand inhabitants is used as an indicator, conditions in Bristol and Belfast appear very different. The death rate in Belfast was always higher than Bristol falling slowly from 23.5 to 22.1 over the years 1881 to 1905 compared with Bristol's figures of 18.1 and 16.0 for the same period.[32] A more specific indicator of the general health within a community is the infant mortality rate, as this is affected by general standards of housing and nutrition. According to the 1910 report on infant and child mortality Bristol had an infant mortality rate of 100 per 1000 live births (the Medical Officer of Health admitted to 102) compared to 139 in Belfast.[33] This is typical of longer term trends which show that Belfast's mortality was consistently higher than Bristol's.[34]

Although Bristol's infant mortality appears low this conceals the fact that in some areas of the city the rate was far higher. In 1908 the infant mortality figure for the city as a whole was 126. However the crowded central ward registered 163 and St Philips 162; in contrast upper class Clifton had a rate of 91 and rural Westbury 86.[35] In simple terms the children of the very poor were less likely to survive than those whose parents had escaped the inner city slums. It is also possible to trace a relationship between density of population and health conditions in Bristol before the First World War. In 1913 the densely populated St Philips ward (82.7 persons per acre) reported 20 per cent of the city's pulmonary tuberculosis cases and 15.1 per cent of all notifiable diseases. In contrast Westbury (2.6 persons per acre) reported only 1.5 and 2.5 per cent of these infections.[36] Again it was the crowded inner-city areas which suffered the highest rates of disease.

Belfast, like Bristol, displayed considerable local variation in death rates, as was shown by a government enquiry of 1914. Dispensary area five, which lay between the Shankill and Falls roads (population density 112 per acre) had a crude death rate of 23.15. In contrast dispensary area twelve, which lay to the south of the Lagan and east of the Connswater (population 36 per acre) had a death rate of 17.2.[37] Again the highest death rates were in the areas of highest population density. However, there was a significant local variation, in that linen workers, who were not the poorest, suffered very high death rates. The effects of the industry on workers' health was a subject of government enquiries as well as frequent comment from the factory inspectors[38]: '. . . the dust is so injurious that Dr Whitaker of Belfast states "If a girl gets a card at 18, her life is generally terminated at 30". . . On the average 16.8 years of work in this process kills.'[39]

Perhaps the greatest single killer in this era was tuberculosis. In Belfast the illness was common among linen workers where the hot humid conditions in the mills created ideal conditions for the spread of infection. In 1914 it was found that rates of pneumonia, respiratory disease and pulmonary tuberculosis were far higher amongst Belfast mill workers than the rest of the city's population.[40] Between 1881 and 1900 the death rate from phthisis (pulmonary tuberculosis) in Belfast was twice that in Bristol.[41] In Bristol TB deaths again occurred disproportionately in the poorest areas of the city. In 1885 180 per 100 000 inhabitants died in the St Philips district compared with 119 in Clifton; by 1910 the rate had fallen dramatically but the difference remained, the relevant rates being 100 and 55.[42]

In 1908 the Bristol School Board examined 3081 school children and found 24 cases of phthisis and 17 of other forms of TB (1.33 per cent). This seems to have shocked the authorities into action as the following year 15 161 children were examined with 81 confirmed cases of phthisis discovered and another five suspected.[43] Treatment for TB victims was fairly limited during these years. A Tuberculosis Sub-Committee of the Bristol City Council's Health Committee, met regularly. Its work consisted of awarding sanatorium places or nourishment grants (usually in the form of a quart of milk a day) and dispensing burial grants of ten shillings.[44] In November 1903 the Health Committee decided to donate £4000 in capital and £1040 a year to the new Winsley sanatorium, in return for which they received the exclusive use of sixteen beds.[45]

The medical inspection of school children, which began in Bristol in 1909, was to have long-term effects on standards of health. It was not however an entirely paternalistic development; there were widespread fears that factory life and urban conditions were seriously affecting the quality of manpower available to the armed forces after 1900.[46] The problem was presented in uncompromising terms by the Chief Medical Officer of the Board of Education in his report of 1909.

It may, however, be stated generally that, in respect of the six million children in the Public Elementary Schools of England and Wales, about 10 per cent of them suffer from serious defects of vision, from 3 to 5 per cent suffer from defective hearing, 1 to 3 per cent have suppurating ears, 8 per cent have adenoids, or enlarged tonsils, of sufficient degree to obstruct the nose or throat and to require surgical treatment, 20 to 40 per cent, suffer from extensive and injurious decay of the teeth, 40 per cent have unclean heads, about 1 per cent suffer from ringworm, 1 per cent are affected with tuberculosis of readily recognisable form, and .5 to 2 per cent are afflicted with heart disease.[47]

During the first year of the Act's operation, 3081 school children aged from 3 to 15 years were inspected in Bristol. Of these 1213 were found to have 'defects' of various kinds, 68 of which were found to be so serious as to require 'A' cards, (unfit for school) and 387 'B' cards (needing medical attention).[48] In 1913 15 603 children were inspected by the Education Committee's staff: of these 1571 were in need of medical treatment, 1324 had defective teeth and 512 had problems with their eyes. A year later it was found that no action had been taken in 49.2 per cent of those cases where medical treatment was necessary, but this compared favourably with those needed dentists or opticians where the non-treatment rates were 71.3 and 74.6 respectively.[49] Only 3240 children (29.6 per cent) were found 'free of defects' although it was pointed out that this was a distinct improvement on previous years. The most common problem was bad teeth, with only 6224 out of 10 995 children examined having 'sound' teeth. However, the picture was not wholly negative. In terms of nutrition and cleanliness conditions were good and even improving. In 1913 only 2.5 per cent of those examined were 'dirty as regards body' and 7.4 were infected with nits (mainly girls). Only 7.9 per cent of children examined in 1913 were suffering from 'nutritional deficiency' and in only 0.55 of cases was nutrition actually 'bad'. Of those examined between 1909 and 1913 89–91 per cent were said to be enjoying a 'normal' diet.[50]

Belfast was not covered by the Medical Inspection of School Children Act, the School Medical Service being established only after the corporation assumed responsibility for education in 1923. The problems faced by the education services in the city can be seen from an early report of the Medical Director Dr Fulton. Of 197 school buildings under his supervision only 16 were 'good' and one 'enlarged and improved' from the point of view of hygiene.[51] Systematic inspection of entrants and leavers began in 1924, the average time taken being five minutes with those children with problems being re-examined later.[52]

The need to assist those children whose families, for whatever reason, could not provide a 'normal' diet was recognised at an early date in Bristol. There existed an extensive charity organisation which by 1904 supplied 69 514 breakfasts and 29 126 dinners a year to orphans or the children of the sick or unemployed.[53] A 'Provision of Meals Act' was introduced at the same time as the 'Medical Inspection of School Children Act' for broadly similar reasons. The changes were not always welcomed by those who supplied charity meals in the past, on the grounds that such government intervention might make matters worse by 'lessening parental responsibility'.[54] Regardless of these fears by 1914 the central kitchens in Narrow Weir supplied 174 795 dinners with a further 107 357 being supplied by other means.[55] The menus used provide an interesting view of what was considered a 'suitable' diet.[56]

Week One

Monday	Stewed Beef with peas and Bread
Tuesday	Cocoa and Raisin Bread with Cheese
Wednesday	Irish Stew with Bread
Thursday	Cocoa and Pressed Beef with Bread
Friday	Boiled Fish with Parsley Sauce and Bread

Week Two

| Monday | Pea Soup with Dumplings and Bread |

Tuesday	Lentil Soup with Dumplings and Bread
Wednesday	Hashed Beef with Vegetables and Bread
Thursday	Haricot Soup with Bread
Friday	Cocoa and Raisin Bread with Cheese

The number of meals provided by the School Board soon far exceeded the number previously supplied by charitable bodies.[57]

Once again the legislation allowing provision of meals for school children did not initially include Ireland; although there was enabling legislation in 1914 no action was taken.[58] In Belfast school meals, as with medical inspection, were only introduced after the corporation assumed responsibility for education. During 1926 a system of 'dining centres' was inaugurated which supplied 254 619 meals from 14 centres in 1926–7, and 418 177 from 19 centres in 1928–9.[59]

The question of public health was a vexed one in Bristol which, unlike Belfast, at the start of this period had few effective local controls. As late as 1845 only Liverpool and Manchester of the English urban districts had higher mortality rates than Bristol. In that year it was reported that only 5000 people in the city had piped water compared to the 73 000 dependent on wells whose supply was 'often too filthy for washing let alone drinking'.[60] Three years later it was noted that 34 sewers discharged into the floating harbour in the middle of the city depositing no less that 20 000 tons of solid matter yearly.[61] Improvement was a slow process and understandably those working to achieve it were sometimes angry at what they saw as ill-informed criticism.

> Recently a clever writer among us, according to the fashion of the hour, has been making a round of visits amongst the lowest class of our population and has been publishing his experiences in a local paper, giving, in grabbe-like fashion and in powerful language, the painful details of improvidence, drunkenness, thriftlessness, poverty and vice which are unfortunately found in all large centres of population ... I sincerely wish that the writer had borne in mind a trite old English adage about a certain very necessary operation not be done in public.[62]

The reports of the Medical Officer of Health show a steady increase in activity through out these years. Private wells were closed and houses connected to piped water supplies, pigs and other public nuisances removed and increasingly fumigation and disinfection were used on houses and clothing to prevent infection.[63]

What medical facilities were available to the 'working class' of each city and how did they survive periods of illness? A vice-regal commission in 1906 noted that Belfast had twelve hospitals under private management, in addition to the corporation fever hospital at Purdysburn and the Port Authority's intercepting hospital.[64] The availability of hospital beds in Bristol was always much lower than in Belfast, amounting in 1891 to only 1070 beds in nine institutions, not counting specialist institutions such as the Eye and Lock Hospitals.[65] In July 1900 the Medical Officer of Health reported to the Council that they had only 147 beds available for infectious disease cases, and the Port Authority another 24. This he pointed out gave only one bed per 2300 inhabitants of the city, rather than one to every 1000 recommended by the Local Government Board.[66] Later he pointed out that this was possible by allowing 1000 cubic feet per patient at the Novers Hill Hospital rather than the recommended 2000.[67] By 1905 the only additions to general hospital capacity in the city were the Clifton Cottage Hospital (established 1894) and Cosham Hospital in Kingswood (being built).[68]

A major advantage enjoyed by Irish cities, including Belfast, was the extensive system of dispensaries established under the Medical Poor Relief (Ireland) Act of 1851.

> Ireland stands in a very different position to England. Here we have an older system of dispensaries, and it is considered that the dispensaries combined with benefit societies, actually meet the requirements of medical assistance for the workers to a far larger extent than in England.[69]

Until 1911 Bristol, and Britain in general, lacked any national system of medical provision to match the Irish one. Even after the National Insurance Act there was nothing to compare with the highly organised Irish dispensary system, although in Bristol there were a number of charitable institutions, some of considerable antiquity.[70] In most cases Bristolians obtained medical assistance as out-patients at one of the hospitals, a practice not always approved of.

> Provident Dispensaries, as an alternative to much of the gratuitous out-patient hospital treatment.
> The difficulty of establishing dispensaries on a provident basis in face of the 'competition' of a huge free system is obviously great, but the Council are not without hope that some much-desired reform in this direction may be effected before long.[71]

The scale of dispensary activity in Belfast was said by Dr Brian O'Brian to have reached 45–50 000 treatments a year by 1914.[72] In the same year according to the Bristol Insurance Panel Doctors' Report, there were 106 704 persons covered by the scheme and a thousand prescriptions were being issued each day.[73]

Prior to 1911 all Bristolians had to pay for medical treatment, and even after that date many still had to. How were these costs met? What facilities existed other than the Poor Law to support the sick worker and their families during periods when they could not earn a living? Prolonged sickness could be disastrous for a working person in this period, particularly the low paid. Mary Galway explained to a government inquiry in 1913 that girls under 21 received only five shillings a week from the union in sick pay and that this did not even cover the cost of medical treatment and a doctor's certificate.[74] The various benefit societies acted as personal insurance against such a situation. A wide range of groups such as Foresters, Shepherds, Druids, and Oddfellows provided medical and unemployment benefits in both Bristol and Belfast. Some unlikely organisations offered their members such facilities as one Belfast worker recorded.

> When I obtained work in the city (1898) I immediately joined the Mechanic' LOL (Loyal Orange Lodge) 1200 in Clifton Street Orange Hall...A benevolent fund was formed and the members had free medical attendance and medicine with sick benefit of 10/- per week. For this the doctor was paid 2/6 per member per annum.[75]

A Dictionary of Bristol published in 1906 lists 26 'benefit societies' of various kinds in the city.[76]

During the winter of 1905–6 7.4 per cent of those claiming relief from the Bristol Distress Committee were members of friendly societies. However, 11.1 per cent of those claiming relief had friendly benefits as part of the trade union membership.[77] The provision of medical and unemployment benefits was one of the great attractions of trade unionism for the semi-skilled or unskilled worker. For the unions providing such services could often present serious problems.

> I have been secretary of a trade union with about 500 members and we have been in the habit of paying the doctor 2/6 per head per annum. Now the doctors want to raise the 2/6 to 8/6, and we could not possibly pay that without increasing very considerably the contributions of our members. As a matter of fact we have been obliged to discharge the doctor entirely, and add 3/6 to the amount

that a man who is sick will receive per week. That will allow him at least one visit from a doctor, and as we think a fair price for a certificate, 1/-.[78]

The Workers Union, representing unskilled workers, produced a circular in Belfast which emphasised the optional sick and out-of-work benefits offered by the union at threepence a week each.[79] The success of such schemes can be gauged by the employer-sponsored Belfast Labour Bureau, offering membership of its own sick club at cut-price rates.[80]

It is impossible to compare living conditions in these cities without looking at wage rates. There were clearly differences between Bristol and Belfast but these were not as great as is sometimes suggested.[81] More significant in the case of both Bristol and Belfast, when looking at living standards, are household or family income levels rather than adult male wage rates (see Table 8.1). To illustrate this point a male

Table 8.1 Weekly wage rates in Belfast and Bristol, 1905[82] (shillings/pence)

		Belfast	Bristol
Building	Bricklayer	38s. 3d.	40s. 6d.
	Plumber	38s. 3d.	40s. 6d.
	Mason	38s. 3d.	40s. 6d.
	Carpenter	38s. 3d.	40s. 6d.
	Plasterer	38s. 3d.	40s. 6d.
	Painter	36s.	38s. 3d.
	Labourer	16–19s.	27–28s.
Engineering	Fitters	37s.	36s.
	Turner	38s.	36s.
	Smith	37s.	36s.
	Pattern-maker	39s.	38s. 3d.
	Labourer	15–18s.	20–22s.
Printing	Compositor	34s.	31s.
Furnishing	Cabinet-maker	36–37s.	
	Upholsterer	36s.	34–38s.
	French-polisher	36s.	31s. 6d.

worker in Fry's chocolate factory in Bristol in 1912 earned 25s. a week, a fairly low male wage for either Belfast or Bristol at this time.[83] However, in either city, it is probable that other members of the family would also be working either full or part time and supplementing the

Table 8.2 Hypothetical family earnings in Bristol, 1914[84]

Mother	Sewing corsets as an outworker 6 dozen pairs a week.	5s. 3d.
Daughter	17yrs, working in clothing firm as machine sewer (time rate)	4s. 11d.
Son	15 yrs, working as van boy	6s.
Son	14 yrs, attending school and working 30 hours for grocer	3s. 6d.
Son	10 yrs, attending school and works in private house odd jobs	2s.
Total income excluding father		21s. 6d.

family income (see Table 8.2). Although clearly not every family would conform to this pattern the opportunities for employment of women and young persons would have greatly increased 'family' incomes.

After rent, the next major element in a family's budget was food. What did the 'working classes' of Bristol and Belfast eat and did the cost of food vary greatly between the two cities? Diet tended to be similar, consisting mainly of imported foodstuffs with 'local' products added for quality not price. There was considerable variation in the price of basic foodstuffs between the two cities.[85] However, the critical point is not the basic price of a commodity but rather the quantity brought. This varied according to income and personal preferences, but some writers have tried to quantify the diet of the 'working classes'.[86] In a study where a detailed week-by-week account of the type of food brought by a number of households was kept, the results were so diverse that an 'average' shopping basket could not be determined.[87] With this limitation in mind, I looked at the cost of food based upon the Board of Trade figures for 1905. This rather artificial method of calculating expenditure shows considerable variation in food costs between Bristol and Belfast. The 'average' shopping list of a worker earning 25–30s. a week would have been 12s. 3d. in Bristol and either 13s. 4d. or 15s. 6d. in Belfast depending on the worker's choice of 'Irish' or 'English' diets.[88] What is surprising is that Bristol food costs are lower than Belfast's, due mainly to cheaper meat and bread.

What were the 'working classes' eating in the years before the First World War? A French visitor to Birmingham commented upon the diet of a prosperous small tool maker and his family and then made some general points about the British worker's eating habits.

In the Brown household, as in all English working-class households, there are several meals. In the morning, before seven o'clock there is breakfast, consisting of coffee, bread and butter, and meat, generally bacon; about twelve there is dinner, consisting of some kind of meat, beef or mutton, with the unvarying boiled potatoes; at four o'clock tea, one or two cups of tea with bread and butter; and in the evening, about eight or nine o'clock, there is supper, which is not so solid a meal as dinner, but which brings meat on the table for the third time.

Of course all Birmingham workmen do not live as well as this. Many do not eat meat every day, or eat it only once a day, but in that case they think themselves on short commons. Their standard diet tends towards what I have just described; they adopt it as soon as their means permit, not as a luxury, not as a matter of taste, but as a normal, reasonable and understandable thing.

...This 4lb. loaf represents the consumption of seven persons for a day making a little over half a pound a head. A French family would need twice as much, but in England bread is little more than an excuse for eating butter.[89]

There is nothing particularly new in this observation, Engels having noted a similar dietary division as early as 1844.[90] The carnivorous tendencies of the working class were also noted by observers such as Edward Cadbury, Maud Pember-Reeves and Arthur Bowley.[91] Such habits were to cause concern among some observers of contemporary social conditions.

The factory operatives are great flesh eaters. It would seem that their utter severance from the soil by machinery has taken out of them all agricultural instincts and vegetarian likings by spoiling their appetites...Probably this excessive flesh eating has a tendency to make the people carnivorously cruel and selfish, and has its effects on morals as well as health.[92]

Whatever vegetarian social reformers thought of their diet the workers in British cities ate increasingly similar foodstuffs. Bread, the staple, was increasingly produced from American grain imports which rose dramatically.[93] In 1880 the first cargo of frozen beef and mutton arrived in London aboard the ss *Strathleven* and by 1902 56lbs a year of frozen or chilled meat was being consumed per head of the population.[94] It is noticeable that American cheddar was the only cheese included in the Board of Trade's 1905 and 1912 price surveys. American and Canadian bacon were included in the 1912 Dublin price survey. Bristol bacon was usually Canadian while Belfast had a preference for Irish 'green' cured.[95] By 1902 imports of dairy products had reached £47 700 000 including £9.3 million of Danish butter and £4.3 million of Canadian cheese.[96] By 1909 the Co-operative Wholesale Society was importing almost £7 million of foreign goods, mostly foodstuffs.[97]

Burnett argues that the years after 1880 were a period marked by falling food prices due to imports, and rapid improvement in the standard of living of the 'working class'.[98] It is probable that this process began rather earlier with imports of foodstuffs increasing from the 1860s.[99] The diet of the urban worker not only improved during these years but became increasingly uniform. Although there were inevitably differences due to levels of income the types of food consumed by workers in Bristol and, perhaps to a lesser degree, Belfast, became increasingly similar to that in other British cities.[100]

Education was a feature of 'working class' life in both Bristol and Belfast: compulsory in both, it was seen by some as the great social leveller. The period 1880 to 1925 was to see a huge increase in both student numbers and school attendance in the city of Bristol's elementary schools. In the years 1880–4 the average number of pupils registered in Bristol's schools were 30 195 per annum which steadily increased to 62 271 in 1905–9 before beginning to decline. The average daily attendance was 73.9 per cent at the start of the period increasing to 89.1 in the years immediately before the First World War.[101] The increasing proportion of children attending school each day was due to the increasing value placed upon education by society in general, and to the prosecution of truants and their parents.[102] However as the Inspector of the Irish Board of Education found in 1904 conditions in schools in Irish cities seemed unlikely to encourage scholars.

> In the ordinary schools in Dublin or Belfast the great majority of the scholars are taught in a single large room 50 feet, or even more in length, and 25 to 40 feet in breadth ... even to maintain order under such conditions requires considerable skill on the part of the teachers.[103]

Not all government officials were as sympathetic to the problems faced by teachers and managers in Belfast.

> As a rule the children prefer the factory to the school, and, indeed this is not surprising, at least during the winter months, when we

compare the cold, dull schoolrooms, the enforced silence, the irksome task, and the ever present fear of a light cane applied by an expert and ready hand, with the warm and well lighted factory with its life and bustle and the freedom of tongue and action which is permitted there.[104]

In Belfast the school system failed to keep pace with the increase in population and by the early twentieth century a crisis had been reached. Reports of the School Inspectors indicated that up to 80 of the city's schools were in unfit buildings and that they were overcrowded by nine to ten thousand pupils. More seriously it was claimed that fifteen to twenty thousand children of school age were unable to find places in the city.[105] Belfast suffered not only a poor standard of school accommodation but also, according to the School Inspector, poor teacher performance. The teachers' union was quick to point out that this had more to do with the attitude of the inspectors than conditions in the schools.[106] In Bristol, where the city rather than a national authority controlled education, there were 73 elementary schools in 1891, only 19 of which were directly managed by the schools board. The others were controlled by various religious denominations. Although critical, the Fabians recognised that there had been progress.

Bristol stands well, so far as its School Board is concerned, with respect to its Day Industrial Feeding School, which feeds and educates 210 poor children; its two swimming baths for Board School children, with swimming instructors; its pianos in the larger schools; and its provision of special instructors for pupil-teachers, as well as classes for deaf, dumb and blind children.[107]

The expansion in the city's school system, as outlying areas were absorbed, meant that by 1914 the number of children who could be accommodated had increased from 37 098 to 61 152 and children on the registers from 35 846 to 58 919.[108] Few Bristolians left school with more than a basic education, those going to secondary school being basically those who could afford it.[109] In May 1913, 3150 pupils were examined to gain scholarships at secondary schools. Of these 1429 passed the exam but only 60 scholarships were awarded (35 boys and 25 girls) plus 66 free places in the municipal secondary schools.[110]

However, education did not end on leaving school. In 1891 the Fabians noted that only 32 per cent of school leavers in Bristol enrolled in evening classes and only half of those actually attended.[111] In 1912,

4050 Bristol school leavers were supplied with cards allowing them free access to evening schools, of whom 1095 entered the classes in 1912–13.[112] A committee investigating the employment conditions of van boys was told 'small' numbers of these juvenile workers attended evening classes in Bristol and 'very few' in Belfast.[113] After a long working day workers were simply too tired for such diversions and sought lighter relief.

Indeed, the factory operatives when their days work is done are too weary and "fagged out" to engage in mental pursuits; they want something exciting, to take with variety the eye that is tired of monotony, to rouse the jaded body, and to plunge into the noisy pleasures of stimulants and singing-rooms.[114]

Despite the apparent lack of interest it was felt by many that education was critical to the 'improvement' of the working classes. The formation and success of the Workers Education Association was to demonstrate that there was a demand for adult education. However, the question of education could be highly controversial, notably as to what form it should take for the 'working class'. In 1910 the Belfast Trades Council's delegates to the Irish TUC opposed the extension of technical education, which provoked an acrimonious debate on their return.[115] A month later a report to the council was to show that they saw education in broader terms than vocational training. In a joint deputation with the ILP and the Co-op they requested that the Queen's University establish 'tutorial classes for working class students at convenient centres in the city'.[116] In Bristol the trades council took an active role in trying to further educational facilities for adults.[117] They were involved in the WEA and helped establish the Bristol University Tutorial Classes Joint Committee in 1912–13 which sought to extend university style education to the masses.[118]

Unemployment was a feature of Belfast and Bristol in the years before the First World War; as in all British cities, it could take many forms. General depressions in trade could mean all industries reducing employment. Some industries, such as construction, were seasonal with high levels of unemployment at certain times of year. Alternatively other groups such as dock labourers faced an employment market which by its very nature was casual and unpredictable. Exact figures on unemployment for the early part of the period do not exist, and data which has been published represents no more than some skilled unions' unemployment rates.[119]

In Bristol seasonal unemployment in the building trades and amongst dockers was a long-standing feature of the labour market.

> September has come and gone, leaving behind pleasant memories of nature's kindness, and grim reminiscences connected with the problems of poverty and unemployment. The problems are the children of selfishness and greed ... each night many thousands of children have gone supperless to bed why? Because the problems of poverty and unemployment have entered their homes. Before going supperless to bed many young children fed themselves with the glowing colours outside the windows, wondering, as children will, if greedy selfishness went hungry to bed.[120]

It has been claimed that the introduction of the steam vessel had the effect of spreading the trade of ports over the year and thus reducing seasonal unemployment.[121] However, the evidence given by the City Council to the Poor Law Commission relating to employment in the docks suggests there was considerable seasonal variation in employment as late as 1903–5.[122] This seasonal variation was particularly marked in the grain trade which was an increasingly important element in Bristol's trade in these years.

In Belfast the economy was heavily dependent on engineering, linen and shipbuilding. Any slump in demand in these sectors could create serious unemployment. During the winter of 1904–5 due to a depression in industry as a whole 19 per cent of Belfast shipyard workers were unemployed and 13 per cent of engineering workers.[123] There was to be a second slump in 1908–9 mainly due to limited demand in the shipbuilding sector. Bristol, as was noted by A.J. Pugsley, was not dependent upon a single industry or manufacturer with the result that it was less susceptible to such slumps in demand than Belfast.[124] However, this was not enough in itself to protect the Bristol worker from fluctuations in the wider economy as the yearly unemployment rates show. Unemployment was a feature of both Bristol and Belfast in the pre-war years but at it peak, during the winter of 1909–10, less than 2 per cent of the total labour force was claiming public relief.[125]

The situation in Dublin cannot be compared with either Bristol or Belfast in these years. Population growth which was such a major feature of development in the other two cities was very limited in Dublin. In 1841 the city had 233 000 inhabitants (265 000 if the suburbs are included) rising to 305 000 by 1911 (404 000 with the suburbs).[126] When compared to Belfast's 452.8 per cent growth or Bristol's 187.9 in these years, Dublin and suburbs grew by only 52.5, and the city itself by only 30.9. In Dublin in these years, it was the 'middle' and professional classes who could move out of the city to suburbs, causing an actual fall in population within the city itself in the 1860s and 1870s. Whereas the suburbs of Bristol and Belfast became characterised by working class housing, the Dublin working class moved into town houses abandoned by the wealthier classes. The old city centre as a result was increasingly characterised by overcrowded tenements and poverty.

Some of the houses in Russell Street were privately owned and oc- cupied by their owners. Others were rented out in floors or rooms, with a mixture of clerks, tradesmen and working men living in them. At the end of the street there was an elegant mansion in which the manager of the Phoenix Bottling Company lived, and in the houses almost directly opposite the Behans, a civil servant, a master baker and a fortune teller lived. On the other hand, a prostitute plied her trade from a room directly under the Behans, and a travelling man next door kept his donkey in the room with him until after many attempts to eject him, the house had finally to be demolished around him.[127]

The private company that ran Dublin's trams was again the subject of much criticism; although an investigating American team com- mented that the Dublin Tramways were well run and efficient.[128] The fares were, said critics, even higher in Dublin than the penny a mile charged in London. Although cheap workman's fares were introduced in 1884 most tram routes ran through middle class rather than working class districts.[129] The trams were even used to score political points between Belfast and Dublin.

A penny tram ride in Belfast is much longer than a penny tram ride in Dublin, but whereas the penny tram ride in Dublin will take you out of the taxable area of the city, a two penny tram ride in Belfast will still leave you within the city limits.[130]

Compared to the other two cities the Dublin Tram Company operated a huge mileage of track linking the outlying suburbs to the centre. Dublin had a track mileage of 107.5 and a population of 3685 per mile of track, compared to 73.14 and 4767 in Belfast and 52 and 6885 in Bristol, this giving the highest overheads per head of population of the three cities, greatly increasing costs.[131]

The improving housing conditions in Belfast and Bristol serve only to make the contrast with Dublin even more stark. The housing conditions in Dublin were notorious, and the report of the Departmental Committee on the problem showed that the reputation was well deserved.[132] The journalist Arnold Wright used the report as the basis of a chapter in his history of the 1913 lockout entitled 'Conditions of Life and Labour'.

> The Dublin slum, in fact, is a thing apart in the inferno of social degradation. Nowhere can there be found concentrated so many of the evils which are associated with the underworld of our modern civilisation. To say that men and women live like beasts of the field is the merest truth. In buildings old, rotten, and permeated with both physical and moral corruption, they crowd in incredible numbers.[133]

If there are villains in the story of Dublin housing they are, as so often in Irish history, the landlords. The absence of new building in the city created a serious housing shortage as population grew. In 1905 landlords owning over 600 houses and tenements admitted increasing their rents by an average of 22 per cent between 1880 and 1900.[134] As a result compared to the workers of Bristol and Dublin those of Dublin were not just appallingly housed but paid higher rents for the privilege. In 1901 almost a quarter of Dublin families were living in a single room compared with less than half living in dwellings of four or more rooms. Rents were also high with some tenants paying as much for a single room as they would have done for a modest four-room house in Belfast or Bristol.[135]

The authorities in Dublin did make progress in improving conditions, as they informed the 1900 enquiry into public health in the city. In 1879 there had been 9760 tenements in the city, 2300 of which had been unfit for habitation; these had been reduced to 6585 by 1900.[136] There had been no system for the removal of domestic refuse in 1880, but from 1882 they had begun the daily cleaning of tenement yards and 440 men were so employed by May 1885.[137] The enquiry was also told that water closets had become almost universal, public baths had been established and street cleaning and paving improved.[138] However, the sheer scale of the housing problem was simply beyond the resources of the City's Council.

In order to try to improve housing conditions the authorities in Dublin, unlike Bristol and Belfast, carried out public housing projects. The largest of these, begun in 1905, comprised 460 tenements between Montgomery Street and Purdon Street. 'The single-roomed tenements are let to widows and to married people with no more than two children, those having larger families occupying the two-roomed.'[139] These 'improved' tenements cost between 2s. and 3s. 3d. with 76 per cent of them being single rooms, in which up to four people were living. The council and other bodies housed some 20 000 people in such accommodation but, as with so much else, Dublin lacked the resources to meet demand.

The housing conditions made Dublin a far less healthy place to live than either of the other two cities. The crude death rate remained at approximately 27 throughout the period 1881 to 1905 while infant mortality was over 170 during the 1880s and 1890s falling to 158 during the early years of the twentieth century.[140] In 1910 the Report on Child Mortality recorded a death rate of 145 per thousand live births in Dublin compared to 139 in Belfast and only 100 in Bristol.[141] The link between poverty, poor housing and bad health was recognised by contemporary observers: 'A one-roomed tenement breeds twice as much tuberculosis as two rooms. Housing was the key not just to health but morale.'[142]

Although the TB rate in Dublin was lower than Belfast it was far higher than Bristol in these years.[143] As in Bristol and Belfast the poor suffered most from TB with the family of a labourer being eight times more likely to suffer infection than those of a member of the professional classes in 1912.[144] In view of the poor health conditions it is as well that the city was comparatively well supplied with hospitals.

> A parliamentary grant of £15,850 is annually voted in support of eleven Dublin hospitals and the Corporation contribute about £5,500 to twenty-two hospitals, including the Meath Hospital (or County Dublin Infirmary). There are also hospitals at Kingstown (St Michaels) and Monkstown, Co Dublin, both under private management.[145]

The diet of the Dublin slum dweller was poorer than Belfast or Bristol's working classes and more expensive. The 'average' weekly food bill was 12s. 2d. in Bristol but 15s. 5d. in Dublin due mainly to higher cost of bread and meat and greater consumption of milk and potatoes.[146] In general the school system was much the same as Belfast's, although as Mary Daly points out the social conditions in the city were even less conducive to academic improvement.[147] The movement towards adult education so much a feature of Bristol and Belfast made little progress. The WEA was not successful in establishing itself in Dublin, and university extension had made no progress as late as 1918.[148]

Not only were rents and food costs higher in Dublin than Bristol or Belfast, but wages tended to be lower for many sectors of the labour force.[149] The employment structure in Dublin offered very limited opportunities for female or child employment compared to the other cities. As a result the adult working male wage is far more likely to represent total family income in Dublin than in either Bristol or Belfast. Membership of benefit and friendly societies appears to have been lower than amongst the better paid industrial workers in the other cities. In the winter of 1905–6 the clerk of the Dublin Distress Committee was to report that there was only one trade unionist and four members of benefit societies amongst the 1345 applicants for relief.[150] Although this was dismissed as merely showing the 'incompleteness' of Irish record keeping, the 0.4 per cent figure for Dublin would seem to indicate a far lower density than the 18.5 per cent reported in Bristol.

However, the problem of unemployment in Dublin went far beyond the normal seasonal variation in labour demand; there were critical structural aspects to the city's problems.

> The really important fact which emerges from an examination of the census figures is that no fewer than 45,149 persons belong to the unskilled labourer class, or about one-seventh of the total population. The significance of this fact is too obvious to need elaborate demonstration. It is the root factor in the economic situation.[151]

The contrast between Dublin and Belfast was made clear by Cyril Jackson in his report on conditions in the two cities during 1908. Dublin was suffering from 'considerable depression' increased by an influx of men from the country whilst Belfast was 'extremely flourishing' and 'no steady man need be out of employment'.[152] Although unemployment was a feature of both Bristol and Belfast before the First World War, demand for labour was generally high in both cities. In Dublin the problem of unemployment was aggravated by widespread under-employment amongst a casual labour force with limited employment opportunities. Certainly more sought assistance under the Unemployed Workman's Act during the Winter months than in either Bristol and Belfast.[153]

CONCLUSION

When the living conditions of the populations of the three cities covered by this study are compared it is possible to see that Belfast and

Bristol shared characteristics not found in Dublin. Whilst adult male wages were fairly similar in all three cities the opportunities for female and child employment produced higher 'family' incomes in Belfast and Bristol. When compared to the slum dwellers of Dublin the 'working classes' of the other two cities were better housed and fed, enjoyed better standards of health and paid cheaper tram fares. Even this brief overview shows how difficult it is to try to compare living standards between cities of this period, as there are so many variables. However, none of the cities were healthy places, as the government committee on 'physical degeneration' concluded in the early years of the twentieth century.[154] There was a slow improvement in the conditions in Britain's cities, but as the experience of the First World War was to show it would take generations rather than years for the reforms to be effective.

It was largely in consequence of our being such a town-breed race that during the war were regarded as C3 people. Medical examination of recruits at that period showed that there was just cause for us to be so considered, for only 36 per cent of recruits for the army could be placed in grade 1: in other words, only one out of every three men examined were found to be physically fit and capable of bearing arms. Previously to the recent war there was a belief that the social condition of the working classes had been improving and that owing to cheap food they were better nourished, but the results of the medical examination during the war did not quite support this contention . . . it takes a considerable time before the physical defects which afflict a people for one or two generations can be got rid of.[155]

Having established that in social terms Belfast can be compared with Bristol, I will now look at the topic which has traditionally been seen as setting Belfast apart from British working class experience, sectarianism.

9 Sectarianism

If any feature set Belfast apart from Bristol and Dublin it was the tradition of intercommunal violence which continues to this day. Other cities had a reputation for sectarianism but nowhere was it on a scale to match Belfast. The improving living conditions within the city did nothing to reduce violent sectarian divisions.

> The town is, in its present proportions, of very recent growth; and the result is that the poorer classes, instead of, as in other cities, occupying tenements in large houses, reside mainly in separate cottages and small houses. The western district of Belfast is covered with these small dwellings of the artisan and labourer; and this district was in the main the theatre of the riots of 1886.
> The extremity to which party and religious feeling has grown in Belfast is shown strikingly by the fact that the people of the artisan and labouring classes, disregarding the ordinary considerations of convenience, dwell to a large extent in separate quarters, each of which is almost entirely given up to persons of one particular faith and the boundaries of which are sharply defined.[1]

Sectarianism was not confined to a single sector of society. Norman Townsend, a District Inspector of the Royal Irish Constabulary, believed even the city's magistrates were sectarian in their attitudes.[2] The Belfast Chamber of Commerce was overwhelmingly Protestant/ Unionist in its opinions. In 1893 John Burke, a shipping agent, objected to remarks opposing Home Rule 'but' he admitted 'I know there would be little use in this chamber of carrying my protest further'.[3] The city saw repeated outbreaks of violence in working class districts, triggered by the provocative behaviour of one side or the other.[4] Elaborate efforts were made to discover, or conceal, the religious affiliation of individuals in the workplace.

> "What is his religion?" when a stranger comes to work in a place in which there is a crowd, that is the first question that they all think of. And, of course, it is amusing to watch the tricks which are played to get the information. The stranger would not be there long until someone would come and speak to him. As often as not the talk would be about soccer, for if the stranger was a Gael (Catholic), it would not be unlikely he would be a Celtic fan, the only team that

132

are supposed to be "Gaelic". But perhaps the stranger would be on his guard and he would say that he had no interest in the game. If he said so, your man would try another trick. "Can you go home at dinner-time?" he would say, for by that means he would find out what district of the city the other man was living in. The stranger could put the other man off, or perhaps he could say that he had a lunch with him and that he intended to eat it at work. But it was all the same Friday would not go past without everyone knowing his religion. If he was a Gael, it would be noticed that day that he had no meat in his lunch. If he was a Scotsman (Protestant) he would have meat with him on Friday, especially his first Friday in work – even if he didn't have it for the rest of the week.[5]

Such divisions were embarrassing to those who sought to present Belfast as a thriving modern city. Government officials and prominent citizens were equally keen to present the problem as political rather than religious.

It appeared that within the parliamentary boundary of Belfast, there were 202 000 Protestants and 70 000 Catholics, and that the Catholics had not a solitary representative in the municipal council. Mr Wolff M.P. said that the differences between Catholic and Protestant in Belfast were purely political, and in no sense religious, and though the statement is not true of the past, I do verily believe it is true of the Belfast of today.[6]

Yet even this observer saw the attempted solution to these problems in simple sectarian terms of Catholic and Protestant.[7]

There had not always been religious conflict in the city. In the 1780s radical Presbyterians in Belfast's volunteer movement argued, unsuccessfully, at the Convention of February 1782 that Catholics should be given the vote. The following year they formally invited Catholics to enlist, the first such body in Ireland to do so. In May 1784 the Volunteers attended the opening mass at St Mary's, the first Catholic church in Belfast, which had largely been built by subscriptions from the Presbyterian community.[8] At this time Catholics formed about 8 per cent of the population but immigration from rural areas was to increase this proportion dramatically in the course of the century.[9]

In rural Ulster relations between Catholic and Protestant were increasingly embittered by competition for land. In Country Armagh Protestant tenant farmers formed a secret society called the 'Peep o' Day Boys' which attacked Catholic tenants and weavers. In response

the Catholics formed the 'Defenders' initially as a purely self defence
organisation but which was soon to become more radical in its political ambitions. By the mid 1790s a civil war was raging in this area,
culminating in the 'Battle of the Diamond' and the formation of the
Orange Order in September 1795.[10]

This development of rural sectarian violence coincided with the
growth of the town of Belfast during the development of the cotton
industry. In 1757 the town had a population of 8000 which grew to
13 000 in 1782 and 20 000 in 1800.[11] Migration fuelled growth and,
these 'immigrants' were critical to the industrial success of Belfast.
However, they brought problems.

> Presbyterian radicalism wilted before the mounting self-confidence
> of organised Irish Catholicism. Sectarian antagonism – although
> most certainly aggravated by a new devotional and evangelical fer-
> vour in Catholic and Protestant churches alike – was drawn into
> eastern Ulster by thousands of migrants from west of the Bann in
> search of work in the Lagan Valley mills.[12]

By 1797 the Orange Order was active in Belfast, although they found
recruitment there less easy than in rural areas.[13] The United Irishmen's
rebellion of 1798 served to convince many Presbyterians that radical-
ism was dangerously uncertain. Increasingly conservative they were
attracted to the Orange Order and unionist politics. On the evening of
the 12 July 1813 there was a violent clash between marching Orange-
men and the Catholics of the Hercules Street area which left two dead
and four injured: the Belfast riots had begun.

The Orange Order perhaps more than any other institution is seen as
representing the sectarian divisions within Belfast. Its growth like that
of Belfast was a feature of the second half of the nineteenth century. In
1851 there were only 35 lodges containing 1335 members. A separate
Grand Lodge was established in 1864 and by 1868 there were four
districts, increasing to five the next year and six in 1870.[14] By 1889
there were 144 Orange Lodges in the city with a membership of 5316.[15]
In 1911 there were 229 chapters of the closely related Royal Arch
Purple Order in the Belfast Area.[16] In Belfast the Orange Order was a
very 'working class' institution performing the functions of a benefit
society as well as social and political roles.[17] Rosemary Harris demonstrates an underlying egalitarianism in the movement, the as-
sumption that 'All Brethren are Equal' making it almost impossible for
middle class members to assume control. Indeed the very fact that the

Orange Lodge was an arena where those of lower status could speak out to their 'betters' was one of its great attractions.[18]

Why did such inter-communal antagonism, based upon rural problems, continue in the urban industrial environment of Belfast? The conflict developed on grounds of religion and was fuelled by subsequent waves of migration into the city. Was Belfast different to other industrial cities of this era? The violence of 1832, 1835, 1841, 1843, 1852, 1857, 1864, 1872, 1880, 1884, 1886, 1898, 1907 and 1909 prove conclusively that Belfast had serious problems.[19] But, were these religious/social tensions to be found elsewhere in Britain at this time?

In British industrial cities during the early decades of the nineteenth century Irish immigrants formed a distinctive subgroup, marked off by religion and poverty, frequently in violent conflict with their neighbours.[20] In Newcastle and Sunderland large Irish communities, attracted by unskilled labour in the shipyards, were established by 1850s in the face of local prejudice.[21] Glasgow was notorious for its violent divisions, although one recent historian suggests these were largely imported from Ireland.[22] Branches of the Dockers Union in Liverpool were divided along sectarian lines. Although Taplin says 'Evidence of religious strife at the waterfront is negligible', foremen tended to employ those of their own persuasion.[23] Men such as 'Captain' Tupper who led the attacks on the Cardiff Chinese in 1911, during a campaign by the National Transport Workers Federation against cheap labour, could claim 'England's conscience wasn't bothered'.[24] For obvious reasons few unions are willing to admit that their past leaders held such views. However, in the official history of the National Union of Printing, Bookbinding and Paper Workers there are recorded events which may have been more typical. In 1899 the retiring General Secretary D. Sharp sent a postcard to a member in Belfast, in which he said of Kelly, the leading candidate to replace him, 'It should be made known that the Manchester man is R.C. Do your best for Powell'. Kelly was elected, and Sharp was severely censured by the union for his actions.[25] How often did similar behaviour go undiscovered or unrecorded?

Most analysts who seek to demonstrate that Belfast was/is a sectarian city look at employment patterns. Coughlan suggests that Catholics were seriously disadvantaged in the better paid shipbuilding and engineering sectors and over-represented in the lower paid linen industry.[26] This view of Catholic industrial employment appears to be supported by the census data for these years.[27] However, Catholic under-representation was also a feature of white collar and local government employment, with only 3.6 per cent of the elected members and 4.5 per cent of the employees of five public bodies being catholic. In 1922 Belfast Corporation had to admit that out of 681 paid officials earning a total of £17 233 per year only 33 were Catholics earning a total of £637.[28] It was also noted by Kenna that the Catholics held low status jobs, the eight working at the asylum, for example, being only attendants and the two working for the Corporation drew only £265 between them a year.[29]

How much sectarianism was there within Harland & Wolff? Edward Harland told the 1886 Riot Commission that he had threatened to close the yard in 1864 to prevent the expulsion of Catholics and that relations were good in the yard.[30] During 1920 William Pirrie tried to resist the expulsion of workers from the yard, but his efforts were ineffectual and dismissed as 'quite contemptible' by the main Catholic historian of these events.[31] Outbreaks of sectarian violence often began in Workman Clark's yard where the management was Unionist in sympathy.[32] Certainly the Orange Order had significant support in the yards, sufficient to justify the establishment of a separate district there in 1871.[33] In 1886 a police officer estimated that only 500 of the 3500 employed in the Queens Island Shipyards were Catholic.[34] At the same time Edward Harland admitted only 225 out of 3000 workers were Catholics both skilled and unskilled.[35]

Catholics were under-represented in the yards but this was not just a matter of religious prejudice. The industry was dependent on a high proportion of skilled labour and as it expanded in Belfast it was necessary to import skilled labour from Scotland and Britain, areas where the Protestant faith was dominant. Recruitment of apprentices into the skilled labour force tended to be from the sons of those already employed within the skilled trades. The result was the creation of what Patterson calls a 'predominantly Protestant elite' in the Belfast working class.[36] What is important to recognise is that such elites were self-perpetuating and were a feature of all British cities; in Belfast the religious differences simply made this division more conspicuous. It was not impossible for a Catholic to gain an apprenticeship in the shipyards. The company's history notes that the only workers who did not return after the 1920 expulsions 'seem to have been 120 apprentices'.[37] Most of these would have been Catholics and this would have represented about 6.7 per cent of the 1784 apprentices listed in Harland & Wolff's Belfast yards in August 1920.[38] This may however be an overestimate as the expulsions had begun on the 21 July 1920 and thus the total for August was probably already reduced.[39] Whatever the exact figure it is fairly clear that while it was possible for a Catholic to obtain an apprenticeship in the yards, comparatively few did.

In the last decades of the nineteenth century the sectarian climate in Belfast was exacerbated by the development of the political demand for Home Rule. The political sensitivity of the issue was to influence the Irish labour movement, and their relations with the wider British movement.[40] Robert McElborough recorded that Will Thorne almost caused a riot at a meeting in Ormeau Park by wearing a green sash specially made for his trip to Ireland. A member of the audience demanded to know if he was a member of the Fenian Society which, McElborough claims, Thorne thought was a local trade union.[41] Such ignorance did not impress Belfast working-class Unionists.

I have been in England more times than I care to remember and I have been in many discussions with English people on the Irish Question, and the majority of them were like Will Thorne who thought when he appeared in a green sash that all Irishmen would welcome him. But he like other Englishmen who visited Ireland a few times and talked with the people found out there were two Irelands.[42]

On the other hand some in the Belfast labour movement, such as William Walker, saw labour representation as offering an opportunity to heal the political divisions of Home Rule.

What attitude is Ireland going to adopt in respect of this question? are we going to stand aloof with our prejudices and our partisanships, or are we going to welcome and participate with it in the struggles of the future... No country in the world requires so much the care and attention to social wants that Ireland demands at the hands of her representatives. Is she getting that care and attention now? only a bigoted partisan would answer this in the affirmative, the keen party political warfare that she is continuously plunged in prevents even moderate attention being paid to her industrial condition.[43]

Others found no difficulty in mixing unionism with their trade union activities.

When the unionist party brought groups of workers from England to see through Ireland travelling from the south to finish their trip in Belfast, we arranged to meet them at their hotels, and impress on them that the workers of the north were strongly opposed to Home

Rule. At the Whitsuntide holidays, a large number of these visitors were entertained and addressed by Unionist trade union officials including myself, and most left for home with changed political views.[44]

The situation in the wider community could be highly volatile, for example the defeat of 1886 Home Rule Bill triggering four months of sporadic rioting which left 32 dead and 371 injured.[45] The introduction of the Second Home Rule Bill in 1893 resulted in the expulsion of Catholic shipyard workers and ugly incidents during the TUC congress held in the city that year.[46] Unionist orators were willing to mix religion, nationalism and economic threats in their appeals to the Belfast industrial working class. In 1886 Hugh 'Roaring' Hanna, a Presbyterian Minister of Unionist Politics, gave a perhaps rather tongue-in-cheek speech on the effects of Home Rule in Belfast.

There is a ragged little urchin selling newspapers, and crying every morning the *Morning News*. That ragged urchin under the new code is to be Marquis of Donegal. There is a Nationalist riveter on Queen's Island, and he is to be successor to W.J. Perrie, and Mr Perrie, for some service he has shown to the nationalists, is to be relegated to the superintendence of a little smithy in Connemara; and Paddy O'Rafferty, a ragman, resident in the slums of Smithfield, is to succeed Sir Edward Harland as the next mayor of Belfast.[47]

However, migration of labour, and hostility to migrants was not unique to Belfast. The Irish in other areas of Britain were often seen as intruders and resented by local populations. In his study of Dundee Walker points out that Irish migrants were subject to prejudice even if there was a relative lack of sectarianism compared to other cities.[48] In Sheffield the Irish formed a distinctive community and outbreaks of violence were not unknown.[49] The Irish were said to number 'nine of twelve' workers in the London docks in the 1860s and Liverpool's dockers were notorious for their irreconcilable religious divisions.[50] There was considerable resentment of Irish migrants among English brush-makers in the 1840s because they were willing to set 30 knots per penny rather than the English standard of 20.[51]

The dislike of the Irish as economic competitors soon acquired a racial element as the number of Irish in England and Scotland increased dramatically during the famine decade.

As England was experiencing a series of violent economic fluctuations throughout the third and fourth decades of the century, there was real cause for complaint as Englishmen and Irishman often competed for the same work. As the Irish integrated themselves into the economy, other sorts of real and imagined competition created fresh antagonism. Pressure on house room, pressure on work and pressure on access to higher social status combined to throw a considerable burden of discrimination on these immigrants, as they did the Jews some forty years later.[52]

In some areas the Irish did little to make themselves popular, acting as strike breakers in industrial disputes.

In a famous cotton strike in Preston in 1854, for instance, the employers 'imported persons from a distance to take the place of the strikers, and a number of the Irish who are now [1912] in the town are the children of parents who came to Preston in 1854'.[53]

In Bristol the Irish were seen as an anti-social element from an early date, a view encouraged by migrant Irish labourers coming to the city claiming to be paupers and seeking repatriation to Ireland at the expense of the local Poor Law.[54] However, it was not only the Irish who were attracted to Bristol by industrial employment. Rural labourers from the surrounding counties constantly moved into the city, depressing unskilled wages and providing a willing pool of strike breakers. In 1889, for example, the Bristol Gas Company sought to break a strike by importing labourers from Exeter.[55] In 1892 the cash wages of agricultural labourers in the counties surrounding Bristol (Somerset, Gloucestershire and Wiltshire) were 10–15s. a week.[56] This compared to $6\frac{1}{2}$d. an hour paid to casual dock workers or 6d. an hour to building labourers in Bristol. Beyond this there was the possibility of regular work on the railways or perhaps the gasworks where stokers were paid 35s. for a seven-day week.[57]

As late as 1911 over a third of Bristol's population had been born outside the city, Atkinson argues that the proportion of adult male workers was even higher.[58] Such migrants were seen as a threat as can be seen from a resolution sent to the Corporation by the Trades Council.

That as men residing in the city and contributing to its rates have the first claim on municipal employment the Committees of the Corporation be requested to issue instructions that in future preference for employment be given to Bristol citizens.[59]

The Health Committee on receiving this resolved that 'the request embodied in the resolution be complied with so far as this Committee is concerned'.

In Belfast the migrant, either skilled or unskilled, tended to settle in the city permanently. Indeed the demand for labour was so great that employers actively encouraged migration to the city.

One of the directors of a large textile factory in the north informs me he recently brought up at his own expense a number of families from the south, but after the time, trouble and expense of teaching them the work, and although in receipt of good wages. I am informed in a letter I have from the director, 'only one family has remained, and this one largely lives on charity'.[60]

In Bristol, as in Dublin, the migrants were often moving from the impoverished hinterland prior to moving again to other industrial areas.[61] Between 1913 and 1922 almost thirty per cent of children leaving Bristol schools did so as having 'emigrated or moved to another district'.[62] In his 1897 enquiry into wage variations, F.W. Lawrence noted that many trades in Bristol were composed of travellers who regarded the city as a temporary stopping place.[63] Many of the older trade unions had developed structures to allow surplus skilled labour to migrate from one centre to another depending on employment conditions.[64]

Internal migration was not always an effective way of dealing with unemployment. According to Frank Shepherd it was often the case that when a man went looking for work he left his family in Bristol. He quoted the example of a couple with eight children. The man had been out of work for six months, and went to Wales to find work.

His wages were $5\frac{1}{2}$d an hour. It is broken weather, which means broken time. He can only send home a few shillings, for he must feed himself and pay his lodgings. The wife at home gets into difficulties: she sells everything that is saleable for food and rent, and when no more rent is forthcoming an ejectment order is lodged against her and she is turned into the street one morning with her eight children.[65]

As in this case, local charity or the Poor Law Guardians had to assist the families of migrants, placing additional strain on resources rather than reducing it.

The free movement of labour was of critical importance in the development of both Belfast and Bristol as industrial towns and provided a critical safety valve for Dublin. It was not only skills that were required from the migrants as a government enquiry heard in 1904.

The effect of certain conditions of town life on the weaker members of the community and the selective tendency of certain classes of employment which creates a demand for men of greater physical efficiency than is to be found as a rule in a town-bred population, as constantly drawing upon the resources of the rural districts, and it is presumably the men of the most energy and possibly of finer physique that respond to the allurements offered them.[66]

In evidence to the committee Dr D.J. Cunningham said that migration of rural labour was a feature of Belfast but not Dublin.[67] Sir Charles Cameron the Medical Officer of Health for Dublin commented on migration into Belfast.

Q. Has not the increase of the population of Belfast been largely due to Scottish immigration?
A. The greater number of the inhabitants of Belfast are not Scotch. In fact it is a comparatively small number. They are recruited from the northern counties of Ireland.[68]

In Dublin, however, craftsmen arriving in the city were a constant threat to the established local trade societies. A good example of this was the demand of the Dublin Master Builders Association in 1905 that they should be free to hire bricklayers or stone masons belonging to any recognised trade union. The Dublin Society was forced to concede this demand after a four-month strike and gained only a concession, worthless in a casual industry, that new employees had to join the Dublin union after twelve months.[69]

The working class in Dublin included a considerable number of Protestants. Mary Daly has pointed out that these workers were underrepresented in most sectors of employment, but were over-represented in printing and machinery manufacture.[70] Martin Maguire estimates that the Protestant working class in the city and county of Dublin remained at about 10 000 between 1881 and 1911.[71] As in the other cities the skilled workers were able to retain a large proportion of apprenticeships for members of their own families.[72] However, they did not form an 'aristocracy of labour' although they were considerably less likely to be members of the unskilled mass that was such a feature of Dublin.[73] Their politics tended to be Unionist and Conservative and they were willing to display them openly through organisations such as the Dublin Protestant Operative Association and the Dublin Conservative Workingmen's Club.[74] The important difference compared to Belfast however was their skilled base combined with small numbers meant they were never perceived as a threat by the majority population.

However, the resentment towards unskilled Irish labour in Bristol as well as Belfast was not simply economic: there was also an element of religious prejudice.

Do I say that a Liberal ministry could, in 1868, have done justice to Irish Catholicism, or that it could do justice to it now? "Go to Surrey Tabernacle" say my Liberal friends to me; "regard that forest of firm, serious, unintelligent faces uplifted towards Mr Spurgeon, and ask yourself what would be the effect produced on all that force of hard and narrow prejudice by a proposal of Mr Gladstone to pay the Catholic priests in Ireland, or to give them money for their houses or churches, or to establish schools and universities suited to Catholic, as England has public schools and universities suited to Anglicans, and Scotland such as are suited to Presbyterians. What would be Mr Gladstones chance of carrying such a measure?" I know quite well, of course, that he would have no chance of carrying it.[75]

Arnold saw the two most influential classes in England as being opposed to Irish Catholicism for different reasons. The upper classes 'who have not the prejudices and passions of our middle class' were fearful about Irish claims to the land. The middle classes who 'might be expected to sympathise with the Irish in their ill-usage by the grantees of confiscation' disliked 'popery'. The result was that 'each class forbears to touch the other's prejudice too roughly, for fear of provoking a like rough treatment of its own'.[76]

Bristol in the late nineteenth century was a city where religion was taken very seriously. Historically non-conformist groups had always been significant and some saw it as their duty to convert Catholics to the 'true' faith. In his study of the origins of American Nativism, Billington noted that the Bristol Reformation Society was one of 'A number of societies concerned principally with missionary work among the natives of Ireland'.[77] This body, and several others, was to continue to operate until the First World War.[78] The Bristol Itinerant Society, established to support preachers to work in the city's outlying villages left little doubt of their attitudes when they called their centenary volume *Bristol's Heathen Neighbours*.[79]

The Catholic church faced strong prejudice in Bristol during the eighteenth century but a slow growth occurred with the city's first Catholic chapel opening in 1790.[80] The controversy of the Reform Bill of 1831, climaxing in the riots of October that year was, in part, sectarian. The anonymous author of a pamphlet printed in Bristol warned his readers that,

> A numerous body thus concentrated, thus united by the close ties of political party and by the still closer ties of uncompromising and relentless superstition, will not fail, in the shifting and windings of public events, to secure to itself and to Ireland, almost any objects at which popish policy and ambition may grasp, or for which the arts of agitators may excite the clamour of the ardent but ignorant population of their ill-fated country. Let Protestants of all denominations, well know the consequences.[81]

However, in the 1890s the Catholic Church was not seen as the main threat by Nonconformists in Bristol. They were able to describe Monsignor Clarke as the 'ablest exponent' of segregated education on the School Board and admit that he was 'Honest and Conscientious in pursuing' it.[82] Despite such magnanimity intolerance could be displayed on matters such as the demand for public inspection of convent premises.

> The time has arrived when Protestants should seek to know how far such a condition of things. For all the occasional anti-catholic feeling the main as Edith O'Gorman has declared to be existent are true in general practice. Apart from religious feeling, in which we would gladly be tolerant than otherwise, the question rests on the lower and common ground of morality. This we are told, and for want of refutation we are forced to believe, is at the lowest ebb in the cloisters.[83]

Religious animosity in Bristol, as in most areas of England, was mainly between Nonconformist and Anglican. In the introduction to the 1906 edition of *John Bull's Other Island* Bernard Shaw, an Irish Protestant living in England, explained.

> The distinction between church-man and dissenter, which in England is a class distinction, a political distinction, and even occasionally a religious distinction does not exist (in Ireland)... It is true that they talk of church and chapel with all the Anglican contempt for chapel; but in Ireland chapel means the Roman Catholic church, for which the Irish Protestant reserves all the class rancour, the political hostility, the religious bigotry, and bad blood that generally in England separates the Established from the non-conforming

Protestant organizations. When a vulgar Irish Protestant speaks of a 'Papist' he feels exactly as a vulgar Anglican vicar does when he speaks of a Dissenter.[84]

In Bristol, religious rivalry was a feature of local politics, with appeals being made to support Nonconformist candidates.[85]

The issue of Irish Home Rule was a difficult one for English Nonconformists after the Liberal Party adopted it in 1886. Arnold believed that Nonconformist opinion on Ireland was shaped by a fear of Catholicism.[86] In the preface to the 'Home Rule Edition' of *John Bull's Other Island* Shaw claimed that such prejudice was still significant in 1912.

> The only considerable body of Englishmen really concerned about Home Rule except as a Party question, as those members of the Free Churches vulgarly called Dissenters or Nonconformists, who believe the effect of Home Rule would be to deliver Ireland into the hands of the Roman Catholic Church, which they regard as The Scarlet Woman. It is clearly not a very deeply considered apprehension, because there is not a country in the world, not even Spain, where the people are so completely in the hands of the Catholic Church as they are in Ireland under English Rule and because of English Rule.[87]

The difficulties created by this conflict of interest were considerable as a letter from a Bristol Liberal to a Nonconformist paper shows.

> Is it that some of them (Leading Liberals) are separated from their old colleagues on the Irish question, that they therefore will not lift a finger on those other questions in which free churchmen are interested? If so, it would amount to betrayal that I cannot as yet believe possible on the part of men who have lectured and laboured for principles which some of us have learnt of them and now expect to see carried out.[88]

Amongst Bristol's Nonconformist community the attitudes to Irish Home Rule were mixed. The *Bristol Christian Leader* carried a rather critical obituary of Parnell and stated that the Irish problem had no place in the pulpit.[89] Later in the year their coverage of the 'Irish Question' in the General Election was far from positive.[90] Some observers even felt that the Irish were receiving preferential treatment at the expense of English workers or employers. In April 1899 a speaker informed the Chamber of Commerce that he sometimes felt it was 'a misfortune that England was not also a conquered country'.[91] In

November 1910 the Webbs addressed a meeting in Bristol on the effects of the Poor Law and the need for change. They argued that the answer to urban poverty was for people to return to the land.

> Let them see what had happened in Ireland. Millions of money spent there had enabled the people to get back to the land. What was good enough for Ireland in this matter was surely good for England too. (hear hear) Millions of pounds had been voted to help the Irish with 6 000 000 people and England with its 36 000 000 had a miserable quarter of a million, and in a country where they had more millions near starvation than the whole population of Ireland. (hear hear).[92]

The strength of this anti-Irish feeling, and the strong element of religious prejudice involved, is shown starkly in the December 1918 Election in East Bristol. The constituency had always been Liberal, and had been held by Charles Hobhouse since 1900, but his active support of Home Rule as the *Western Daily Press* warned had created problems.

> The great strength of radicalism in East Bristol has hitherto lain in the large and small Dissenting congregations in the division. Many of these people regard the Roman Catholic with an intensity of repugnance which is quite out of character with the indolent broad-mindedness which is typical of the age. Their attitude is not the less strenuous, however, because it happens to be old-fashioned, and from what we have heard they are sorely disquieted by the Home Rule Bill, and the prospect which it unfolds of a Roman Catholic supremacy in Ireland. Such people take their politics very seriously, and they will give the Right Honourable Gentleman a great deal of trouble.[93]

Hobhouse was not intimidated and replied that Home Rule had to be introduced on the grounds of Irish support for the First World War, and because the government had pledged its honour on the matter. He recognised that partition was inevitable but felt that this would only be a short term matter and that 'in a very few years the whole population would desire to be governed from an Irish centre'.[94] Hobhouse won the election, with a reduced majority, in part at least because Labour had also pledged themselves to support Home Rule.

The labour movement in Bristol drew much of its support from the Liberal/Nonconformist community and thus inevitably was influenced by their views and prejudices. In 1889 Hugh Holmes Gore, was elected to the Bristol School Board as the first 'socialist' rather than 'labour' representative in the city.[95] However, in 1894 he was to cause a serious scandal when he objected to the employment of a school teacher solely on the grounds that she was Jewish. Despite the violent objections of the socialists at the next election Gore was to head the poll, his opinions and actions being approved of by Bristol's voters.[96] Anti-Semitism and anti-Irish prejudice were a feature of English working class thought and shared similar origins.[97] The Jewish community in Bristol was established by 1750 as was the case with a number of other provincial ports.[98] Initially merchants or pedlars the community acquired a wealthy leader with the arrival of the glass-maker Lazarus Jacobs from Frankfurt-on-Main in 1760.[99] By 1850 the community numbered about 300 and included the shipping and insurance family of Alexander and the wine importers Abrahams.[100] By 1845 the community had established its own charitable societies to care for and educate poor members of the faith.[101]

Why should this prosperous and self-contained community be the subject of such prejudice? There are two main reasons, the first of which was well demonstrated by a cartoon in a Bristol newspaper. Two stereotypical Jewish businessmen are in conversation: '"What is he like?" "I would let him marry my daughter!" "Alright, but this is serious I'm talking about money!".'[102] The Jews were seen as shop owners or unscrupulous exploiters. This preconception was to be found at all levels, even government reports, with the Jews being blamed for 'sweating' in the clothing trades.[103] The House of Lords Committee on the Sweating System was so anti-Jewish in tone that William Hoffman was provoked to reply.

Infant and child labour and female labour is more prevalent amongst English finishers than it is amongst the Jews. It is very often the case amongst English finishers, who are not spoken of as sweaters, that families are employed by them.[104]

However unpopular Jews were as employers, it was as competitors for work that they were most resented. The migration of at least 120 000 impoverished eastern European Jews to Britain stimulated a growth in the community from 46 000 in 1882 to 300 000 in 1914.[105] The migrant Jews formed a low paid stratum within certain industries and threatened the status and earnings of workers in them.

Polish Jews and English women will do any work, at any price, under any conditions ... the Jew ... is unique in possessing neither a minimum nor a maximum; he will accept the lowest terms rather than remain out of employment; as he rises in the world new wants stimulate him to increase intensity of effort, and no amount of effort causes him to slacken his indefatigable activity.[106]

As with the Irish before them, the Jews were accused of living on the bare minimum, thus lowering the standard of life for all workers. At the 1894 Trade Union Congress Jewish workers were accused of working fifteen hours a day and subsisting on 'cold coffee and bread and cheese'.[107] The British worker might feel a degree of sympathy for the Jews as persecuted refugees, but none at all for them as workers or employers.

This migration had little long-term effect on the Bristol Jewish population: as one historian of the community put it 'it helped slightly to top-up the size of the community and eventually changed its composition'.[108] The limited extent of Jewish immigration to Bristol in these years was demonstrated by the city's reply to a circular seeking details of 'foreigners now in receipt of relief' in the city. Only five persons were in receipt of outdoor and three of indoor and in the case of those on outdoor payments they had been in the city between nine and 33 years. Bristol was hardly being swamped by migrant poor from Eastern Europe.[109] However, this did not prevent considerable local anti-Semitism and determined efforts by local groups to convert the Jews to Christianity. The Society for Promoting Christianity among the Jews, was in existence by 1883 and later amalgamated with the British Society for the Propagation of the Gospel among the Jews.[110] However, as their annual meeting was told in 1892:

> Missionaries, at home and abroad, labour under peculiarly difficult circumstances in endeavouring to bring the Jews to acknowledge Jesus as the true messiah, and exercise saving faith in him. The natural and national pride of the Hebrew race seem to present an insuperable barrier in the way of success.[111]

If the Jews were numerically unimportant in Bristol at this time they were even less so in Ireland. Dublin's community, the first outside London, was traditionally re-established by Portuguese settled in the city by Cromwell.[112] By 1850 the community numbered 150–200 who seem to have been mainly involved in craft manufacturing rather than merchants or shopkeepers.[113] Some European migrants settled in Dublin and by 1921 the population had increased to 3500.[114] In Belfast there was no Jewish community until the 1870s when poor migrants began to settle there; by 1921 there were 1200 Jews in the city.[115] In the 1894 report on immigration from Eastern Europe, Ireland was said to have 12 900 resident 'foreigners': 7499 were said to be American compared to only 1111 Russians and 35 Poles.[116] Despite the relatively low numbers there was still prejudice as can be seen in the evidence of the Bishop of Ross to a government enquiry in 1904.

Is there any compensating immigration into Ireland? — *There is immigration of Jews*
Only Jews? — *Yes*
Where do they come from — *I think they arrive in Ireland from England. How they have traversed Europe I do not know.*
They do not come into the rural parts of your diocese? — *Yes a few go round and do very great harm, they go round peddling.*
Gombeen Men? — *Yes; they sell tea of the vilest character; they go to the doors of the peasantry and sell them the tea and other articles. It is nearly impossible to keep the people from dealing with them. That is one of the causes of physical degeneration, because they are getting the vilest stuff from the Jews.*
Are they foreigners? — *Yes, there are no Irish Jews.*[117]

Like the Jews, the Irish in Bristol established their own societies and welfare organisations.[118] However, they also brought their politics to Bristol: in the 1870s Irish Nationalists were already meeting regularly at the 'Coach and Horses' in Broadmead.[119] Later a highly active branch of the Irish National League was established in the city and most of the leading nationalists of the day addressed meetings there.[120] Unionism also found supporters in Bristol; in March 1908 there was a well attended meeting in North Bristol addressed by J.H. Campbell and H.T. Barrie.[121] In 1910 Herbert Shaw of Dublin established the first Unionist Party 'regional office' in Bristol. Until that time activities had been controlled from Dublin or Belfast.[122] Home Rule was certainly an important local issue during the two 1910 elections and both unionists and nationalists were active in trying to present their cases.

Belfast's 'Peculiar Institution' the Orange Order was also to be found in Bristol. In 1830 there were six lodges in the Bristol district.[123] In 1836 the Grand Lodge of England was dissolved and two competing bodies emerged which combined in 1876 to form the Loyal Orange Institution of England.[124] In 1905 there were three lodges of this body in Bristol which claimed to be a benefit society.[125] Whilst Bristol's three branches cannot be compared to the vast organisation that existed in Belfast this organisation, often seen as typical of Ulster, could be found in Bristol. The history of freemasonry in Bristol noted the singular Irishness which 'frequent intercourse' with that country had created compared to most English centres.[126]

However, despite these links, anti-Irish feeling still ran high, sometimes taking a form which it was argued was 'only a joke'. In 1924 the *Wills' Works Magazine* carried a series of cartoons under the heading 'Brightening up the Office: some suggestions'. The Irish section it was said could be 'brightened-up with the aid of national costume'. Two shillelagh-swinging figures in tail coats sat at a desk one saying to the other 'Just see to the pig, Pat, and then we'll get on again'.[127] However as the minutes of the Bristol Advisory Committee for Relief of Distress show, there were new prejudices already developing:

> Mr Andrews and his wife, these are coloured people, and owing to racial trouble the man has been unable to obtain employment. Representations were made to the Board of Trade, and an allowance of 28/- per week was obtained for him pending repatriation. This being delayed it was felt that if Andrews could get to Cardiff he would stand a better chance of obtaining employment.[128]

CONCLUSION

Sectarianism had been a feature of Belfast since the early nineteenth century, and the period 1880 to 1925 is marked by repeated outbreaks of violence. This has inevitably affected the labour movement in the city. However, similar prejudices existed in both Bristol and Dublin during these years. The sectarianism of Belfast may have differed in scale but similar processes were at work in Bristol.

Violence was not a feature of Bristol, not because the city was inherently more peaceful or liberal in its attitudes, but because the migrants were perceived as less of a threat. The Belfast industrial worker saw his livelihood being undermined by unskilled migrants and fundamentally threatened by the political threat of Home Rule. The Bristolian or the Dubliner may not have liked outsiders but they did not pose a threat to the established status quo in the city. The absence of riots should not be taken as signifying greater tolerance, rather a greater sense of security.

10 War and Rebellion

Although there were considerable differences between Belfast and Bristol in the period 1880 to 1912, similarities between these cities become clear when they are compared with Dublin in the same period. Their experience begins to diverge in the years after 1912 as political and social unrest, war on an unprecedented scale and severe economic depression affect all three cities. There was still considerable similarity, but this was a period of political and social change. It is these years which see Belfast finally categorised, much against its will, as an Irish city rather than a British one. It would be wrong to present British society prior to 1912 as being in a peaceful and stable condition. As Dangerfield suggests, trade unionists, women and supporters of 'labour' politics were already agitating for change.[1] Social and political disruption was a feature common to all three cities in this era. The Home Rule Crisis of 1912, however, marked the beginning of a period of far-reaching political and social change.

The political origins of the 1912 Home Rule crisis are well recorded and lie beyond the scope of this study.[2] However, these events polarised Irish society, affecting the labour movement in the years before the First World War. Opposing factions in the national political debate could disrupt local proceedings and arouse hostility between branches and central officers. For example, the National Union of Paper Mill Workers had been successful in winning recognition in a dispute in Ballyclare in 1911 but by 1912 was seen as the enemy by unionist workers. The General Secretary of the union received an anonymous letter stating he would be killed if he went to the town again 'as they wanted no Home Rulers there'.[3] Refusing to be intimidated he went to investigate and was told by the local police that there would be a riot if he tried to hold a meeting. However, he was determined to proceed.

Finding it was the intention of the General Secretary to go on with the meeting, the sergeant consulted the leading branch officials. When he reported their agreement that, on account of the bitter party feeling that had been stirred up, it would not be safe, or of any use, Ross (the G.S.) abandoned the attempt, and wired the Larne members to arrange a meeting there. Waiting for the train to Larne, he was 'assaulted by five of the paper mill workers, and but for the prompt appearance of three of the police, would have been badly mauled'.[4]

Similarly, the Workers Union which had been very successful in the Belfast region, withdrew its full time official in 1913 in the face of 'local prejudice' which had caused the near collapse of the union.[5] While the chairman of Belfast Trades Council condemned the expulsion of ship-yard workers and other sectarian activity,[6] seven weeks later he had to admit that few unions had taken any action to stop such incidents within the workplace.[7]

Others within the Belfast labour movement opposed the Trades Council's attempts to introduce a 'labour' perspective to the Home Rule Question. As Joseph Cunningham put it,

> The Trades and Labour Council with very little support from the trade unionist, were sending reports across the water that only the employer class were opposed to Home Rule, the workers were not interested . . . when I had arrived home from work one evening, the District Secretary of the Shipwrights, T. Donald, called from the shipyard to ask if I was satisfied at the misrepresentation. I informed him that I was prepared to do anything to correct same, we were then encouraged to form all trade union officials into a loyalist emergency committee.[8]

Labour supporters found themselves faced with making the choice between Unionism and Nationalism. In an interview Joseph Cunningham's widow told of John F. Gordon, a unionist MP for County Antrim and later Minister of Labour. An active trade unionist he 'scoffed at the UVF and mocked their drilling by parading up and down with a broomstick on his shoulder'. It was only under the influence of William Grant, again a trade unionist and later Minister of Health, that he joined the Unionist rather than the Labour Party.[9]

The events in Belfast spilled over into Bristol to a degree where Home Rule become an important political issue. The Unionist Party had a full time agent in the city who was highly active as early as the second election of 1910.[10] In Dublin the response of Irish nationalists was to prove as extreme as that of the Unionists and soon both sides were raising private armies.[11] The Dublin labour movement was caught up in this upsurge of national feeling at a time when they were themselves undergoing critical changes. As organised labour faced the struggle of the 1913 Dublin Lock Out labour politics were becoming increasingly marginalised. The trade unionist in Dublin, as in Belfast, was forced to place the 'labour' question in a secondary position to the 'national' one. By 1913 even a socialist such as James Connolly was becoming increasingly 'anti-Orange' and anti-partition in his writings.[12]

Thus on the eve of the First World War the labour movement in
Dublin and Belfast was hopelessly entangled in the wider struggle of
Irish Nationalism and Unionism.

After the industrial unrest of 1911 Bristol was to enjoy comparative
tranquillity compared to the Irish cities. However, this was to change
in August 1914 when Britain found itself drawn into a vast European
conflict. The war was to affect economic and social conditions in each
city in a different manner and it is this I shall concentrate upon. Unlike
the Second World War neither Bristol nor Belfast were to suffer the
effects of direct military action and although Dublin saw widespread
fighting during Easter 1916, all three cities were comparatively safe
areas. In Bristol there was some fear of air-raids, and street lighting
was reduced as a precaution. However, as Stone noted, at the end of
1915 the only visible signs of war were the uniforms on the streets, and
the streets 'less brilliantly illuminated at night then they were eighteen
months ago'.[13] In February 1916 as a result of Zeppelin raids on
London, Bristol was subjected to a 'blackout' from an hour and a half
after sunset until an hour and a half before sunrise, but this was mild
compared to restrictions on southern and eastern counties.[14] The men-
ace of U-boat attacks was a matter of concern but heavy patrols, dangerous currents and comparative inaccessibility made the Irish Sea and
Bristol Channel unattractive hunting grounds. There were losses in
these areas, notably in late 1917 to mid 1918 but these were relatively
minor compared to losses off the south and east coasts.[15]

As the Bristol Civic League was to report, at first the war appeared
to have a negative effect on employment, at least amongst female
workers.[16] However, Bristol soon found itself developing new industries and expanding old ones to meet the needs of the war. The
shipbuilding industry, which had almost vanished by 1914, was re-
vitalised by government grants and wartime orders.[17] The ship re-
pairing trade also increased, with the firms of Charles Hill and G.K.
Stothert being active in the city, and J. Jefferies and J. Shearman at
Avonmouth.[18] The Bristol corrugated iron industry switched from
roofing material and prefabricated building to more military products.[19] The Douglas Engineering Co, established to manufacture
boot-making equipment in Kingswood was successfully manufacturing cars and motorbikes by 1913.[20] The war was to create a massive
demand for their motorbikes, particularly a 2.75 horse-power model
produced in accordance with a War Office specification of which
25 000 were produced.[21] Bristol quickly acquired a significant chemical
industry which included plant transferred from Rotterdam in the early

days of the war. By 1915 this plant was producing 80 per cent of the UK supply of toluol, the main ingredient in many explosives.[22] However, the most spectacular growth was in aircraft production which had employed 400 workers in 1914, but was providing work for 3000 by the end of the war.[23]

The demand for labour was immense, particularly as the need for military manpower became more pressing. According to some observers even army enlistment could lead to an improvement in a family's conditions. As a Bristol school teacher from a working class district reported,

... the children have never been better looked after than since the war broke out. Under the earlier normal conditions the family exchequer was often ill-provided, owing sometimes to irregular work, at others to unwise expenditure on drink; the war by calling away the breadwinner, has secured those remaining a dependable allowance.[24]

Some indicators do seem to support this claim, for example, the number of children receiving free school meals fell dramatically during the war years.[25]

The wartime shortage of labour became particularly acute when large numbers of men enlisted during 1915. By October the local Factory Inspectors organised a conference to convince local employers in the wood-working trades to introduce female labour.[26] By the end the year women and school children were becoming increasing important in the Bristol labour force.[27] The Bristol Aeroplane Company which had previously employed no women, was by 1918 so dependent upon them to perform some semi-skilled tasks that they formed 80 per cent of the labour force in some sections.[28] A similar development occurred in the Motor Construction Works of the Bristol Tramways Company where there were 127 men, including 21 disabled soldiers, as opposed to 614 women in a range of semi-skilled jobs.[29] In addition to this replacement of male labour, there was expansion in largely female-employing industries such as chocolate and tobacco further boosting female employment.

In other sectors, such as boot and shoe making, machinery was adopted to try and replace scarce labour.

It was not until 1917 that the first record appears of the purchase of a 'Grimson Consol Laster with knife attachment' and in the following year three 'British Unites C.H.M. McKay Lasting Machines' were installed. This was an ominous development for the outdoor hand makers whose numbers, by the early years of the 'Kaisers war' had grown to nearly 150, machine production had begun.[30]

Some companies appear to have simply run their machinery at full capacity throughout the war. In October 1918 the Chief Engineer at W.D. & H.O. Wills wrote to the management committee listing machinery that was worn out and in need of replacement. He warned that the 'first instalment' would consist of 100 standard cigarette machines and 160 other items of production and packing machinery.[31] The comparative prosperity created by the demand for labour meant that there were few examples of labour unrest during the war. Those which did occur tended to be caused by the refusal of employers to increase wages to match increasing wartime prices.[32] Union membership was to increase considerably as the unskilled, semi-skilled, and particularly women sought to improve their working conditions.[33]

Politically, and in line with socialist principles of internationalism, the labour movement in Bristol, as throughout the rest of Europe, tried to oppose the war. Ernest Bevin called a mass meeting on the Grove in Bristol Docks on 2 August 1914 to condemn the war and call for British neutrality.[34] The Independent Labour Party adopted a policy that the conflict was one between capitalists which no socialist could support.[35] As a result, out of touch perhaps with the views of their own membership, the ILP found itself marginalised by popular support for the war and its membership collapsed.[36] A similar drop was to occur in other 'labour' organisations such as the WEA: of the eighteen branches in the western district ten were to close in the early days of the war.[37]

In Dublin the labour movement was also shocked by the failure of socialists and trade unionists across Europe to oppose the war. The passive acceptance of the conflict by the 'working class' profoundly affected leaders such as James Connolly.

> What then becomes of all our resolutions; all our protests of fraternisation; all our threats of general strikes; all our carefully built machinery of internationalism; all our hopes for the future? When the German artilleryman, a socialist serving in the German army of invasion, sends a shell into the ranks of the French army, blowing of their heads; tearing out their bowels, and mangling the limbs of dozens of socialist comrades in that force, will the fact that he, before leaving for the front 'demonstrated' against the war be of any value to the widows and orphans made by the shell he sent upon its mission of murder?[38]

It is widely believed that it was the disappointment of this failure of internationalism, combined with his view that the British labour movement had failed to support the Dublin strikers, which turned Connolly's thoughts from internationalism to Irish nationalism.[39] Certainly within a few weeks his views on the war appear to have changed considerably.

The Germans are in Boulogne, where Napoleon projected an invasion of Britain. To Ireland is only a twelve hour run. If you are itching for a rifle, itching to fight, have a country of your own; better to fight for your own country than for the robber Empire.[40]

The Irish Nationalist Party of John Redmond joined with the Unionists in support of the war, and encouraged Irishmen to enlist in a conflict to 'protect the rights of small countries'. The bulk of those who rejected this appeal did so on grounds of nationalism, rather than any moralistic objection to war itself, refusing to fight what they regarded as an 'English' war. To Unionists, on the other hand, support for the war was seen as a test of loyalty and opposition, regardless of reason, was interpreted as disloyalty. In these circumstances, pacifism as a separate political issue ceased to exist in Ireland, submerged in wider politics. After 1916 the division between Nationalist and Unionist on the question of the war became complete, as Nationalist opinion, increasingly under Sinn Fein influence, rejected the war completely.[41]

In Bristol pacificists remained active, despite verbal and often physical assaults, especially after the introduction of conscription early in 1916.[42] The labour movement in the city was split on the issue, with leaders such as Frank Shepherd supporting the war, while the trades council announced a policy of assisting conscientious objectors in April 1916.[43] The campaign in support of those who refused to accept compulsory military service was pursued with great vigour. 'The fight for conscience is the one fight whatever the battleground. Trade Unionists must guard against all and every attempt to flinch from us our freedom whether of conscience, of speech or of political action.'[44]

The Independent Labour Party remained a vocal opponent of the war, presenting very definite ideas about why it was being fought and who were responsible.

As they plunged their nations into war, the rulers prated loudly of God and Freedom and Self Defence, but in their hearts they were thinking of power and domination and fresh markets for their shoddy.[45]

The most important anti-conscription group in Bristol was the Joint Advisory Committee for Conscientious Objectors, established early in 1916. By August 1916 a newsletter was being circulated in the city giving details of Bristolians arrested and sentenced for opposition to the Military Service Acts.[46] By June 1917 complaints were made concerning the treatment of those held at Horfield Barracks and accusing the military of usurping the powers of civil magistrates.[47] In the aftermath of the Russian Revolution the committee published a list of thirty Bristolians 'Imprisoned for their Opinions'. This included Walter Ayles, the ILP's full time officer in Bristol, and a member of the city council.[48]

If the war was to be marked in Bristol by economic boom, political disruption, large scale employment of female labour and heavy handed conscription what were the effects on the other two cities? In the case of Belfast there was initially some economic dislocation as industries adapted to the demands of the military. The linen trade was hit by both the loss of continental markets and falling demand for 'luxury' goods such as table linen, but this was replaced by demands for aeroplane fabric, shirts, haversacks and army bedding.[49] The shipbuilding industry was also thrown into some disorder by the outbreak of war but soon recovered and adapted to war conditions.[50] Politically the issue for Belfast, as Dublin, remained Home Rule. Support for the British war effort, particularly after the events of Easter 1916, became a potent symbol of loyalty. Demands by Unionist politicians for the introduction of conscription were unpopular among Belfast workers, and even pro-unionist writers such as Cunningham had to admit the UVF did not enlist 'en masse'.[51] Belfast never faced the serious shortages of labour that Bristol did during the war years.

In evidence to a government enquiry Mr Hill of the Belfast tobacco firm of Gallaher's admitted that in Ireland it had not been necessary to substitute women for the male work force.[52] Understandably, in view of the financial sacrifice involved, most skilled men preferred to stay at home; as late as August 1917 there were 150 unemployed joiners seeking work in Belfast.[53] A hostile witness was later to claim that it was doubtful if 5% of the shipyard workers enlisted during the war.[54] Certainly Harland & Wolff was not forced to employ women on a large scale, and as late as July 1916 there were only 151 women in a shipyard labour force of 8962.[55] As in Bristol, Belfast in these years saw comparative industrial peace and an increasing unionisation of those elements within the labour force which had previously been poorly organised.[56] This was also the case in Dublin, although the wartime boom was not as extensive as in the two more industrialised centres. Wages increased as prices rose and even such traditionally low payers as the Dublin Laundry Company were forced to increase wage rates.[57] In general terms, recruiting in Dublin was lower than Belfast, due mainly to nationalist views of the conflict as an 'English' fight not an Irish one.

It can be argued that the main event in Dublin in the years 1914–18 was the Easter Rising of 1916 which has entered into the mythology of Irish Nationalism. The week's fighting in central Dublin resulted in 500 dead and 2500 wounded, a trifling cost compared to the carnage taking place on the Western Front.[58] However, the use of artillery in the city centre, and savage house-to-house fighting resulted in up to 179 buildings being totally destroyed and many others damaged, rendering over 5000 families homeless.[59]

> All that was necessary was to blockade the Post Office until its microcosmic republic was starved out and made ridiculous. What actually happened would be incredible if there were not so many living witnesses of it. From a battery planted at Trinity College (the Irish equivalent of Oxford University) and from a warship on the Liffey, a bombardment was poured on the centre of the city which reduced more than a square mile of it to such a condition that when, in the following year, I was taken to Arras and Ypres to show me what German artillery had done to those cities in two and a half years, I laughed and said "You should see what the British artillery did to my native city in a week." It would not be true to say that not one stone was left upon another; for the marksmanship was so bad that the Post Office itself was left standing amid a waste of rubbish heaps; and enough scraps of walls were left for the British Army, which needed recruits, to cover with appeals to the Irish to remember Belgium lest the fate of Louvain should befall their own hearths and homes.[60]

At first Irish public opinion, even in Dublin, was heavily against the rebels who were seen as irresponsible if not actually treasonable in their actions. British troops had to protect captured rebels from the hostility of the Dublin poor who had suffered during the fighting. It appeared that the whole venture was a disastrous error which would damage irretrievably the hopes of physical force Irish Nationalism.

However, two errors were made on the part of the British: the execution of sixteen of the defeated rebel leaders and the outlawing of the innocent and ineffectual Sinn Fein party, allowed the initial damage to the extreme nationalist cause to be repaired.

In Belfast, as in Bristol, the Easter Rising was seen as appalling treachery to the men fighting at the front, and the fate of its leaders was regarded as no less than was deserved for plotting with the country's enemies in time of war. Subsequent events were to reinforce such feelings. On 1 July 1916, on the first day of the Battle of the Somme the 36th (Ulster) Division suffered 5500 killed, wounded or missing out of a full strength of 20 000. Unionists were to compare the loyalty of the 36th with the treachery of the Dublin rebels. Although it was pointed out at the time that 'some thousands' of Catholics served in the 36th, in popular mythology it became a wholly Protestant and Unionist formation.[61] The result of this was a hardening of Unionist attitudes towards Irish Nationalism and an increasing opposition to Home Rule.

Dublin after 1916 was increasingly gripped by extreme nationalist ideologies, and anti-war attitudes became even more hardened. By the time of the anti-conscription campaign of 1918 almost the whole of Irish society, outside Ulster, was opposed to the war.[62] In Bristol, the cost of living increased rapidly during the war years which, combined with increasing shortages, led to growing discontent in the city. Conscription was to affect over 17 000 men from Bristol where the tribunals appear to have been very sparing in granting exemptions.[63]

The effects of the war on British society as a whole were disastrous. 745 000 were killed and 1 600 000 were permanently disabled to some degree physically or mentally. In round terms 9 per cent of the male population between 18 and 45 were killed and 19.3 per cent suffered some degree of disability.[64] The social effects of such carnage were immense, and not being restricted to any single class, created long-lasting ramifications.

A medical friend of mine who has two grown up daughters informs me that his daughters have recently gone into professions, for they have lost in the war many of their male friends, some of whom were likely to be aspirants for their hands in marriage. Out of eighteen young men, prospectively of the marrying type, fourteen had been killed in the war; and if this has been the experience of one small social circle, what must it be in all ranks of life as regards the chances of women marrying when their numbers so far exceed those of men.[65]

The sense of social injustice was equally strong, many feeling in the words of the old army song, it was 'The rich what gets the pleasure and the poor what gets the pain'. In March 1924 the *Western Daily Press* carried an article on the 'King's Roll', an attempt to assist unemployed or disabled soldiers.

> There is a vast army of men for whom the war has not yet ended; who are engaged day by day in looking out from the trench of unemployment over no-man's land of despair. And the Armistice came in 1918.[66]

The post-war years were to prove as difficult for the three cities as the war had been. The problems they faced were not the same but they changed the social and economic structures of these three cities and set them on differing routes.

In the immediate post-war period Belfast experienced an unprecedented demand for the products of its industries; the shipyards, factories and mills were never busier.[67] The first crisis to grip the city was not political but industrial: in January 1919, a demand for a 44-hour week with pay increases to ensure that earnings levels remained unaffected, resulted in widespread strike action.[68] It appeared that, at last, the old division between Catholic and Protestant had been forgotten and that all workers could now make common cause.[69] It was reported that the Trades Council was not only looked to for leadership in the dispute but 'had control of the movement of goods in the city', effectively acting almost as a soviet.[70] The strike was settled with an agreement of 47 hours after serious divisions emerged between extreme socialists and more conservative elements in the face of increasing military intervention.[71]

During the next few months this alliance of workers was to be shattered by a revival of sectarian animosity which was in part created by the employing class and in part a reaction to events elsewhere in Ireland. In the December 1918 election Sinn Fein secured 73 out of Ireland's 105 parliamentary seats, although it was significant that they gained only one seat in the six north-eastern counties.[72] Four days before the start of the Belfast 44-hour strike, a group of newly elected Sinn Fein MPs assembled in Dublin and issued a declaration of Irish independence. On the same day, at Soloheadbeg in County Tipperary a local unit of Irish Volunteers ambushed a consignment of explosives going to a local quarry. Two policemen were killed in this incident, which is generally seen as the first action of the Irish War of Independence.[73] Belfast found itself being declared part of an 'independent'

Ireland by a 'government' none of whose members had been elected in the city. In an atmosphere of growing violence the Unionists reformed the UVF and again prepared to resist Home Rule whether imposed by London or seized by Dublin.

In Dublin the period 1919–21 was to see civil war as Sinn Fein attempted to operate an underground national government based in the city, with the Irish Volunteers fighting a prolonged guerilla war on the streets against police and troops.[74] What was the role of the labour movement in the struggle for Irish Independence during these years? Mitchell says that relations between the Irish labour movement and the national movement were 'close but unofficial' with labour playing 'only a subordinate, supporting role in the struggle'.[75] Thornley suggests that militant labour as represented by the Irish Citizen Army established by Connolly had declined by 1921 to the point where it could not even maintain a chain of command, and that labour made no independent contribution to the struggle.[76] A certain amount of Anti-Unionist and Anti-British propaganda was carried out under the auspices of the Irish Labour Party but no anti-nationalist views were expressed.[77] Other authors try to emphasise the importance of labour within the broader nationalist alliance, but in general it was the case that labour was no longer capable of formulating or pursuing a distinctive policy.[78]

The attitude of the British labour movement was however of great importance in the Irish conflict, developing as it did into one of support for Irish independence.[79] As early as 1919 Arthur Henderson wrote that the Irish should be allowed to elect a government of their own who should create a constitution which should protect 'minorities'.[80] This was, admitted Henderson, fully in accord with the policy of Sinn Fein. The partition of Ireland was seen as impractical by British socialists such as Shaw, who argued that the unity of Irish workers would not allow the 'Ulster capitalists' to cut themselves off from those of the south.[81] However, perhaps the most damaging propaganda from the point of view of the British government and Irish Unionists was the report of a Labour Party Commission sent to Ireland in 1921. Their research was hardly impartial or complete, as its authors admitted 'our enquiries were confined to Dublin and neighbourhood and the south-west of Ireland'.[82] The report itself was highly critical of the behaviour of the security forces on the ground and British policy in Ireland in general.[83]

Understandably both Ulster Unionists and Ulster Labour supporters found such uncritical acceptance of Sinn Fein as the legitimate representatives of all the Irish people infuriating. As a result the Ulster Unionist Labour Association, established in 1917, became increasingly the representative body of Belfast Protestant labour. Although at times written off as a front organisation of the Unionist Party, it was capable of adopting a distinctive labour position, as during the 44-hour strike of 1919.[84] This body published an 'analysis and criticism' of the Labour Commission to Ireland's report, which made some very valid comments, but which was largely ignored outside Ulster.[85]

Tragically, trade unionists were to play an active role in perhaps the most disgraceful event of these years, the expulsion of thousands of Catholic and non-Unionist Protestants from their jobs in Belfast. By July, 1920 the situation in the southern area of Ireland had created considerable tension in Belfast. On the 12th Edward Carson made a speech, in which he discussed the 'labour question' which could at best be called ill-considered, and easily be seen as an incitement to sectarian violence.[86] On the 21 July, following further deaths in the south and serious rioting in Derry, a meeting of unionist workers at Workman Clark's shipyard developed into what is known as the Belfast expulsions.[87]

Only one history of these events was written and the author suppressed most copies of it as he felt it would only serve to provoke further hatred and resentment.[88] In a letter to Dublin Evening Telegraph on 11 November, James Baird, Town Councillor of Belfast, Protestant and expelled worker, told what had happened.

> Every Roman Catholic – whether ex-service man who had proved his loyalty to England during the Great War, or Sinn Feiner who claims to be loyal to Ireland alone – was expelled from the shipyards and other works; . . . Almost 10,000 workers are at present affected, and on several occasions men have attempted to resume work only to find the 'loyal' men still determined to keep them out. I am informed that one catholic has been permitted to start on the Queen's Island – one out of thousands, assuming the report is true.[89]

Although in this case the Catholic workers were the main focus of attention it should be remembered that 'rotten prods' formed almost a quarter of those expelled.[90] On the day of the expulsions sectarian killings began which over the next two years were to result in 455 deaths and over 2000 injuries.[91]

The response of the labour movement to these developments did them little credit. The Amalgamated Society of Carpenters and Joiners did attempt to force eight firms to reinstate expelled workers by calling on their members to strike, but this was largely ignored.[92] The actions of the 'loyalist' community appeared to be endorsed in November 1920 when many of the unofficial Unionist vigilante groups were consolidated into the Ulster Special Constabulary.[93] The political consequences of allowing the Unionist population to effectively police their own areas were to profoundly affect the formation and policies of the new Northern Ireland State.[94]

Although Bristol was not to see civil war or sectarian outrage, the post-war years were not a happy period for many Bristolians. The legacy of the war and rising levels of unemployment were to create serious social and economic problems. By 1921 the situation was approaching crisis.

> Creeping paralysis is reported in other trades. The big boot-making centre at Kingswood is suffering keenly. Engineering is slack. Short time is being worked at the tobacco factories and the big cocoa works. The Employment Exchange reports 13,600 persons wholly out of work and 7,400 working three days or less a week, and the position is worsening.
>
> What are the employers doing about it? They are doing little more than waiting for trade to revive, and they freely admit their helplessness. "Doncherno, my boy," said one jocose individual who had just paid a dinner bill of 22s. 6d., "we're up against the law of supply and demand".[95]

By September the frustration of the unemployed led to organised protest; on 9 September the Committee for the Unemployed staged a march to St Peter's Hospital.

> A large crowd of men and women marched to Peter Street and assembled outside the front gates of St Peter's hospital, bearing a red flag and banners. Whilst the Committee for the Unemployed was endeavouring to see the Guardians, a man named Goodman, who was afterwards arrested, pinned a medal on the flag saying "this is what the government gives us for fighting since 1914" this was followed by shouts from the crowd, and the singing of what I understand to be "The Red Flag".[96]

The meeting was eventually dispersed by the police in such a manner as to lead to accusations of brutality.[97] The authorities feared revolution, and some reports seemed to indicate that this was indeed being planned.

I got into conversation with a man, one of the unemployed, ... I said "Well they had nothing to defend themselves with" he replied "Oh! yes they did, some had service revolvers, and one man I know had a Mills bomb."[98]

Much of this unrest occurred in that area of central Bristol where poverty was most severe and where, according to a police inspector, 'the majority of the residents are of a very low character' and 'the crowd are invariably hostile to the police'.[99]

Unemployment amongst ex-soldiers was seen as a particularly serious problem, both because it was felt they were owed a degree of consideration for their war service and because they would have made dangerous revolutionaries. Bristol City Council's Advisory Committee for the Relief of Distress, and bodies such as the King's Roll, paid particular attention to the needs of this group.[100] However, more general answers were also being sought as a report from the Bristol Association for Industrial Research noted 'the only satisfactory cure for unemployment is employment'.[101]

Mass unemployment was to have serious repercussions on the economy of Bristol, as it did on Britain as a whole. In September 1921 the Co-operative Wholesale Society announced that it had made a loss of £3.5 million on the previous year's trading. The reasons were explained by an official:

"The Co-operative Wholesale Society" he said "depends for its support almost solely on the working classes. Unemployment, partial employment and labour disputes have reduced their incomes to such an extent that they have been able to buy only the bare necessities of life, and have had to bar luxuries severely. There has been practically no demand for furniture, drapery, boot and shoes, and clothing generally."[102]

Falling demand also affected Bristol's brewers who, in June 1922, cut their worker's wages by between five and ten shillings a week.[103] The Transport and General Workers Union objected strongly to this cut on the grounds that it was being made to ensure high profits and dividends rather than to protect jobs. Certainly the Bristol brewers' dividends at this time appear to justify the union's complaints.[104]

By October 1925 when Neville Chamberlain visited Bristol, the council were able to report that it was trying to relieve unemployment through public works. In addition to a vast programme of house building intended to reduce the problems created by the war, two very large road-building schemes had been undertaken.[105] However, such projects could do little more than relieve the worst of the suffering, and unemployment was to be a major problem in Bristol during the interwar years.

Although the experience of Bristol and Belfast in the years 1912–25 appears very different, some similarities are evident. Both cities suffered a decline in their previously high standards of housing during the war and the immediate post-war years. In 1914 Bristol City Council prepared a local housing scheme, abandoning its earlier dislike of municipal housing because of the shortage of low rent housing of good quality in the area south of the New Cut. The project enjoyed the support of local trade union branches, but was opposed by the local rate payers' association on the grounds of cost.[106] Unfortunately, as the Bristol Civic League was to report in December 1914, the scheme was placed in abeyance on the outbreak of war when private house building also ceased.[107] The effect of the War on Bristol's housing stock was dramatic as the city engineer was to demonstrate in his report for the year 1925–6. House construction had declined in the years before the war, from 1372 in 1906 to 218 in 1913; as a result the number of vacant houses declined from 4800 in 1909 to 3400 in 1913. House building almost ceased during the war years with only 254 houses being completed in 1915–18 and in consequence the number of vacant houses fell to 756 by 1918.[108] In January 1920 the Bristol Photographic society heard a lecture illustrated with photographic slides on housing conditions in the city; the club suggested that those councillors responsible for housing should see the evidence. The council's reply shows how serious the problem had become.

> The Committee will be pleased to avail themselves of the opportunity of inspecting the photographs referred to at some date, but they can see no advantage in doing so now as they are at present powerless to deal with such properties owing to the shortage of housing accommodation.[109]

Exactly the same process appears to have occurred in Belfast, and a serious overcrowding problem emerged in this city once famed for the quality of its working-class housing. Compared to 1911 by 1926 the number of families living in one room had increased from 488 to 2682, those in two rooms from 3205 to 8178 and those in three rooms from 3898 to 10 226.[110] By 1923 the Bristol House Famine Campaign could quote cases of 29 persons living in a seven-room house or 18 in five rooms; they claimed that there was a shortage of 7270 houses in the city and an urgent need to build 8–10,000.[111] In the years 1920–5 a total of 3048 houses were built, 1253 by private enterprise and 1795 by the local authority.[112] However, this was insufficient to improve the basic housing position and the number of empty houses continued to fall to a figure of 204 in 1923 before increasing to 380 in 1925.[113]

But the working classes of Bristol and Belfast not only faced problems in housing, the cost of living had risen substantially during the war years and wages had not fully kept pace. The *Labour Gazette* of October 1922 was quoted by the Belfast Branch of the Electrical Trades Union to show that there had been a 121 per cent rise in prices during the war period.[114] The cost of food had gone up even further: the cost of the weekly food ration of a third-class officer in the Belfast Union increased by 157 per cent between July 1914 and October 1921.[115] It was not only the cost of the necessities of life that increased. Imperial Tobacco noted that, due largely to the increase in the duty on raw tobacco in the war years, the price of tobacco had increased by 25 per cent and cigarettes by 50 per cent.[116] In September 1919 the patternmakers at Harland and Wolff requested a pay rise in part to cover the increase in the cost of tools, which had doubled during the war years.[117]

Perhaps most painfully in both cities unemployment, which had been a seasonal or cyclic feature, now became a permanent feature of industrial life. Although the figures are not strictly comparable, the financial assistance supplied to the unemployed by the Bristol Public Assistance Committee and the Belfast Poor Law Guardians shows something of the scale of unemployment (Table 10.1).

CONCLUSION

The years 1912 to 1925 were to see enormous changes throughout the world and the cities of Bristol, Belfast and Dublin were not exempt from this. Dublin, although now once again a capital city, still suffered serious problems of poor housing and under-employment which would only be effectively tackled long after this period. Belfast and Bristol, both of which expanded and developed in the latter half of the nineteenth century, found the first quarter of the twentieth century a time of difficulty and hardship. The sub-committee established by Bristol City Council's Health Committee to look into badly needed reform of the city's health services, met once and reported that the city's financial situation was such that reorganisation was impossible at that time.[119]

Table 10.1   Unemployment in Bristol and Belfast[118]

		Bristol	Belfast
1920			794
1921			1 052
1922	1 January	9 377	913
	1 July	10 625	
1923	1 January	9 758	1 005
	1 July	9 659	
1924	1 January	9 987	1 531
	1 July	8 660	
1925	1 January	8 869	1 821
	1 July	6 336	
1926	1 January	8 780	4 087
	1 July	8 751	
1927	1 January	10 731	6 446
	1 July	8 401	
1928	1 January	9 533	997[*]
	1 July	6 318	
1929	1 January	5 554	2 195
	1 July	4 034	
1930	1 January	3 041	1 379
	1 July	1 497	
1931	1 January	2 095	4 165
	1 July	1 891	
1932	1 January	6 073	14 345
	1 July	8 999	
1933	1 January	7 517	21 387[**]

[*] Belfast Guardians refuse relief to able-bodied.
[**] Peak figure in Belfast.

The years between the wars were to be a stark contrast to the period before 1914 in both Bristol and Belfast, the growth and confidence of the earlier period being replaced by decline and uncertainty.

11 Conclusion

Belfast in the first two decades of the twentieth century was perhaps the most 'industrialised' city in the British empire. Its mix of industries, giving employment to both men and women, created high levels of employment. A larger proportion of Belfast's population was employed, in non-white collar jobs, than in such centres as Glasgow or Newcastle. Women formed a major element of the labour force employed in the manufacturing sector rather the domestic service.[1] Yet Belfast was an Irish city, located in a region normally presented as under-industrialised or even rural in character. In an attempt to explain this anomaly it has often been stated that Belfast was 'different' simply a deviation from the Irish 'norm'. Certainly if compared to Dublin, and if Dublin is accepted as typical of Irish urban conditions, Belfast was very different indeed. However, was Dublin really a suitable comparison for the industrial city on the banks of the Lagan?

Bristol and Dublin between 1880 and 1925 appear rather odd comparators and H.V. Morton, the travel writer, left descriptions suggesting little, if any, similarity between the three cities by the 1930s.

Everything in Belfast is on the big size. All the cliches are applicable to it. It is a "hive of industry", its chimneys "tower". Its mills are "mammoth", its workers "pour out" of factories. Its docks could, and let us hope soon will, "hum" with activity. It is, therefore, thoroughly comprehensible to most people. There is no mystery about it. It is as serious as a child playing a game.[2]

My trouble in Bristol is that I cannot leave the by-ways. It is a city as fascinating as London; and in the same unselfconscious way. Bristol hides itself up alleys just as London does. It gives nothing to him who does not search; but to the explorer Bristol is generous with the unexpected; with sudden glimpses of old things: queer old buildings; old steps; alluring doorways, and – always – the sight of a ship lying landlocked between two streets.[3]

Dublin in the early morning, with the sun shining, is a city the colour of claret. The red-brick Georgian mansions, with fine doors, fanlights, and little iron balconies at the first floor windows, stand back in well bred reticence against wide roads, quiet and dignified, as if the family has just left by stage coach. Dublin shares with Edinburgh the air of having been a great capital.[4]

The description of Belfast appears reasonably accurate, a city created by its industries and proud of their scale and success. Even today its long roads of red brick houses give Belfast the feel of a prosperous Victorian industrial town. At the peak of its success even a virulent critic such as James Connolly or the indomitable Miss Martindale had to admit that living conditions in the city were good. Visitors could find the city an uncomfortable mix of brash self-confidence and nouveaux riches attitudes and tastes.

Red brick in the suburbs, white horse on the Wall,
Eyetalian marbles in the City Hall:
O stranger from England, why stand so aghast?
   May the Lord in his mercy be kind to Belfast.

This jewel that houses our hopes and our fears.
Was knocked up from the swamp in the last hundred years;
But the last will be first and the first will be last:
   May the Lord in his mercy be kind to Belfast.[5]

Morton presents Bristol as an old-fashioned town wallowing in centuries of history and almost detached from the modern world. He fails to recognise, or chooses to ignore, that by 1930 the city was a major industrial centre which could boost 150 industries from Aeroplanes to Zinc Smelting.[6] Morton like other contemporary visitors was struck by the ships moored in the old docks in the very centre of the city. However, he did not visit the new port facilities at the mouth of the river which handled most of the city's trade. Bristol may give 'nothing to him who does not search' but Morton was looking for the old and quaint not the modern and industrial.

In Dublin Morton was greatly impressed by the hospitality and conversation of the residents he met. He claimed that their relaxed lifestyle, riding to hounds or shooting grouse, gave the city a singular quality: 'a balanced sanity. She is an ancient capital with the health of a county town. She is Georgian not only in her architecture but in her attitude to life.'[7]

He ignored the fact that the Georgian houses he admired so much comprised some of the worst housing conditions in Europe. Those whom he met and talked to were not the casually employed inhabitants of the slums but the social elite of the city. He may have found that 'through Irish life and conversation there runs a bitter spitefulness that at first puzzles you until you understand that it is a national gift'[8] but he did not come in contact with the black humour of the slums.

> Says my old one to your old one
> We've got no beef or mutton
> If we went up to Monto Street
> We'll get a treat for nothing
> Here's a nice bit of advice
> I got from an old fishmonger
> If food is scarce and you see the hearse
> You know you've died of hunger
>
> *What'll you have?*
> *I'll have a pint!*
> *I'll have a pint with you Sir!*
> *And if one of us doesn't order soon*
> *We'll be chucked out of the Boozer* [9]

The three cities in this study are of course very different to each other. A range of factors dictate this; urban conglomerations, like people, are products of their environment and origins. In the introduction I posed the question was Belfast Irish or British in character? The answer must inevitably be that the city, in terms of social organisation and economic development, had more in common with British centres such as Bristol than Dublin. This is not to say that it is not an Irish city simply that it developed in the form it did within a wider United Kingdom economic structure. The political implications of this 'Britishness' lie beyond the scope of this study. However, the economic integration of the north-east of Ireland and the rest of the British economy was amongst the most persuasive arguments of the Unionists. The 'similarities' between Bristol and Belfast become increasingly clear when they are compared to Dublin.

The economic structures of the three cities were totally dissimilar, and this inevitably influenced social developments. Belfast was a mature industrial city by 1880, its main industries were well established and expanding. As population grew, employment in linen, engineering and shipbuilding expanded steadily to absorb the growing labour force. A further range of industries building, transport and food processing were stimulated by the very growth of the city and its population. The concentration on a relatively narrow range of employment was to prove a source of strength in good times but disaster when depression hit the city's basic industries.

For Bristol 1880–1914 were years of development and change, new or previously minor industries forming the basis of expansion. In comparison to Belfast the city's employment was made up of a patchwork of industries none of which really dominated the city's economy. This gave Bristol a very different, but no less 'industrial' economic structure. Alfred Pugsley, the pioneering economic historian of the city, saw this as giving definite advantages: 'the names of Fry and Wills are known the world over, but Bristol would still be an important manufacturing centre without these great concerns.'[10]

Pugsley argued that such a structure, while unlikely to produce the vast prosperity of more specialised cities, was less likely to suffer the devastating effects of industrial slump.

In the case of Dublin it is difficult to escape Mary Daly's conclusion that the city was trapped by its former status as a capital city. Dublin was not an industrial city but rather an administrative and transport centre serving the whole of Ireland. The manufacturing industries that did exist were very limited and in the main consisted of small units catering for the domestic market. Those large scale export based firms such as Guinness, Jacobs and the distilleries employed only a tiny proportion of the labour force. Other sectors such as building, transport and tailoring trades were mainly seasonal or casual employers and could not absorb the labour surplus in the city.

The employment structures of the cities, as might be expected in view of their differing industrial bases, were very distinctive. Belfast needed a mixed labour force as the industries upon which its prosperity was based were very diverse. Shipbuilding and engineering were wholly dependent upon highly skilled males while the linen industry required a constant supply of low paid female workers. Bristol developed industries which employed large numbers of comparatively low skill workers in food processing, ready made clothing, footwear and transport. Skilled labour was vital in the engineering and printing trades but in numerical terms the skilled labour force was less important than Belfast's. Dublin possessed a surplus of labour and as a result the unskilled suffered serious problems of underemployment or unemployment. At the other extreme, the city had a large affluent white collar workforce in government and the professions, a hangover from its capital city status.

The consequences of these differences in employment structure are very evident when trade unionism is compared in the three cities. In Belfast the labour movement is dominated by those unions representing the skilled male workers, despite challenges from unions representing semi-skilled or unskilled labour at various times. In Bristol the emergence of unions representing such semi-skilled workers as seamen, railwaymen, gasworkers, dockers and miners was to lead to a shift in power within the labour movement away from the old skilled bodies. In Dublin the weak position of the unskilled labour force mean that the craft unions were not seriously challenged until the emergence of the ITGWU in the years before the First World War.

An important difference between Bristol or Belfast and Dublin was the type of trade union which emerged to represent workers. In Bristol and Belfast national or 'amalgamated' unions became increasingly important throughout these years; Dublin to a greater degree is typified by small local societies. This is not to say that local bodies were not important in Bristol and Belfast or that the 'amalgamates' did not establish themselves in Dublin. The reasons for this are partly political, partly social and partly economic: Dublin craftsmen saw outsiders as a threat; those of Bristol and Belfast saw themselves in many cases as part of a wider labour market. The trade union movements in all three cities did share certain experiences and difficulties, women and white collar workers were hard to recruit and there was an increase in militancy, notably among transport workers after 1906. However, the labour movements of Bristol and Belfast have more in common with each other than they do with Dublin.

This similarity and difference becomes clearer when the wider labour movement is examined. All three cities have trades councils, although the Dublin body was formed quite late, and bodies such as the Fabians and the ILP are to be found in each of them. However the Co-operative movement in Dublin was minuscule compared to those of Belfast and Bristol. Dublin's Suffragists belonged to a quite different, and basically nationalist body, to that found in both Belfast and Bristol. In Belfast and Bristol bodies such as the WEA, Clarion League and Socialist Sunday School could be found, all of which failed to establish themselves in Dublin. The labour movement in Belfast, like that of Dublin, was forced to adapt its organisation and policies to the basically nationalist/unionist political environment in Ireland. However, the Belfast labour movement still appears to have more in common with Bristol than Dublin.

The major factor in shaping both the economic structure of Belfast and that city's labour movement was the success of the shipbuilding industry. The growth in this sector and its dependence upon highly unionised skilled labour was to have a profound effect upon the Belfast labour movement. It is significant that as the industry declined in the years after the First World War the labour movement in the city became progressively weaker. The unions in the shipyards represented workers who may not have been irreplaceable, but were certainly difficult to replace. For this reason their negotiating position was stronger than those bodies representing unskilled labour in the city and immeasurably better than trade unions in Dublin.

The heavy dependence upon skilled labour within the British shipbuilding industry gave the unions great potential strength. However, they faced serious problems which prevented them exploiting their position to the full. There were too many unions within the industry and relations between them were often antagonistic rather than fraternal. Demarcation disputes between unions were a costly and damaging feature of both the industry and trade unionism within the industry. There was enormous potential for internecine strife as the unions representing the trades of wooden shipbuilding were forced to yield their dominance to those whose members worked in iron or steel. Skilled workers faced a constant threat from new technology and semi-skilled labour if wage demands or working practices were seen as a threat to profit or efficiency. Relations between management and workers were shaped by such considerations and divisions.

There were many possible responses by employers to the emergence of organised labour within British industry, and being as individual as trade unionists they varied considerably in their attitudes. In all three cities it is possible to find employers who were responsible and paternalistic in their relations with workers. In 1905 Meakin wrote his *Model Factories and Villages* to draw attention to the best examples of employers caring for their workers. The examples he quotes include Guinness and Jacobs in Dublin, the Ropeworks and Sirocco in Belfast and Frys in Bristol.[11] Equally, employers whose behaviour was exploitive or provocative can be found in all the cities.

There was good reason for a Belfast or Bristol employer to treat his workers well; labour was in short supply in both cities. Skilled or experienced workers were vital to the success of most industries and could easily find employment elsewhere if they needed to. In these circumstances a degree of paternalism, or at least moderation in industrial relations made good business sense. There were frequent industrial disputes and some employers such as those in the Bristol Boot and Shoe or the Belfast 'Putting out' trades were sometimes high-handed in their dealings with their employees. However, even in these cases the employer was seldom in a position to dismiss workers who resisted his demands. In Dublin labour was plentiful and employers had less need to be considerate in their treatment of workers. There was a marked tendency to end industrial disputes, even amongst the semi-skilled or skilled, by replacing the strikers with new workers. This tactic was less prevalent amongst the employers of the other two cities, not because they were more liberal, but because they had no pool of under-employed labour to draw upon.

Employers federations, Free-Labour associations and local arbitration boards can all be seen as responses by employers to an increasingly unionised labour force. Employers' federations were not necessarily seen as negative by organised labour but rather as an 'organisation' representing the other 'side' which made collective bargaining easier. Free Labour bodies were invariable 'union busters', and their activities could generate great bitterness in industrial disputes. In contrast the attempt to establish and operate arbitration panels can be seen as an attempt to remove, or at least reduce, bitterness in employer/union relations. The type of unions involved, the personalities of the employer and the union leader, availability of labour and the general condition of the industry were all factors in industrial relations. It is pointless to try and establish a typical employer/labour relationship when they varied from mutual respect and co-operation to uncompromising conflict.

It is difficult to see the Belfast shipyard worker as anything except a member of an elite stratum within the city's labour force. When they, along with workers in engineering and printing, are compared to other workers in the city their wages are better, employment more regular and status superior. Bristol had a similar, but much smaller elite, composed of workers in the engineering and printing trades. However, semi-skilled workers in boot and shoe making, clothing, mining and transport were more significant in Bristol's labour history. Despite these differences in both cities demand for labour was great and whole families could find employment, ensuring a considerable degree of prosperity. Dublin is a particularly painful contrast: with a saturated labour market underemployment was endemic and family earning power was consequently limited. This was particularly the case for women and juveniles, who had very limited opportunities in Dublin, but formed a critical element in the labour force of both Bristol and Belfast.

The comparative wealth of Bristol and Belfast is clear from the living conditions of their populations. There were problems, Bristol was short of hospital accommodation and Belfast had poor schools, but compared to Dublin conditions were incomparably better. In general the Belfast and Bristol working man enjoyed low rents, lower food bills, better public transport, lower unemployment and better health than the Dubliner. Indeed Bristol and Belfast enjoyed some of the best housing conditions in the United Kingdom.[12]

One feature of Belfast which appears to set it apart from Bristol, and indeed other British cities, is its unenviable history of inter-community violence. Belfast has not always been a sectarian battleground. In the late eighteenth century it was famous for its moderation in religious matters rather than its bigotry. Sectarianism grew in parallel with industry in the city, and like industry it was fed by migrants. The migrant worker is seldom a popular figure, and the unskilled migrant competing with the existing unskilled labour force is even less likely to be welcomed. In the case of Belfast the migrants were often of a different religious persuasion to the 'natives' and came from areas with an established tradition of inter-community violence. British cities were not immune to such pressures: there were strong elements of anti-Irish, anti-Catholic and anti-Semitic bigotry within British society before the First World War. It is notable that the Irish Home Rule Bill was as politically contentious in the rest of Britain as it was in Belfast, and the language no less extreme.

Inter-communal riots were not a feature of Dublin or Bristol, although there was occasional personal violence and general antagonism. The reason for this is not that the other cities were reasonable or liberal places to live, but because the religious minorities were so much smaller and subsequently not perceived as a threat. In both Bristol and Dublin there was considerable resentment against migrants in general, regardless of their religion. However, this did not develop into riots because most migrants either moved on or were absorbed into the community within a generation. In Belfast religion marked the newcomer as a threat even if they were the produce of generations within that city.

Why has it become the practice to simply write off Belfast as 'Irish but Different' rather than looking at it in terms of the wider British situation? In part this is political, a consequence of the British government's desire to have as little as possible to do with Ireland after 1922. It is also the case that social and economic conditions in Bristol and Belfast begin to diverge during the First World War. The years 1880 to 1912 were generally marked by social and economic similarity between Belfast and British cities; the war and the creation of the 'statelet' of Northern Ireland changed much of this. There were still many similarities between Bristol and Belfast but they are less conspicuous, and in the changed conditions of the inter-war years both begin to appear more like Dublin.

Bristol and Belfast up until 1914 can be seen as 'similar' although there were considerable differences between them. The degree of similarity is only really apparent when they are contrasted with Ireland's other major city. Dublin cannot be compared in real terms with the other cities; the better comparisons would be other 'capital cities' such as London and Edinburgh. Belfast on the other hand can only be compared with ports or industrial centres such as Cardiff, Barrow or Birmingham. All these urban centres grew rapidly in size and population in the latter half of the nineteenth century due to the development of engineering, shipbuilding and other localised industries, and enjoyed good housing and living conditions.[13]

If Belfast is compared to other centres that are undergoing a similar process of expansion and change, it is still a rather singular place. However, there is enough similarity to say that Belfast followed broader patterns discernible in other British cities. The periodic expulsions of Catholics from the shipyards and the savage outbursts of inter-communal violence appear to set Belfast apart. It was a singular city with problems and character created by a unique combination of historical, political, economic and social factors. But equally it was part of a wider British economic and cultural environment which equally shaped its development. The socialists in Ormeau Park, despite the shipyard expulsions, are no more an anomaly than they would be in any other British port/city of this era.

Notes

Location of material: See list of abbreviations in the bibliography, page 225.

1 INTRODUCTION

1. Photographic collection of the Ulster Museum. See Hill, M. & Pollock, V., *Images and experience: Photographs of Irishwomen* (Belfast 1993), p. 161.
2. Reports Annual Co-operative Congress. Bradford 1911, Lancaster 1916, Scarborough 1921, Belfast 1926, Bournemouth 1931.

Irish retail co-operatives

	Retail co-op	Membership	Belfast	% Total
1911	25	12 463	7 000	56
1916	38	24 453	14 200	58
1921	53	44 892	24 800	55
1926	34	45 889	29 500	64
1931	29	56 221	43 200	77

3. Clarkson, J.D., *Labour and Nationalism in Ireland* (New York 1926), p. 26.
4. O'Connor, E., *A Labour History of Ireland: 1824–1960* (Dublin 1992), pp. 202–3.
5. Judge, J.J., 'The Labour Movement in the Republic of Ireland' PhD thesis NUI (1955), appendix II.
6. Cummings, D.C., *Historical Survey of the Boilermakers and Iron and Steel Shipbuilders Society* (Sunderland 1905), p. 296.
7. Askwith, G., *Industrial Problems and Disputes* (London 1920), p. 296.
8. Schneider, F.D., 'British Labour and Ireland 1918–21' *Review of Politics*, Vol. 40 Pt 3 (1978), pp. 368–91.
9. Budge, I. & O'Leary, C., *Belfast Approach to Crisis* (London 1973), p. 89.
10. Boyd, A., *Holy War in Belfast* (Tralee 1970), pp. 119–21.
11. Mortimer, J.E., *History of the Boilermakers Society* (London 1973 & 1982).
12. Dougan, D., *The Shipwrights* (n.p. 1972); Jefferys, J.B., *Story of the Engineers* (London 1945); Tuckett, A., *The Blacksmiths Story* (London 1974).
13. Stevens, W.C., *Story of the E.T.U.* (1952), p. 100.
14. Higgenbottom, S., *Our Society's History* (Manchester 1939), pp. 226–9.
15. Lynch, M., *Scotland a New History* (London 1994), p. 395; Taplin, E., *The Dockers Union* (Leicester 1985), p. 23; Thompson, E.P., *Making of the English Working Class* (Harmondsworth 1968), pp. 469–85.

2 BELFAST, BRISTOL AND DUBLIN

1. Johnson, T., 'Social Conditions in Belfast prior to 1917', Gaughan, J.A., *Thomas Johnson 1872–1963* (Dublin 1980), Appendix 4, p. 414.
2. Beckett, J.C. & Glasscock, R.E., *Belfast Origin and Growth of an Industrial City* (Belfast 1967), pp. 111,128; Bardon, J., *Belfast an Illustrated History* (Belfast 1982), pp. 125–37; Beckett, J.C. et al., *Belfast Making of a City* (Belfast 1983), p. 171.
3. Census of Ireland.
4. Boyle, E., 'Linenopolis: The Rise of the Textile Industry', Beckett, *Belfast*, pp. 51–5.
5. Coe, W.E., *The Engineering Industry in Northern Ireland* (Newton Abbott 1969), pp. 47, 53, 63, 73, 92, 103, 112, 118–9, 121; McCutcheon, W.A. *The Industrial Archeology of Northern Ireland* (Cranbury 1980), pp. 134, 235, 301.
6. Pollard S. & Robertson P., *The British Shipbuilding Industry 1870–1940* (Harvard 1979), pp. 153–4.
7. Moss, M. & Hume, J.R., *Shipbuilders to the World* (Belfast 1986).
8. Inspector of Factories and Workshops (1889) (Cd 6720) BPP 1890 XX, p. 606.
9. Beckett & Glasscock, *Industrial City*, pp. 111, 128; Bardon, *Belfast*, p. 137; Beckett, *Belfast*, p. 171.
10. Bardon, *Belfast*, pp. 139–41.
11. Postgate, R.W., *The Builders History* (London 1923), p. 333.
12. The Bristol Construction Industry:

	1881	1891	1901	1911	1921
Building contractors	121	156	201	184	147
Employed in industry	6200	6270	11300	9520	6830
% Male labour force	11.2	10.0	12.0	9.1	5.9

The number of contractors is taken from *Mathew's Directory* for each year and the labour force from Bristol Industrial Museum's unpublished analysis.
13. Daly M.E., *Dublin: the Deposed Capital* (Cork 1984), pp. 55, 120.
14. Ibid, pp. 63, 117–23.
15. *Census of Britain and Ireland.*
16. Ibid.
17. Ibid.
18. Ibid.
19. Inspector of Factories and Workshops (1913) (Cd 7491) BPP 1914 XXIX p. 76.
20. Way J.P., *A Short History of Old Bristol Pottery and Porcelain* (Bristol undated 1920s).
21. Somerville J., *Christopher Thomas: Soapmaker of Bristol* (Bristol 1991), pp. 18, 53.
22. Weedon, C., 'The Bristol Bottlemakers', *Chemistry and Industry*, June 1978, p. 381, and 'The Bristol Glass Industry', *Glass Technology*, Oct 1983, p. 244.

23. Farr, G., *Bristol Shipbuilding in the Nineteenth Century* (Bristol 1971), pp. 13–22, and *Shipbuilding in the Port of Bristol* (London 1977), pp. 48–51, 64–5.

24. Buchanan A. & Cussons, N., *Industrial Archeology of the Bristol Region* (Bristol 1969), pp. 67–8; and Harvey, C. & Press, J.,'Industrial Change in the Economic Life of Bristol', in C. Harvey & J. Press, eds, *Studies in the Business History of Bristol* (Bristol 1988), pp. 5–6.

25. Davis, P., Harvey, C. & Press, J., 'Locomotive Building in Bristol in the Age of Steam', Harvey & Press, *Business History*; Rolt, L.T.C., *A Hunslett Hundred* (Dawlish 1964); Lee, M.J., 'Peckett & Sons Ltd: A Brief Memoir', *Industrial Railway Record*, April 1974.

26. Pugsley, A.J., 'Modern Growth in Cities', *Bristol Times and Mirror*, 1 March 1922.

27. Anon, *Work in Bristol: a Series of Sketches of the Chief Manufactures in the City* (Bristol 1883).

28. Data from UK Census 1881 and 1921.

29. Royal Commission on Labour: Employment of Women (Cd 6894) BPP 1893–4 XXXVIII p. 35.

30. Census.

31. Inspector of Factories and Workshops (1899) (Cd 233) BPP 1900 XI p. 397.

32. Census.

33. *Commercial*, 1 March 1928.

34. Betty, J.H., *Bristol Observed* (Bristol 1986), p. 62.

35. Data taken from an unpublished analysis of census undertaken by the Bristol Industrial Museum.

36. Daly, *Dublin*, pp. 5–6.

37. Port of Bristol Authority, *Port of Bristol: History Trade and Facilities* (Bristol 1959).

38. Ibid. The fourteen commodities were grain, feeding stuffs, oil seeds and oil nuts, petroleum products, timber, paper, wood pulp, ores, tobacco, frozen meat, butter, cheese, bananas and citrus fruit.

39. Census.

40. Royal Commission on the Port of London (Cd 1153) BPP 1902 XLIV pp. 855–78.

41. Wells, C., *A Short History of the Port of Bristol* (Bristol 1909), p. 321; Port of Bristol Authority, *Facts and Figures Relating to the Port of Bristol* (Bristol 1928), pp. 10–11; Sweetman, R. & Simmons, C., *The Port of Belfast* (Belfast 1985); Gribbon, S., 'An Irish City: Belfast 1911', Harkness D. & O'Dowd M. (eds), *The Town in Ireland* (Belfast 1981), p. 215.

42. O'Connor, U., *Oliver St John Gogarty : a Biography* (London 1963), p. 134.

43. Wright, A., *Disturbed Dublin: the Story of the Great Strike of 1913–14* (London 1914), p. 15.

44. Daly, *Dublin*, pp. 21.

45. Meakin, B., *Model Factories and Villages* (London 1905), pp. 197, 276, 284.

46. Daly, *Dublin*, p. 33.

47. Ibid, pp. 26–30.

48. Ibid, pp. 33–41.

49. Census.

Employment in retail and food processing industries

	1881	1891	1901	1911
Dublin				
Labour force	16 591	17 829	19 945	18 614
% labour force	13.1	14.6	14.0	12.6
Bristol				
Labour force	10 988	14 177	23 752	32 934
% labour force	12.2	13.9	16.2	20.1
Belfast				
Labour force	10 353	12 035	15 297	15 688
% labour force	11.9	11.4	10.8	10.2

50. *Belfast and Ulster Trades Directory* 1903.
51. Report of the War Cabinet Committee on Women in Industry (Cd 135) BPP 1919 XXXI p. 115.
52. *Retail sector in Bristol*

	1881	1891	1901	1911	1921
Bakers	183	225	280	267	197
Butchers	169	191	236	236	225
Fishmongers	33	58	54	80	83
Grocers	535	592	692	658	493
Public houses	1018	1184	1114	1180	1004

Figures from *Mathew's Directory* for each year.
53. UK Census for 1881, 1891, 1901, 1911. Final figure from *Commercial* 1 March 1928.
54. Inspector of Factories and Workshops (1901) (Cd 1112) BPP 1902 XII p. 4.
55. Minute Books of the W.D. & H.O. Wills Management Committee, 28th July 1905, BRO 38169/M/6(a).
56. W.D. & H.O. Wills, Letter Book 1904–6; BRO 38169/C/1(h).
57. Diaper, S., 'J.S. Fry and Sons', Harvey & Press, *Business History*, p. 43.
58. Bristol Chamber of Commerce and Shipping, *Report of the Council and Proceedings of the Annual General Meeting of 25 April 1900*, p. 11.
59. *Fry's Works Magazine: Bicentenary Issue* (1929) p. 9.
60. Census.
61. Census.
62. Royal Commission on Labour (Cd 6795) BPP 1892 XXXVI Pt 2 Questions 16,300–16,307.
63. Board of Trade Strikes and Lockouts (1892), (Cd 7403) BPP 1894 LXXXI strike 270 p. 50.
64. Board of Trade Strikes and Lockouts (1900), (Cd 495) BPP 1901 LXXIII strike 15 p. 58.

65. Stewart, M. & Hunter, L., *The Needle is Threaded* (London 1964), p. 156.
66. Inspector of Factories and Workshops (1891), (Cd 6720) BPP 1892 XX p. 11.
67. Fox, A., *A History of the National Union of Boot and Shoe Operatives 1874–1957* (Oxford 1958), p. 99.
68. Inspector of Factories and Workshops (1888), (Cd 5697) BPP 1889 XVIII p. 81.
69. Boot and clothing industries in Bristol

	1881	1891	1901	1911	1921
Wholesalers (boot and shoe)	33	78	94	44	46
Clothing manuf.	9	12	17	16	23
Shoe workers*	4 780	4 860	6 350	4 730	3 150
Clothing workers**	10 370	10 870	14 980	17 200	9 420
% of total Workforce	16.8	15.5	14.7	13.4	7.2

  * Does not include workers in Kingswood district; in 1911, for example, 3000 can be added.
  ** Includes both factory and outworkers.
  Figures for wholesale firms from *Mathew's Directory*. Employment figures from Bristol Industrial Museum.
70. Board of Trade Report, *Standard Time Rates of Wages*:
 1900 [Cd 317] BPP. 1900 LXXXII;
 1906 [Cd 3245] BPP. 1906 CXII;
 1910 [Cd 5459] BPP. 1910 LXXXIV;
 1914 [Cd 7194] BPP. 1914 LXXX.
71. Webb, P.J., 'The Industrial Geography of the Port and City of Bristol since 1861' (MA thesis London 1967).
72. Inspector of Factories and Workshops (1886), (Cd 5002) BPP 1887 XVII pp. 8–9.
73. Inspector of Factories and Workshops (1887), (Cd 5328) BPP 1888 XXVI pp. 19–22.
74. De Rousiers, P., *The Labour Question in Britain* (London 1896), pp. 82–3.
75. Connolly, J., 'The Reconquest of Ireland' *Collected Works* (Dublin 1987) Vol. 1, p. 214.

3 TRADE UNION GROWTH: A COMPARISON

1. Fyrth, H.J. & Collins H., *The Foundry Workers* (Manchester 1959), p. 32.
2. Pelling, H., *A History of British Trade Unions* (Harmondsworth 1976), pp. 33–5.
3. Rule 12 of the Belfast Sailmakers Society, quoted in Hirsh, M., 'The Federation of Sailmakers of Great Britain and Ireland 1889–1922: a Craft Union in Crisis'(MA thesis Warwick 1976), p. 3.

4. Pelling, *Trade Unions*, p. 36.
5. Jones, T., *First Annual Trade Union Directory* (1861 reprinted Farnborough 1991), pp. 4, 8, 23.
6. Cummings, D.C., *A Historical Survey of the Boilermakers and Iron and Steel Shipbuilders Society* (Robinson & Co 1905), p. 33.
7. Blankenhorn, D.G., 'Cabinet Makers in Victorian Britain', (MA thesis Warwick 1978), p. 1.
8. O'Brian, J.V., *Dear Dirty Dublin* (University of California 1982), pp. 299–304.
9. Dougan, D., *The Shipwrights* (1972), p. 92.
10. French, J.O., *Plumbers in Unity* (London 1965), p. 53.
11. Atkinson, B., *Trades Unions in Bristol* (Bristol 1992), p. 6.
12. Rules of the West of England and South Wales Operative Trade and Provident Society. (Bristol Records Office 32080/TC4/10).
13. Atkinson, *Trades Unions*, p. 6.
14. Rules of West of England Provident Society

Age	Entrance fee	Weekly contributions by class of membership		
		1st	2nd	3rd
16–20	2s	$6\frac{1}{2}$d	6d	n/a
20–25	2s 6d	$6\frac{1}{2}$d	6d	n/a
25–30	3s	7d	6d	n/a
30–35	4s	$7\frac{1}{2}$d	$6\frac{1}{2}$d	6d
35–40	5s	8d	7d	$6\frac{1}{2}$d
40–42	7s	n/a	$7\frac{1}{2}$d	7d
42–43	8s	n/a	8d	$7\frac{1}{2}$d
43–44	9s	n/a	$8\frac{1}{2}$d	8d
44–45	10s	n/a	9d	$8\frac{1}{2}$d
Sick benefit (first 20 Weeks)		14s	12s	10s
(second 20 Weeks)		7s	6s	5s
(third 20 Weeks)		3s 6d	3s	2s 6d
Funeral benefit (Member)		£12	£10	£8
(wife)		£ 8	£ 7	£6

15. *Bristol and Clifton Trade Directory 1893; Annual Report of the Bristol Trades Council 1894.*
16. Atkinson, *Trades Unions*, p. 6.
17. Bristol Incorporated Chamber of Commerce, *Report of Annual Meeting – 11th April 1888*, p. 41.
18. Atkinson, *Trades Unions*, p. 7; *Annual Report of the Bristol Trades Council 1891.*
19. Fox, A., *A History of the National Union of Boot and Shoe Operatives*, (Oxford 1958), pp. 137, 138, 164, 167, 179.
20. Ibid., p. 179.
21. *Annual Report of the Bristol Trades Council 1891.*
22. Marsh, A. & Ryan, V., *Historical Directory of Trade Unions* Vol. 2 (Aldershot 1984), p. 208.

23. Atkinson, *Trades Unions*, pp. 7–9; *Annual Report of the Bristol Trades Council (1891)*.
24. Ibid.
25. *Annual Report of the Bristol Trades Council 1892*; Marsh & Ryan, *Historical Directory*, Vol. 3, p. 161; Bagwell, P.S., *The Railwaymen* (London 1963), p. 132.
26. Atkinson, *Trade Unions*, p. 10.
27. *Annual Report of the Bristol Trades Council 1892*.
28. Large, D. & Whitefield, R., *The Bristol Trades Council 1873–1973* (Bristol 1973), p. 8.
29. Coates, T. & Topham, T., *The History of the Transport and General Workers Union* (Oxford 1991) Vol. 1 Pt 1, p. 125.
30. *Annual Report of the Bristol Trades Council 1892 & 1904*.
31. McKee, A., *The Belfast Trades Council* (Belfast 1983), p. 7.
32. Patterson, H., *Class, Conflict and Sectarianism* (Belfast 1980), p. 30.
33. Taplin, E.L., *The Dockers Union* (Leicester 1985), pp. 168–9.
34. Morgan, A., *Labour and Partition* (London 1991), p. 151; O'Connor, E., *A Labour History of Ireland 1824–1960* (Dublin 1992), pp. 37, 52; Patterson, *Class & Conflict*, p. 24.
35. Clegg, H.A. Fox, A. & Thompson, A.F., *History of the British Trade Unions Since 1889*, Vol. 1 (Oxford 1964), pp. 70, 84.
36. Ibid., p. 84; Patterson, *Class & Conflict*, p. 30.
37. UK and Irish Census.

| *Unskilled as a percentage of the labour force* | | | |
	1881	*1891*	*1901*	*1911*
Belfast	7.7	7.9	9.3	10.8
Bristol	6.2	5.5	3.1	1.8
Dublin	10.5	10.8	10.9	12.8

38. Boyle, J.W., *The Irish Labour Movement in the Nineteenth Century* (Washington 1988), p. 101.
39. Bagwell, *Railwaymen*, pp. 189, 133.
40. Taplin, *Dockers*, pp. 168–9.
41. Redmond, S., *The Irish Municipal Employees Trade Union 1883–1983* (Dublin 1985), pp. 11, 12, 60; Brown, K.D., 'Fireman's Trade Unionism in Northern Ireland' in Bailey, V., *Forged in Fire* (London 1992) pp. 176–7.
42. McKee, *Belfast Trades Council*, p. 7.
43. Patterson, *Class & Conflict*, pp. 29–31, 37–8.
44. Webb, S., Manuscript notes from minute books of Bristol Trades Council (Bristol Record Office 32080/TC1/28); Marsh & Ryan, *Historical Directory*, Vol. 3, p. 276.
45. Transcript of interview with William Hughs, a Belfast carter. Used in production of the radio programme 'Neither Wheel nor Hand' Feb. 1959 (PRONI D3358/1).

46. Coates & Topham, *Transport Workers* Vol. 1, Pt 1, p. 5.
47. The data used in the preparation of this table are from two sources and are not completely compatible, thus the need for a break point in 1902; (1893–1902) 'Royal Commission on Trade disputes and Combinations' (Cd 2825 & 2826) BPP 1906 LVI Appen 1; (1903–1909) Bowley, A.L., *An Elementary Manual of Statistics* (London 1915), p. 164.
48. *Report of the Trade Union Congress 1877.*
49. 'Report of a conference between organisers of trade Bristol employers and others concerned with the industrial employment of women', pp. 3, 5 (BRO 40458).
50. Webb, Manuscript notes, 2 April 1874.
51. Ibid., 7 December 1876.
52. Printed wage demand sent by the NUT to Bristol Education Committee, 11 July 1914. BRO 38773/18/2.
53. Wrigley, C., 'Labour and Trade Unions in Great Britain', *ReFRESH*, No. 13, Autumn 1991, p. 3.
54. Census.
55. Hunt, E.H., *British Labour History 1815–1914* (Atlantic Heights 1982), pp. 300–1.
56. McKee, *Belfast Trades Council*, pp. 13–14.
57. Messenger, B., *Picking up the Linen Threads* (Belfast 1980), pp. 207–8.
58. *Bristol and Clifton Directory* 1895–1901.
59. Webb, manuscript notes; *Annual Report of Bristol Trades Council* (1899).
60. Memorandum of agreement between Bristol Master Printers and Allied Trades Association and the National Union of Printing and Paper Workers 5 October 1918, BRO 40145/E/8a.
61. Census.

Percentage of female labour in domestic sector

	1881	*1891*	*1901*	*1911*
United Kingdom	42.5	41.8	38.7	
Bristol	44.6	39.5	33.4	29.5
Belfast	32.5	15.8	16.3	14.2
Dublin	48.1	40.0	42.7	36.6

62. Hearn, M., *Below Stairs* (Dublin 1993), pp. 86–7.
63. Hoffman, P.C., *They also Serve: the Story of the Shopworker* (London 1949), p. 5.
64. *Select Committee of the House of Lords on Early Closing of Shops* [Cd 369] BPP 1901 VI, Questions 2385, 2767.
65. Marsh & Ryan, *Historical Directory*, Vol. 1, pp. 6, 131; *Annual Reports of Bristol Trades Council.*
66. *Annual Report of Bristol Trades Council (1905); UK Census 1901.*
67. *Souvenir of the 21st Annual Delegate Meeting of the National Union of Shop Assistants, Warehousmen and Clerks* pp. 45–7, BRO 32080/TC4/18.

68. Whitaker, W.B., *Victorian and Edwardian Shopworkers* (Newton Abbot 1973), p. 173.
69. Typed manuscript 'The Clerks and the TUC' BRO 32080/TC4/15.
70. Hughes, F., *By Hand and Brain: The Story of the Clerical and Administrative Workers Union* (London 1953), p. 14.
71. Ibid, p. 38; Marsh & Ryan, *Historical Directory*, Vol. 1, pp. 34–5.
72. UK Census 1911.
73. Wardley, P., 'Edwardian Britain: Empire, Income and Political Discontent', Johnston, P., *20th Century Britain* (Harlow 1994), pp. 68–9.
74. Dangerfield, G., *The Strange Death of Liberal England* (London 1966), p. 176.
75. Bristol Adult School Union, *Facts of Bristol's Social Life* (Bristol 1914), p. 20.
76. Coats & Topham, *Transport Workers*, Vol. 1, Pt 1, p. 262; Atkinson, *Trades Unions*, pp. 17–8.
77. Clegg, H.A., *A History of British Trade Unions*, Vol. 2 (Oxford 1985), chapter 2; Large & Whitfield, *Bristol Trades Council*, p. 12.
78. Atkinson, *Trade Unions*, p. 19.
79. Ibid., pp. 19–22.
80. Ibid., p. 22.
81. McKee, *Belfast Trades Council*, p. 9.
82. Gray, J., *City in Revolt* (Belfast 1985), p. 205.
83. Ibid, p. 58.
84. Keogh, D., *The Rise of the Irish Working Class* (Belfast 1982), pp. 135, 141; Hyman, R., *The Workers Union* (Oxford 1971), pp. 63–4.
85. Johnson, 'Social Conditions', p. 416.
86. Kenny, B., 'The Growth of the Irish Transport and General Workers Union: a Geographer's View', *Saothar*, Vol. 12 (1987), p. 78; Keogh, *Irish Working Class*, pp. 138–41; O'Connor, *Labour History*, pp. 74–5.
87. Belfast Trades Council Minutes, 1 August 1912.
88. Ibid., 5 September 1912, 21 September 1912.
89. Marsh & Ryan, *Historical Directory*, Vol. 3, p. 285.
90. O'Connor, *Labour History*, pp. 76–7; Keogh, *Irish Working Class*, pp. 142–5.
91. Ibid., pp. 138–141.
92. O'Connor, *Labour History*, pp. 74–5; Kenny, 'Growth of the ITGWU' p. 78.
93. Keogh, *Irish Working Class*, p. 141; Redmond, *Municipal Employees*, p. 60.
94. Merrigan, M., *Eagle or Cuckoo: the Story of the ATGWU in Ireland* (Dublin 1989), pp. 19–20.
95. Clegg, *Trade Unions*, Vol. 2, p. 73.
96. Holton, B., *British Syndicalism* (London 1976), pp. 102–3.
97. Ibid., p. 102.
98. Brown, G., *The Industrial Syndicalist* (Nottingham 1974), pp. 94–5, 204–5, 236–7, 314–5, 342–3, 374–5.
99. *Bristol I.L.P. Newsletter 20 December 1913.* BRO 32080/TC/10/2a.
100. Brown, *Industrial Syndicalist*, pp. 314–15.
101. O'Connor, E., *Syndicalism in Ireland* (Cork 1988), p. 46.

4 THE LABOUR MOVEMENT: A WIDER VIEW

1. Backstrom, P.N., *Christian Socialism and Co-operation in Victorian England* (London 1974), p. 196.
2. *Bristol Observer*, 25 Oct 1913.
3. Belfast Trades Council, *Souvenir of the Trade Union Congress at the Grosvenor Hall Belfast* (Belfast 1929), pp. 61–3, 73–8.
4. Wall, J., *History of the Bristol Co-op* (Manuscript) (1893) BRO 37886/ 25; 'Co-op Marks Ninety Years of Progress', *Bristol Evening Post*, 27 July 1973.
5. Belfast TC, *Souvenir of TUC*, pp. 61–3; *Bristol Evening Post*, 25 July 1973.
6. Belfast TC, *Souvenir of TUC*, pp. 61–3, 73–8.
7. *Bristol Evening Post*, 25 July 1973.
8. Jackson, E., *A Study in Democracy: Industrial Co-operation in Bristol* (Bristol 1907), p. 440.
9. Reports of the Annual Co-operative Congresses Bradford 1911, Lancaster 1916, Scarborough 1921, Belfast 1926, Bournemouth 1931.
10. Ibid., p. 441.
11. O'Brian, J.V., *Dear Dirty Dublin: A City in Distress 1899–1916* (University of California 1992), p. 91.
12. Boyle, J.W., *The Irish Labour Movement in the Nineteenth Century* (Washington 1988), pp. 189–191.
13. McInevney, M., 'The Irish Labour Movement' *Hibernia*, March 1963, p. 6; Thornley, D., 'The Development of the Irish Labour Movement' *Christus Rex* 18 (1964), pp. 16–17.
14. O'Brian, *Dublin*, p. 92.
15. Belfast TC, *A Souvenir of TUC*, p. 75.
16. The best description of tensions between the Catholic and the Irish trade unions can be found in Connolly, J., 'Roman Catholicism and Socialism' *Collected Works* (Dublin 1988), pp. 234–8.
17. McElborough, R., manuscript autobiography, Vol. 1, p. 57 (PRONI D770/1/1–4).
18. Patterson, H., *Class, Conflict and Sectarianism* (Belfast 1980), p. 34.
19. Boyle, *The Irish Labour Movement*, pp. 183–8.
20. Morgan, A., *Labour and Partition* (London 1991), pp. 269–70.
21. Bryher, S., *An Account of the Labour and Socialist Movement in Bristol* (Bristol 1929), pp. 33, 43.
22. Bristol ILP, *Souvenir of the Opening of Kingsley Hall, 23–24 Sept 1911*, p. 16, BCL B24623.
23. Ibid., pp. 17–18.
24. Ibid., p. 21.
25. *Bristol ILP Newsletter*, 4 Oct. 1913. The Newsletters of the Bristol ILP that remain have been used as scraps for press cuttings. (BRO 32080/ TC/10/24a–b).
26. Boyle, *The Irish Labour Movement*, pp. 179–80.
27. Pease, E.R., *History of the Fabian Society* (London 1918), p. 240.
28. Bryher, *Labour and Socialist Movement* Pt 1, p. 27; Fabian Society, *Tract No. 18: Facts for Bristol* (London 1891).

29. Pease, *Fabian Society*, pp. 153, 185, 191.
30. *Bristolian*, December 1913.
31. Pease, *Fabian Society*, pp. 237, 252.
32. Boyle, *Irish Labour Movement*, pp. 171–9.
33. Bryher, *Labour and Socialist Movement* Pt 1, p. 18.
34. Ibid., p. 20.
35. Ibid., pp. 23–4.
36. John Wall Papers, List of Publications (BRO 37886).
37. Bristol Socialist Society, *Labour Songs*, pp. 4–5 (BRO 37886/18).
38. Scrap Book relating to 'Liberty Faire' (BCL 27123).
39. Bristol Socialist Society, *Programme of Liberty Faire* (BRO 37886/17).
40. Thomas, C., 'With Paste Pot and Brush: Origins of the Bristol Labour Party' in, Bristol Broadside, *Placards and Pin Money* (Bristol 1986), p. 128.
41. Ibid., p. 130.
42. *Bristol ILP Newsletter*, 20 December 1913.
43. Fraser, W.H., 'Trades Councils in England and Scotland: 1858–1897' DPhil Sussex thesis, 1967.
44. McKee, A., *Belfast Trades Council 1881–1981* (Belfast 1983); Large & Whitfield, *Bristol Trades Council*; Cody, S., O'Dowd, J. & Rigney, P., *The Parliament of Labour: 100 Years of the Dublin Trades Council* (Dublin 1983).
45. Large & Whitfield, *Bristol Trades Council*, p. 10.
46. Large, D. & Whitfield, R., *The Bristol Trades Council 1873–1973* (Bristol 1973), p. 2.
47. Owens, R., *Smashing Times* (Dublin 1984), p. 70.
48. 'Reminiscence' manuscript autobiography of Elizabeth Hutchinson, pp. 10–11.
49. Bax, E.B., 'Some Current Fallacies on the Women Issue' *Essays on Socialism New and Old* (London 1907), p. 119.
50. *Co-operative News* 22.11.1913.
51. Bristol ILP, *Kingsley Hall*, pp. 17–18; Boyle, *Labour Movement*, pp. 289–70.
52. Manuscript in the John Wall Papers. BRO 37886/68.
53. Patterson, *Class & Conflict*, p. 42; Boyce, D.G., *Nineteenth Century Ireland* (Dublin 1990), p. 224; Travers, P., *Settlements and Division: Ireland 1870–1922* (Dublin 1988), p. 98.
54. *Minutes of the Belfast Trades Council* 18.2.1911, 6.4.1912, 1.6.1912.
55. Connolly, 'The Roots of Modern War' *Collected Works*, Vol. 2, p. 25.
56. Clarke, A., *The Effects of the Factory System* (London 1913), p. 120.
57. Bryher, *Labour and Socialist Movement*, pp. 36–7.
58. *Arrowsmith's Dictionary of Bristol* (Bristol 1906), pp. 395–7.
59. *Annual Report of the Belfast Chamber of Commerce* 15 February 1899.
60. Bristol Adult School Union, *Facts of Bristol's Social Life* 1914 (Bristol 1914), pp. 28–9.
61. Turner, M., *A History of the Workers' Educational Association–Western District 1911–1986* (Bristol 1987), pp. 4–12; Nolan, P., *A Brief History– Branch Resource Pack*, Belfast WEA.
62. Mansbridge, A., *An Adventure in Working Class Education* (London 1920), p. 67.

63. Bristol Adult School, *Facts of Bristol*, pp. 28–9.
64. Large & Whitfield, *Bristol Trades Council*, pp. 12–13.
65. Bristol Adult School, *Facts of Bristol*, p. 29.
66. *Newsletter of the Bristol I.L.P.*, 13.7.1914.
67. Ibid., 6.9.1915, 4.10.1915, 3.11.1915.
68. Bryher, *Labour and Socialist Movement*, p. 68; Boyle, *Irish Labour Movement*, p. 188.
69. Pease, E.R., *A History of Socialism* (London 1913), p. 383.
70. Bryher, *Labour and Socialist Movement*, p. 68.
71. Ibid., p. 54.
72. Bristol Socialist Sunday School, subscription card dated Sept 1898. (BCL B19561).
73. Jackson, *Study in Democracy*, pp. 480–2.
74. *Newsletter of the Bristol I.L.P.* 1.2.1915, 1.3.1915.
75. O'Rahilly, A.J., 'The Education System in Ireland' *W.E.A. Handbook 1918* (London 1920), p. 125.
76. *W.E.A. Handbook 1918*, pp. 319–20.

5 BELFAST'S SHIPYARD WORKERS: A STUDY IN ORGANISED LABOUR

1. Pollard, S. & Robertson, P., *The British Shipbuilding Industry 1870–1914* (Harvard 1979), p. 153.
2. *Labour Force of Harland & Wolff.*

	1912 %	1915 %	1919 %	1920 %	1921 %
Skilled & apprentices	50.8	59.2	48.9	54.1	53.9
Semi-skilled	4.9	7.1	6.4	6.9	5.9
Unskilled	44.7	33.7	44.7	39.0	40.2

Harland & Wolff papers, 25 July 1912, 10 March 1915, 27 August 1919, 20 July 1920, 20 June 1921.
3. Harland & Wolff Papers, PRONI, D2805; Memo dated 28 March 1911; Letter to City Clerk dated 19 April 1920.
4. Burgess, K., *The Challenge of Labour: Shaping British Society 1850–1930* (London 1980), pp. 82, 85.
5. Wardley, P., 'Edwardian Britain: Empire, Income and Political Discontent' Johnston, P. (ed.), *20th Century Britain* (Harlow 994), pp. 68–9.
6. Pollard & Robertson, *British Shipbuilding*, p. 158.
7. Dougan, J., *The Shipwrights* (1972), p. 3.
8. Jefferys, J., *The Story of the Engineers* (London 1945), p. 45.
9. Pollard, S. & Robertson, P., *British Shipbuilding*, p. 153.
10. Royal Commission on Labour, Third Report, Evidence of John McIlwain (Cd 6894) BPP 1893–4 XXXII Question 26,474.
11. Report on Strikes and Lockouts by the Labour Correspondent of the Board of Trade:

1890 (Cd 6176) BPP 1890–1 LXXVIII p. 74;
1891 (Cd 6890) BPP 1893–4 LXXXIII p. 83;
1911 (Cd 6472) BPP 1912–3 XLVII pp. 104–5;
1913 (Cd 7658) BPP 1914–6 XXXVI pp. 124–5.

12. Hirsh, M., 'The Federation of Sailmakers of Great Britain and Ireland 1889–1922: a Craft Union in Crisis' (MA thesis Warwick 1976), p. 82.

13. Lovell, J., 'Employers and Craft Unionism: a Programme of Action for British Shipbuilders 1902–5', *Business History* Vol. 34 No. 4 (1992), p. 40.

14. Pollard & Robertson, *The British Shipbuilding*, p. 117.

15. Tuckett, A., *The Blacksmiths History* (London 1974), p. 212.

16. French, J.O., *Plumbers in Unity* (London 1965), p. 61.

17. Minute Books of the Belfast Operative Plumbers PRONI D1050/5/2/1–5.

18. Ibid., 19 June 1890; 29 August 1891; 7 September 1891; 24 September 1891.

19. Ibid., 30 October 1891; 2 November 1891.

20. Ibid., 13 November 1891.

21. Harland & Wolff Papers, 28 March 1911, 19 April 1920; 1911 Census of Ireland.

22. Connelly, T.J., *The Woodworkers 1860–1960* (Manchester 1960), p. 78.

23. Kidd, A.T., *History of the Tin Plate Workers and Sheet Metal Workers and Braziers Societies* (London 1949), p. 169.

24. Marsh, A. & Ryan, V., *Historical Directory of Trade Unions* Vol. 2 (Aldershot 1984), pp. 122–3.

25. Kidd, *Plate Workers*, p. 179.

26. Moss, M. & Hume, J., *Shipbuilders to the World* (Belfast 1986), pp. 170–2.

27. Marsh & Ryan, *Historical Directory* Vol. 3, pp. 21–2, 24–5.

28. Harland & Wolff Papers, April 1911.

29. Fairfield Demarcation, *Boilermakers v. Shipwrights*, 31st July 1899, in Cummings, D.C., *A Historical Survey of the Boilermakers and Iron and Steel Ship Builders Society* (Robinson & Co 1905), pp. 204–7.

30. Mortimer, J.E., *History of the Boiler Makers*, Vol. 2 (London 1982), p. 12.

31. Jefferys, *Engineers*, p. 127.

32. Ibid., pp. 104–5.

33. Moss & Hume, *Shipbuilders*, pp. 171–2.

34. Harland & Wolff Papers, 28 March 1911.

35. Ibid., 15 April 1911.

36. Clegg, H.A., Fox, A. & Thompson, A.F., *A History of British Trade Unions since 1889*, Vol. 1 (Oxford 1964), p. 66.

37. Board of Trade Report on Strikes and Lockouts 1889 (Cd 6176) BPP 1890 LXVIII p. 48.

38. Board of Trade Report on Strikes and Lockouts
1892, May–July, Platers Helpers (680 strikers) (Cd 7403) BPP 1894 LXXXI p. 58.
1893, July–Sept, Platers Helpers (98 strikers) (Cd 7566) BPP 1894 LXXXI p. 83.
1894, Feb–March, Platers Helpers (312 strikers) (Cd 7901) BPP 1895 XCII pp. 108–9.

1897, April–May, Platers Helpers (93 Strikers) (Cd 9012) BPP 1898 LXXXVIII pp. 54–5.
1900, June, Rivet Heaters (120 strikers) (Cd 689) BPP 1901 LXXIII pp. 40–1.

39. Hyman, R., *The Workers Union* (Oxford 1971), pp. 12–13.
40. Interview with Bob Getgood. Transcript with the papers of Sam Hanna-Bell, PRONI D3358/1.
41. Harland and Wolff Papers, 2 December 1911.
42. Ibid., 3 December 1911.
43. Ibid., 21 June 1913.
44. Ibid., 26 June 1913.
45. Bain, G.S., *The Growth of White Collar Unionism* (Oxford 1970), p. 150.
46. Routh, G., 'White Collar Trade Unions in the UK' Sturmthal, A., *White Collar Trade Unions* (London 1966), p. 176.
47. Clegg, H.A., *A History of the British Trade Unions Since 1889*, Vol. 2 (Oxford 1985), p. 1.
48. Routh, G., 'White Collar Trade Unionism', p. 181.
49. Harland & Wolff Papers, Undated (late 1918).
50. Hughes, F., *By Hand and Brain: the Story of the Clerical and Administrative Workers Union* (London 1953), p. 64.
51. Harland & Wolff Papers, 15 October 1921.
52. Ibid., 12 December, 15 December and 22 December 1919.
53. Pollard, S. & Robertson, P., *British Shipbuilding*, pp. 198–200.
54. Harland and Wolff Papers, Late 1918.
55. Pollard, S. & Robinson, P., *British Shipbuilding*, p. 198.
56. Bain, *White Collar*, pp. 84–6; Marsh & Ryan, *Historical Directory*, Vol. 1, pp. 77–8.
57. Mortimer, J.E., *A History of the Association of Engineering and Shipbuilding Draughtsmen* (London 1960), pp. 28, 39.
58. Marsh & Ryan, *Historical Directory*, Vol. 1, pp. 4–5, 40–1, 151.
59. Harland & Wolff Papers, 28 January 1919.
60. Moss & Hume, *Shipbuilders*, p. 168.
61. Ibid., pp. 170–7.
62. Moss & Hume, *Shipbuilders*, pp. 49, 55.
63. Patterson, H., *Class Conflict and Sectarianism* (Belfast 1980), p. 26.
64. Mortimer, *Boilermakers*, Vol. 1, p. 112; Board of Trade Report on Strikes and Lockouts 1888 (Cd 5809) BPP 1889 LXX p. 49.
65. March 1889, platers & Assistants (238 strikers)
    April 1889, shipyard painters
    Sept–Nov 1889, shipyard joiners (300 strikers)
    Feb 1890, shipyard plumbers
    August 1890, shipyard joiners (50 strikers)
    August 1891, shipyard joiners
    May–July 1892, platers' helpers (680 strikers)
    Dec 1892, shipyard carpenters,
    ? 1892, shipyard joiners (H&W) (894 strikers)
    May 1893, riveters, (330 strikers)
    July–Sept 1893, platers' helpers (98 strikers)
    Jan–Feb 1894, riveters, (500 strikers)

Jan–Feb 1894, iron shifters, (35 strikers)
Feb 1894, platers, helpers, (190 strikers)
Feb–March 1894, platers' helpers, (312 strikers)
Feb–March 1894, shipyard labourers (210 strikers)
May–July 1894, french polishers, (30 strikers).

66. Inspector of Factories and Workshops (1892) (Cd 6978) BPP 1893–4 XVII p. 115.
67. Hume & Moss, *Shipbuilders*, p. 75.
68. Dougan, *The Shipwrights*, p. 94.
69. Moss & Hume, *Shipbuilders*, pp. 74–5.
70. Jefferys, *Engineers*, p. 141.
71. Mosses, *Patternmakers*, pp. 59–60, 64, 82, 84, 96, 99–101, 107, 114, 118–19, 124–5, 135, 157, 160–2, 173, 182, 193, 231, 265.
72. *1911, August*, rivet heaters (241 strikers + 331 affected)
1911, November–December, joiners in demarcation dispute H&W (700 strikers)
1912, August unskilled workers in shipyards (700 strikers)
1913, Jan–Feb apprentices in both yards (1300 strikers)
1913, February apprentices (300 strikers)
1913, April platers (300 strikers plus 300 affected)
1913, May–June joiners, H&W (540 strikers)
1913, August–Sept shipwrights, H&W (362 strikers).
73. Boyle, J.W., *The Irish Labour Movement in the Nineteenth Century* (Washington 1988), p. 35; O'Connor, E. *A Labour History of Ireland* (Dublin 1992), p. 35.
74. O'Connor, *Labour History*, pp. 37–8.
75. Pollard & Robertson, *British Shipbuilding*, p. 154.
76. McElborough, R., *My Years in the Gas Industry* (Manuscript) PRONI D770/1/1/1–4, Vol. 1, pp. 100–1.
77. Moss & Hume, *Shipbuilders*, p. 168.

6 INDUSTRIAL RELATIONS

1. Report of the Dublin Disturbances Commission [Cd 7269 & 7272] BPP 1914 XVIII p. 2.
2. Holton, B., *British Syndicalism* (London 1976), p. 124; Pelling, H., *A History of British Trade Unionism* (Harmondsworth 1976), p. 24.
3. Meakin, B., *Model Factories and Villages* (London 1905), p. 300.
4. Sheppard, F., *Labour Unrest and Some of its Causes* (Bristol 1912), p. 3.
5. De Rousiers, P., *The Labour Question in Britain* (London 1896), p. 6.
6. Introduction to the Rule Book of the Irish Transport and General Workers Union (1919).
7. Mrs Gallichan, 'The Truth About Women', quoted in Clarke, A. *The Effects of the Factory System* (London 1913), p. 151.
8. *Socialism a Warning* Free Labour Leaflet No. 464. George White Papers, BRO 35810/LUT/P/6a.
9. Meakin, *Model Factories*, p. 305.

10. See Chapter 3 of this volume; Akinson, B., *Trade Unions in Bristol* (Bristol 1992), pp. 1–12; Large, D. & Whitfield, R., *The Bristol Trades Council* (Bristol 1973), pp. 6–9.
11. Report of the council and proceedings at the annual meeting of members of the Bristol Incorporated Chamber of Commerce and Shipping. 9 April 1890.
12. Powell, L.H., *The Shipping Federation* (London 1950), p. 56.
13. Report of Belfast, Chamber of Commerce (1891), Outgoing Presidents address of Adam Duffin, pp. 20–1.
14. Board of Trade Reports of Strikes and Lockouts 1888–1901.
15. Askwith, G., *Industrial Problems and Disputes* (London 1920), p. 69.
16. Royal Commission on Labour: Textile, Clothing, Chemical, Building and Misc Trades. Evidence of Charles O'Reilly Dublin Trades Council [Cd 6795] BPP 1892 XXXVI Question 16,297.
17. Jones, M., *Those Obstreperous Lassies: a History of the Irish Women Workers Union* (Dublin 1988), pp. 8–9.
18. Paybooks of the Dublin Laundry Co. Ltd, INA BRS DUB/56.
19. Inspectors of Factories and Workshops (1905) [Cd 3036] BPP 1906 XV p. 53–4.
20. Inspector of Factories and Workshops (1904) [Cd 2569] BPP 1905 X p. 43.
21. Bundock, C.J., *The Story of The National Union of Printing, Bookbinding and Paper Workers* (Oxford 1959), p. 163.
22. Considerable correspondence connected with this report can be found in PRONI D1326/26/70.
23. Transcript of interview with Bob Getgood, an official of the Workers Union in Belfast. Sam Hanna-Bell Papers (PRONI D3358/1).
24. Bristol Chamber of Commerce (1891), pp. 88–9.
25. Ibid.
26. Annual Reports of the Belfast Chamber of Commerce Outgoing President's address 1878, 1894, 1896, 1899.
27. 'The Development of Ulster's Prosperity', *The Ulster Bulletin* February 1925 p. 19.
28. Newspaper article by Philip Snowden at the time of the Dublin Lockout; Askwith, *Industrial Problems*, p. 260.
29. Child, J., 'Quaker Employers and Industrial Relations' *Sociological Review* 12 (1964), pp. 293–315.
30. *Bristol Christian Leader*, Dec 1891, pp. 6–7.
31. Inspector of Factories and Workshops (1909) (Cd 5191) BPP 1910 XXVIII p. 156.
32. Keogh, *Irish Working Class*, p. 45.
33. Meakin, *Model Factories*, p. 304.
34. Ibid., pp. 191, 297.
35. W.D. & H.O. Wills Papers BRO 38169/9/11a.
36. Ibid.
37. W.D. & H.O. Wills, Works = BRO 38169/M/6a Jan 1907; Staff = BRO 38169/M/6h Jul 1910.
   A factory worker could retire on a pension of 12/6 p.w. after 25 years' service. For each additional year an extra 6d. was added to a maximum

of 25s. after 50 years' service, (women in factory, half these rates). Staff received a pension of £300 a year after 30 years' service, rising by £10 for each additional year to a max of £500 p.a.

38. W.D. & H.O. Wills Papers, BRO 38169/C/1(i) 5.2.1912.
39. Phelps-Brown, E.H., *Growth of British Industrial Relations* (London 1959), p. 78.
40. *Typographical Circular*, Sept 1912 p. 12.
41. Meakin, *Model Factories*, pp. 193, 197, 276, 284.
42. Gray, J., *City in Revolt* (Belfast 1985), pp. 58–9; Gaughan, J.A., *Thomas Johnson* (Dublin 1980), p. 24.
43. Meakin, *Model Factories*, pp. 196–7.
44. McElborough, R., *My Years in the Gas Industry and my Fight with the Trade Unions*, Vol. 1, p. 20; PRONI D770/1/1.
45. Dr Greville MacDonald, 'Introduction' to Clarke, *Factory System*, pp. xi–xii.
46. Inspector of Factories and Workshops (1901) [Cd 1112] BPP 1902 XII p. 148.
47. Hilton, G.W., *The Truck System* (Cambridge 1960), pp. 7–8.
48. Inspector of Factories and Workshops (1911) [Cd 6239] BPP 1912–3 XXV p. 38.
49. Inspector of Factories and Workshops (1907) [Cd 4166] BPP 1908 XII p. 133; Inspector of Factories and Workshops (1913) [Cd 7491] BPP 1914 XXIX p. 104.
50. Inspector of Factories and Workshops (1901) [Cd 1112] BPP 1902 XII pp. 147–8; Inspector of Factories and Workshops (1907) [Cd 4166] BPP 1908 XII pp. 132–3.
51. Inspector of Factories and Workshops (1903) [Cd 2139] BPP 1904 X p. 36.
52. Inspector of Factories and Workshops (1912) [Cd 6852] BPP 1913 XXIII p. 31.
53. Inspector of Factories and Workshops (1906) [Cd 3586] BPP 1907 X p. 63; Inspector of Factories and Workshops (1909) [Cd 5191] BPP 1910 XXVIII p. 35.
54. Inspector of Factories and Workshops (1898) [Cd 9281] BPP 1899 XII p. 49.
55. Inspector of Factories and Workshops (1894) [Cd 7745] BPP 1895 XIX p. 185; Inspector of Factories and Workshops (1895) [Cd 8067] BPP 1896 XIX p. 250.
56. Inspector of Factories and Workshops (1899) [Cd 688] BPP 1900 XI p. 125.
57. Inspector of Factories and Workshops (1907) [Cd 4166] BPP 1908 XII p. 430.
58. Inspector of Factories and Workshops (1886) [Cd 5002] BPP 1887 XVII (report of Mr Cameron).
59. Inspector of Factories and Workshops (1910) [Cd 5693] BPP 1911 XXII pp. 29–30.
60. Oliver, T., *Dangerous Trades* (London 1902), p. 825.

61. Inspectors were obliged to report cases of anthrax and certain other industrial diseases, for example see, Inspector of Factories and Workshops (1907) [Cd 4166] BPP 1908 XII p. 438.
62. Inspector of Factories and Workshops (1892) [Cd 6978] BPP 1893–4 XVII p. 6.
63. Inspector of Factories and Workshops (1899) [Cd 223] BPP 1900 XI pp. 222–3.
64. Inspector of Factories and Workshops (1904) [Cd 2569] BPP 1905 X pp. 38–9.
65. Inspector of Factories and Workshops (1909) [Cd 5191] BPP 1910 XXVII p. 127.
66. Inspector of Factories and Workshops (1900) [Cd 668] BPP 1901 X p. 170.
67. Minute Book of Bristol Branch No. 3 of the Dock Wharf and Riverside Union, 25 May 1911 BRO 27161 (1).
68. Report of the second annual dinner of the Bristol Master Printers and Allied Trades Association *Typographical Circular* April 1910, p. 3.
69. Coates, T. & Topham, T., *The History of the Transport and General Workers Union*, Vol. 1 Pt 1 (Oxford 1991), pp. 144–9.
70. George White Papers, BRO 35810/LUT3/P/6a *Crack the Nut*, p. 2.
71. Ibid., *Strike Insurance* NFLA recruiting leaflet.
72. Ibid., *Crack the Nut*, p. 1.
73. Ibid., *For and Against*.
74. Ibid., *Crack the Nut*, pp. 5–6.
75. Ibid., *For and Against*.
76. Ibid., *Crack the Nut*, pp. 5–6.
77. Ibid., p. 1.
78. Powell, *Shipping Federation*.
79. Ibid., p. 5.
80. Board of Trade Reports of Strikes and Lockouts:
    Belfast, April–August 1892, 1907
    Bristol, July 1891, May 1892, May 1893, June 1893, 1910
    Dublin, November 1891, December 1898, 1913.
81. Handbill of Belfast Labour Bureau Sick Benefit Club Harland & Wolff Papers PRONI D2805 Box 30.
82. Letter from Belfast Labour Bureau to Harland & Wolff, 9 October 1911 Harland & Wolff Papers PRONI D2805.
83. Mullen, S., 'Sweet Girls and Deal Runners' Bristol Broadsides, *Placards and Pin Money* (Bristol 1986), pp. 112–16.
84. Ibid., p. 112.
85. Ibid., p. 119.
86. Howell, B., *The Police in Victorian Bristol* (Bristol 1989), p. 22.
87. Atkinson, *Trade Unions in Bristol*, pp. 11–13.
88. Ibid., pp. 17–18.
89. City of Bristol Docks Committee, Reports of Officers 1913 Vol. 1, p. 209 BRO (unlisted).
90. Bristol Chamber of Commerce (1890), pp. 69–70. Speech by Sir Michael Hicks-Beach, President of the Board of Trade.

91. Bristol Chamber of Commerce (1895), p. 85.
92. Bristol Chamber of Commerce (1891), p. 26.
93. Belfast Chamber of Commerce (1896), pp. 16–17.
94. *Bristol Conciliation and Arbitration Board*, October 1890, BRO 11172(i).
95. Bristol Chamber of Commerce Annual Reports 1892, 1894, 1896, 1897.
96. Board of Trade, Strikes and Lockouts (1892–4):
    [Cd 7403] BPP 1894 LXXXI
    [Cd 7566] BPP 1894 LXXXI
    [Cd 7901] BPP 1895 XCII.
97. Akinson, *Trade Unions in Bristol*, p. 11.
98. Bristol Conciliation Board (By-Laws) BRO 11172(1).
99. Fox, A., *A History of the National Union of Boot and Shoe Operatives 1874–1957* (Oxford 1958), p. 179.
100. Ibid., pp. 167, 179.
101. *Bristol and Clifton Directory* 1890–1917.
102. De Rousiers, P., *The Labour Question in Britain* pp. 72–3.
103. McCarthy, M.J.F., *Five Years in Ireland 1895–1900* (Dublin 1901), p. 119.
104. Introduction to the Rules of the Irish Transport and General Workers Union (1919 edition).
105. Powell, L.H., *The Shipping Federation*, p. 17.
106. Askwith, *Industrial Problems*, p. 260.
107. Bryher, S., *An Account of the Labour and Socialist Movement in Bristol* (Bristol 1929), pp. 33–4, 47.
108. Moss & Hume, *Shipbuilders*; Gray, *City in Revolt*.
109. McCarthy, C., 'The Impact of Larkinism on the Irish Working Class' *Bulletin of the Society for the Study of Labour History*, Vol. 35 (1977), pp. 12–15.
110. Taplin, E., *The Dockers Union* (Leicester 1985), pp. 71–3.
111. Askwith, *Industrial Problems*, p. 110.
112. Ibid., p. 113.
113. Sam Hanna-Bell Papers: (a) Bob Getgood, Union Organiser; (b) William Hunter, Carter; (c) John Orr, Carter; (d) James Clarke, Docker.
114. Coates & Topham, *History of the TGWU*, Vol. 1 Pt 1, pp. 328–9; McHugh, J., 'The Belfast Labour Disputes and Riots of 1907' *International Review of Social History*, Vol. 22 (1977), pp. 1–20; Merrigan, M., *Eagle or Cuckoo: the Story of the ATGWU in Ireland* (Dublin 1989), pp. 9–15.
115. Coates & Topham, *History of the TGWU*, Vol. 1 Pt 1, pp. 362–3, Vol. 1 Pt 2, p. 541.
116. Powell, *Shipping Federation*, p. 23.
117. Atkinson, *Trade Unions in Bristol*, p. 122.
118. Typographical Circular August 1875, in Musson, A.E., *The Typographical Association: Origins and History up to 1949* (Oxford 1954), pp. 158–9.
119. Price, R., *Masters, Unions and Men* (Cambridge 1980), p. 122.
120. Jefferys, J.B., *The Story of the Engineers* (London 1945), pp. 145–6.

121. Mortimer, J.E., *A History of the Association of Engineering and Shipbuilding Draughtsmen* (London 1960), p. 124.
122. Wilson, H., 'My Stormy Voyage Through Life' Powell, *Shipping Federation*, p. 5.
123. Hume and Moss, *Shipbuilders*, pp. 89–90, 170, 284–5.
124. Harland & Wolff Papers, PRONI D2805; Letter from Clyde Shipbuilders Association to Harland & Wolff, dated 29 September 1911.
125. Ibid., Letter from the Ship Building Employers Federation to the Secretaries of Local Associations, copy to H&W.
126. Bob Getgood, Sam Hanna-Bell Papers.
127. Correspondence of Flax Spinners Association with various unions. Was PRONI D2279, now unlisted and filed with Chamber of Commerce Papers.
128. Ibid., Letter from Sam Kyle, District Organiser of the Workers Union to W.J.P. Wilson of the Linen Merchants Association, 2 May 1919.
129. Ibid., Letter from Harry Midley to Messrs J.A. Lowery 25 May 1920; J.A. Lowery to Harry Midley, 26 May 1920; J.A. Lowery to Household Linen and Piece Goods Association, 26 May 1920.
130. Harland & Wolff Trade Union Papers PRONI D2805. This collection contains several thousand documents in Boxes numbered 29 to 45 covering the period from 1911 to 1925.
131. Askwith, *Industrial Problems*, p. 69.

7 WORKING CLASS OR CLASSES?

1. These issues are raised in: Reid, A., 'Skilled Workers in the Shipbuilding Industry 1880–1920: A Labour Aristocracy' in Morgan, A. & Purdy, B. *Ireland: Divided Nation Divided Class* (London 1980).
2. Gray, R., *The Aristocracy of Labour in Nineteenth Century Britain* (London 1981).
3. Gray, R., *The Labour Aristocracy in Victorian Edinburgh* (Oxford 1976), pp. 98–9.
4. Cadbury, E. Matheson, M.C. & Shann, G., *Women's Work and Wages* (London 1908), p. 47.
5. Ledlow, F., 'The Reform of Felix Marton' *Tales and Sketches of Old and New Bristol* (Bristol 1890), pp. 20–30.
6. Connolly, J., 'Belfast and its Problems' *Collected Works*, Vol. 1 (Dublin 1987), p. 233.
7. Fyrth, H.J. & Collins, H., *The Foundry Workers* (Manchester 1959), pp. 114–15.
8. Jefferys, S.B., *The Story of the Engineers* (London 1945), pp. 66–7.
9. Oliver, T., 'Effects of Concussion on Air' Oliver, T. (ed.) *Dangerous Trades* (London 1902), p. 752.
10. Report to the Secretary of State for the Home Dept on Accidents occurring in Shipbuilding Yards. (Cd 7046) BPP 1913 LX p. 3.
11. Anderson, G., 'Some Aspects of the Labour Market in Britain' Wrigley, C. *History of Industrial Relations 1875–1914* (Brighton 1982), p. 4.

12. Harland & Wolff Papers, PRONI D2805, 17 August 1912.
13. Ibid., early 1915:

1 Box	12s. 0d.	1 Hammer	2s. 0d.
1 Saw	6s. 6d.	1 Caulking Mallet	3s. 6d.
1 Jack Plane	4s. 6d.	9 Caulking Irons	9s. 0d.
1 Hand Plane	3s. 6d.	1 Opening Iron	2s. 0d.
1 Pap Plane	1s. 9d.	1 Maul	3s. 6d.
1 Set Gouges	12s. 0d.	1 Foot Edge	4s. 0d.
1 Set Chisels	14s. 0d.	1 Doling Bit	1s. 6d.
Screw Augers	10s. 0d.	1 Expanding Bit	9s. 10d.
1 Ratchet Brace	7s. 6d.	2 Cutters.	
1 Set Bits	16s. 0d.	1 Spokeshave	3s. 0d.
2 Auger Bits	2s. 9d.		
1 Square	2s. 6d.		

Total Cost of Outfit = *£6.11.4.*

14. More, C., *Skill and the English Working Class* (London 1980), pp. 60–1.
15. Ibid., pp. 160–1.
16. Fox, A., *History of the National Union of Boot and Shoe Operatives 1874–1957* (Oxford 1958), pp. 359–60.
17. Inspector of Factories and Workshops (1891) (Cd 6720) BPP HoC 1892 XX, p. 6.
18. Inspector of Factories and Workshops (1906) (Cd 3586) BPP 1907 X, p. 25.
19. Royal Commission on Depression of Trade and Industry (Cd 4715) BPP 1886 XXII App D pp. 3, 36–7.
20. Keogh, D., *The Rise of the Irish Working Class* (Belfast 1982), p. 27.
21. Musson, A.E., *The Typographical Association* (Oxford 1954), pp. 183–191.
22. Ibid., Chapter XI.
23. Bristol Trades Council Annual Reports 1891–1923; *Bristol and Clifton Directory* 1880–1917.
    Amalgamated Society of Lithographic Printers
    Bookbinders and Machine Rulers Consolidated Union
    Bristol Bookbinders
    Bristol Box and Packing Case Makers Trade Union
    Electrotypers and Stereotypers Federated Society
    Lithographic Stone and Plate Preparers
    National Amalgamated Printers Warehousemen and Cutters
    National Union of Printing and Paper Workers
    Operative Printers Assistants Society
    Society of Lithographic Artists, Designers, Engravers and Process Workers
    Typographical Association.
24. *Typographical Circular*, 1914.
25. Tressall, R., *The Ragged Trousered Philantropist* (1911, edition London 1955).
26. City of Bristol, Report of the Distress Committee, 26 April 1906.

27. Daly, M.E., *Dublin* (Cork 1984), p. 110.
28. Social Service Committee of the Bristol Adult School Union, *Facts of Bristol's Social Life* (Bristol 1914), pp. 11–12.
29. Postage, R.W., *The Builders History* (London 1923), pp. 340, 456–7.
30. UK Census 1911, summary table.
31. UK Census 1911, summery table.
32. Report of Board of Trade Enquiry into the Earnings and hours of labour of work people. [Cd 4924] BPP 1909 LXXX.
33. Bristol Adult School, *Bristol's Social Life*, p. 20.
34. Wills Papers, BRO 38169//M/6(h).
35. Harvey, C. & Press, J., *Sir George White of Bristol 1854–1916* (Bristol 1988), p. 26.
36. Board of Trade Strikes & Lockouts (1901) (Cd 1124) BPP 1902 XCVII; National Free Labour Association *Crack this Nut and you will get to the Kernel of the Whole Question* BRO 3581/LUT/P/6, p. 6.
37. National Civic Federation, *Municipal and Private Operation of Public Utilities* (New York 1907) Vol. 3, p. 51.
38. McElborough, R., *My Years in the Gas Industry and My Fight with the Trade Unions* PRONI D770/1/1, pp. 19–20.
39. Bagwell, S.P., *The Railwaymen* (London 1963), pp. 84–5.
40. McKillop, N., *The Lighted Flame* (London 1950), p. 97.
41. Messanger, B., *Picking up the Linen Threads* (Belfast 1980), pp. 21–2.
42. Protestant male linen worker, born 1900, began work 1914, worked as weaver outside city before moving to Belfast. Messanger, *Linen Threads*, pp. 160, 230.
43. Inspector of Factories and Workshops (1891) (Cd 6720) BPP 1892 XX, p. 11.
44. Hunt, E.H., *Regional Wage Variation in Britain 1815–1914* (Oxford 1973), p. 112.
45. Fox, *Boot and Shoe Operatives*, p. 425.
46. Report of the Board of Enquiry into the Earnings and Hours of Labour of Working People (Cd 4795) BPP 1909 LXXX p. XLIX.
47. Hearn, M., *Below Stairs* (Dublin 1993), p. 30.
48. Report of the Board of Trade on the Money Wages of Indoor Domestic Servants (Cd 9346) BPP 1899 XCII p. 15.
49. Cadbury, *Women's Work and Wages*, pp. 115–16.
50. Whitaker, W.B., *Victorian and Edwardian Shopworkers* (Newton Abbot 1973), p. 174.
51. Details of strike at Glasgow Grocers in 1908. Hoffman, P.C., *They Also Serve: the Story of the Shopworkers* (London 1949), pp. 80–1.
52. Report by Fred Wilson, Inspector, to the Bristol City Council Watch Committee. Minute Books of the Watch Committee BRO 0458 (20) 19 January 1898.
53. Lovell, J., *Stevedores and Dockers* (London 1969), p. 32.
54. Transcripts of interviews carried out by Sam Hanna-Bell of workers who had taken part in 1907 Belfast Docks Strike. i. Joseph Cooper; ii. James Clarke; iii. William Long.
55. Royal Commission on the Poor Law (Cd 4795, 4890 & 4632) 1909 XLIX App XIX

Comparative employment in Bristol's Docks

Department	Permanent workers	Day workers	Casual workers	Total
Day 1 (Busy)				
Grain	41	273	230	544
General	15	45	185	245
Timber	13	22	57	92
Stevedoring	15	111	125	251
	84	451	597	1132
Day 2 (Slack)				
Grain	40	39	4	83
General	15	35	–	50
Timber	15	15	–	30
Stevedoring	15	26	–	41
	85	115	4	204

56. Report of the Bristol City Council Distress Committee to the 31st of March 1906, Table 1 BRO 11172 (2).
57. Royal Commission on Labour – The Employment of Women (Cd 6894) BPP 1893–4 XXXVIII, p. 34.
58. Inspector of Factories and Workshops (1906) (Cd 3586) BPP 1907 X, p. 152; Inspector of Factories and Workshops (1887) (Cd 5328) BPP 1888 XXVI, p. 21.
59. Third Report of the Select Committee of the House of Lords on the Sweating System (Cd 165) BPP 1889 XIII, pp. 679–8.
60. Royal Commission on Labour: The Employment of Women (Cd 6894) BPP 1893–4 XXXVIII, pp. 33–43.
61. Report of the Select Committee on Home Work (Cd 290) BPP 1907 VI Question 560.
62. Report on the Volume and Effect of Recent Immigration from Eastern Europe into the United Kingdom (Cd 7406) BPP 1894 LXVIII, p. 70.
63. Report of the Select Committee on Home Work (Cd 290) BPP 1907 VI Questions 612–618.
64. Anti-Sweating League *Bristol Sweated Industries Handbook* (Bristol 1908) BCL.
65. Bythell, D., *The Sweated Trades* (London 1978), p. 257.
66. Fourth Report of the Select Committee of the House of Lords on the Sweating System (Cd 331) BPP 1889 XIV Questions 26649–50.
67. Stewart, M. & Hunter, L., *The Needle is Threaded* (London 1964), p. 156.
68. Inspector of Factories and Workshops (1887) (Cd 5328) BPP 1888 XXVI p. 20.

69. Inspector of Factories and Workshops (1912) (Cd 6852) BPP 1913 XXIII p. 31.
70. *Belfast Newsletter* 14 May 1910.
71. *Belfast Newsletter* 2 September 1910.
72. *Belfast Newsletter* 14 May 1910.
73. Connolly, J., 'Belfast and its Problems' *Collected Works*, Vol. 1 (Dublin 1987), p. 232.
74. Royal Commission on Labour – The Employment of Women (Cd 6894) BPP 1893–4 XXXVIII, p. 34.
75. Report of the Select Committee on Home Work (Cd 290) BPP 1907 VI, p. 31.
76. Inspector of Factories and Workshops (1881) (Cd 3183) BPP 1882 XVIII, p. 24.
77. Inspector of Factories and Workshops (1904) (Cd 2569) BPP 1905 X, p. 199.
78. Miss Martindale served as 'Lady Inspector' in Ireland in the years 1907 to 1913 when she was moved to the Midlands. Her contributions to the Inspectors' reports for these years provide a detailed, if critical, view of Belfast.
79. Inspector of Factories and Workshops (1908) (Cd 4664) BPP 1909 XXI, pp. 152–3.
80. Inspector of Factories and Workshops (1890) (Cd 6330) BPP 1890–1 XIX, pp. 67–9.
81. Oliver, *Dangerous Trades*, pp. 92, 7.
82. Inspector of Factories and Workshops (1903) (Cd 2139) BPP 1904 X, p. 153; Inspector of Factories and Workshops (1906) (Cd 3586) BPP 1907 X, p. 43.
83. Inspector of Factories and Workshops (1906) (Cd 3586) BPP 1907 X, table 1.
84. Connolly, 'Belfast and its Problems', p. 232.
85. Phelps-Brown, E.H., *The Growth of British Industrial Relations* (London 1959), p. 59.
86. Inspector of Factories and Workshops (1910) (Cd 5697) BPP 1911 XXII, p. 111.
87. Van Boys and Warehouse Boys Committee (Cd 6886 & 6887) BPP 1913 XXXIII Question 6355.
88. Ibid., p. 23.
89. Royal Commission on the Poor Laws, Vol. XIX (Cd 4795, 4890 & 4632) BPP 1909 XLIV, pp. 48–50.
90. 36th Annual Report of the Bristol Charity Organisation Society (1907), p. 4.
91. Hearn, *Below Stairs*, pp. 90–4.
92. John Wall Papers, BRO 37886/63, pp. 2–3.
93. Inspector of Factories and Workshops (1901) (Cd 1112) BPP 1902 XII, p. 36.
94. Report of the Inter-Departmental Committee on the Employment of School Children (Cd 849 & 895) BPP 1902 XXV, p. 495.
95. Ibid., Question 4603–6, Appendix no. 32 p. 401.

96. Ibid., Appendix no. 32, p. 400.

Employment of school children in Bristol March 1901

	Schools	Attendance	Working
Boys Depts	29	8226	1057 (12.8%)
Girls Depts	24	5134	158 (3.0%)
Mixed Depts	14	4504	177* (3.9%)

* 130 boys and 47 girls.

97. First Report of the Vice-Regal Enquiry into Education in Ireland. [Cd 6828] BPP 1913 XXII; The Report of the Bristol Education Committee y/e 31 March 1914.
98. Census data.
99. De Rousiers, P., *The Labour Question in Britain* (London 1896), p. 20.
100. Cadbury, *Women's Work and Wages*, p. 186.
101. Vice-Regal Enquiry into Education.
102. Minute Book of the Irish Protestant National Teachers Union. PRONI D517.
103. Hunt, *Regional Wage Variation*, p. 352.
104. Anderson, G., *Victorian Clerks* (Manchester 1976), p. 109.
105. Anderson, *Victorian Clerks*, p. 2; Bains G.S., *Growth of White-Collar Trade Unionism* (Oxford 1970), pp. 11, 14.
106. Anderson, *Victorian Clerks*, p. 49.
107. Gray, *Victorian Edinburgh*, pp. 98–9.

8   LIVING CONDITIONS AND PROBLEMS

1. Mitchell, B.R. & Dean, P., *Abstract of British Historical Statistics* (Cambridge 1962), p. 25.
2. Hewitt, F., 'Population and Urban Growth in East Bristol 1800–1914'. (PhD Bristol 1965), pp. 109–10.
3. Royal Commission on the Housing of the Working Classes [Cd 4547] BPP 1884–5 XXXI Question 23, 361–6.
4. Ibid., Question 17, 268.
5. Inspector of Factories and Workshops (1899) [Cd 223] BPP 1900 XI, p. 135.
6. Bristol Chamber of Commerce Annual Report (1899) p. 39.
7. *Bristol Mercury* 17 October 1878, quoted in Harvey, C. & Press, J., *Sir George White of Bristol 1854–1916* p. 7.
8. Ibid., pp. 16–17, 23–5.
9. Cooke, A., *Bristol Hovels* (Bristol 1907), p. 14; Harvey & Press, *Sir George White*, pp. 23–4: the complaints against the Bristol Tramway Co. and their reply can be found in the rather acrimonious exchange of correspondence with the Council Tramway Committee in 1913–14 BRO 28787/4.

10. Budge, I. & O'Leary, O., *Belfast: Approach to Crisis* (London 1973), p. 115.
11. Bardon, J., *Belfast* (Belfast 1982), pp. 135, 166.
12. National Civic Federation, *Municipal and Private Operation of Public Utilities*: Vol. 1, p. 448; Vol. 2, pp. 705, 707, 710.
13. For an account of conditions in the Belfast Tram Co. see McElborough, R., *My Years in the Gas Industry* (Manuscript) PRONI D770/1/1, pp. 19–20; Harvey & Press, *Sir George White* p. 26.
14. Royal Commission on Housing, Question 17, 267.
15. Fabian Society, *Facts for Bristol* (London 1891), p. 5.
16. Minutes of the Bristol City Council Sanitary Committee, 14 October 1889, BRO 04904(6).
17. Reports of Bristol Medical Officer (1902–14).
18. Cook, *Bristol Hovels*, p. 11.
19. Burnett, J., *A Social History of Housing 1815–1970* (Newton Abbot 1978), pp. 158–60.
20. Beckett, J.C. & Glasscock, R.E., *Belfast Origin and Growth of an Industrial City* (Belfast 1967), pp. 111, 128; Bardon, *Belfast*, p. 137; Beckett, J.C. et al. *Belfast Making of the City* (Belfast 1983), p. 171.
21. Bardon, *Belfast*, pp. 137–9.
22. UK and Irish Census 1901:

| | *Percentage of population tenants of* | | | | |
	1 Room	*2 Rooms*	*3 Rooms*	*4 Rooms*	*5 + Rooms*
Belfast	0.4	4.7	6.4	29.1	59.4
Bristol	1.6	5.7	7.9	10.5	74.3

23. Reports of a Board of Enquiry by the Board of Trade into Working Class Rents and Retail Prices [Cd 3864] BPP 1908 CVII pp. 117, 568

House rents in Belfast and Bristol 1908

	3 Rooms	*4 Rooms*	*5 Rooms*	*6 Rooms*
	s. d.	s. d.	s. d.	s. d.
Belfast	2. 6.	3. 4.[a]	5. 0.	5. 6.
	to	to	to	to
	3. 6.	5. 0.	6. 3.	7. 0.
Bristol		4. 0.	5. 0.	6. 6.
		to	to	to
		5. 0.	6. 6.	8. 6.

[a] Kitchen-type house. Better class 'parlour' houses would have been 4s. 6d. to 5s. Kitchen and parlour houses are externally similar but in internal layout:
Kitchen house large kitchen at front of house on ground floor with bedroom and scullery at rear. Two bedrooms upstairs reached by stairs from kitchen.
Parlour house parlour at front of house on ground floor, kitchen and scullery at rear. Stairs at end of small separate hallway led to two bedrooms upstairs.

24. Fabian Society, *Facts for Bristol*, pp. 5–7; Cooke, *Bristol Hovels*, pp. 13–4.
25. Bristol City Council, *Bristol as it is Today* (Bristol 1905), p. 11.
26. Minutes of the Health Committee of Bristol City Council, BRO 04883, Vol. 1, 19 December 1899.
27. Ibid., 1 January 1900.
28. Ibid., 2 January 1900, 6 February 1900.
29. Ibid., Vol. 1, 13 February 1900; Vol. 2, 17 June 1902.
30. Report of the Departmental Committee on Humidity and Ventilation in Flax Mills and Linen Factories. [Cd 7433 & 7446] BPP 1914 XXXVI Question 2638.
31. Connolly, J., 'Belfast and its Problems' *Collected Works*, Vol. 1 (Dublin 1987), p. 226.
32. Belfast Health Commission [Cd 4128] BPP 1908 XXXI, p. 13.
33. Report of the Board of Local Government Medical Officer on Infant and Child Mortality [Cd 5263] BPP 1910 XXXIX, pp. 49, 60.
34. Belfast Health Commission, p. 21.

Infant mortality per 1000 live births

	1881–1890	*1891–1900*	*1901–5*
Bristol	141	147	122
Belfast	151	161	146

35. Annual Report of Bristol Medical Officer of Health (1908).
36. Social Service Committee of the Bristol Adult School, *Facts of Bristol's Social Life* (Bristol 1914), pp. 1–2:

Population density and health in Bristol (1913)

	Density (per acre)	*Cases of eight diseases*	*Pulmonary TB*
Ashley	22.5	286	46
Bedminster	31.8	572	89
Central	51.7	242	72
Clifton	32.7	220	51
Knowle	19.8	173	26
St George	29.9	539	68
St Philip	82.7	431	96
Stapleton	10.6	216	17
Westbury	2.6	69	7
Total City	20.7	2748	473

37. Report of the Departmental Committee on humidity and ventilation in flax mills and linen factories. [Cd 7433 & 7446] BPP 1914 XXXVI, App C tables C–E.

38. Report on the Conditions of Work in Flax and Linen Mills as Affecting the Health of the Operatives Employed therein. [Cd 1997] BPP 1904 X; Report of the Departmental Committee on humidity and ventilation.
39. Inspector of Factories and Workshops (1893) [Cd 7368] BPP 1894 XXI, p. 9.
40. Committee on Ventilation and Humidity, tables B–E.
41. Belfast Health Commission p. 32.
42. Report of Bristol Medical Officer of Health (1911) table II.
43. Annual Report of the Chief Medical Officer of the Board of Health (1908) [Cd 4986] BPP 1910 XXIII, pp. 66–7; Annual Report of the Chief Medical Officer of the Board of Health (1909) [Cd 5426] BPP 1910 XXIII, pp. 64–5.
44. Minute Books of the Tuberculosis Sub-committee of the Bristol City Council Health Committee, BRO 04892(1).
45. Minutes of Health Committee of Bristol City Council BRO 04883, Vol. 3, 3 November 1903.
46. Memorandum by the Director General of Army Medical Service, on the physical unfitness of men offering themselves for enlistment in the army. [Cd 1501] BPP 1903 XXXVIII.
47. Medical Officer of Board of Trade (1909), p. 27.
48. Report of the Bristol City Council Education Committee (1910) pp. 50–1.
49. Adult School Union, *Bristol's Social Life*, p. 7.
50. Ibid., p. 8.
51. McNeilly, N., *Exactly Fifty Years* (Belfast 1975), p. 14.
52. Ibid., p. 15.
53. Medical Inspection and Feeding of Children [Cd 2779 & 2784] BPP 1906 XLVIII Question 3224, Report of Committee, p. 41.
54. 36th Annual Report of the Bristol Charity Organisation Society (1907), p. 4.
55. Report of Bristol Education Committee (1914), p. 41.
56. Ibid., p. 42.
57. Number of meals provided by the Bristol Education Committee, Annual Reports 1910–15.

1910	340 501 meals
1911	405 962 meals
1912	433 625 meals
1913	370 627 meals
1914	282 152 meals
1915	302 336 meals

58. McNeilly, *Fifty Years*, p. 17.
59. Ibid., p. 17–18.
60. Large, D. & Round, F., *Public Health in Mid-Victorian Bristol* (Bristol 1977), pp. 1,3.
61. Large, D., 'Records of the Bristol Local Board of Health' in McGrath, P. *A Bristol Miscellany* (Bristol 1985), pp. 125 ff.
62. Report of Bristol Medical Officer of Health (1883) pp. 3–4.

63. Reports of Bristol Medical Officer of Health

	1883–7	*1888–92*	*1893–7*	*1898–1902*	*1903–7*
Wells closed	53	118	113	153	64
Water supplied	118	263	541	533	293
Pigs etc removed	773	513	1 177	766	693
Houses fumigated	1 015	2 868	5 641	9 638	11 172
Clothes disinfected	40 640	1 05 927	1 90 208	2 45 690	2 65 332

64. Report of the Vice-Regal Commission on Poor Law Reform in Ireland. [Cd 3202] BPP 1906 LI, pp. 166–9.
65. Fabian Society, *Facts About Bristol*, pp. 4, 18.
66. Bristol City Council Health Committee, Vol. 1, 17 July 1900.
67. Ibid., Vol. 2, 7 May 1901.
68. *Arrowsmith's Dictionary of Bristol* (Bristol 1906), pp. 217–25.
69. Report of the Committee Appointed to Consider the Extension of Medical Benefit under the National Insurance Act to Ireland. [Cd 6963] BPP 1913 XXXVII Question 1949.
70. *Arrowsmith's Dictionary*, pp. 217–25.
71. Annual Report of Bristol Charity Organisation Society (1907), p. 3.
72. Royal Commission on Venereal Diseases [Cd 7474] BPP 1914 XLIX Question 8001.
73. Stone, G.F., *Bristol Chronology 1915* (Bristol 1916), 1 February 1915.
74. Committee on Extension of Medical Benefits, Question 866.
75. Cunningham, J., *Particulars of my Life* (manuscript) PRONI D1288/1A.
76. *Arrowsmith's Dictionary*, pp. 17–20.
77. Royal Commission on the Poor Laws [Cd 4795, 4890 & 4632] BPP 1909 XLIV, p. 444.
78. Committee on Extension of Medical Benefits, Question 885.
79. Prospectus of the Workers Union 1914. Copy in the Harland & Wolff Papers, PRONI D2805.
80. Belfast Labour Bureau: Sick Benefit Club. Copy in Harland & Wolff Papers, 9 October 1911.
81. Cullen, L.M., *An Economic History of Ireland* (London 1987), p. 160; O'Grada, C., *Ireland: A New Economic History* (Oxford 1994), p. 272.
82. Report of an Enquiry by the Board of Trade into Working Class Rents, Housing and Retail Prices. [Cd 3864] BPP 1908 CVII pp. 115, 560, 566.
83. Notes on male wage rates and hours of work. Fry's Archives 913.2 Acc. No. 001119.
84. The wages quoted here are all taken from government reports of this period.
   Mother: Report of the Select Committee on Home Work [Cd 290] BPP 1907 VI, Question 561.
   Daughter: Report of the Board of Trade Enquiry into the Earnings and Hours of Labour of Work People [Cd 4545, 4844 & 4924] BPP 1909 VI; p. 105
   Son (A): Van Boys and Warehouse Boys Committee [Cd 6886 & 6887] BPP 1913 XXXIII, p. 23.

Sons (B+C): Report of Inter-Departmental Committee on the Employment of School Children [Cd 849 & 895] BPP 1902 XXV, p. 401.

85.   Board of Trade Working Class Rents, Housing and Retail Prices (1908 & 1913).

86.   The original attempt to do this can be found in Statistical Tables and Charts [Cd 2337] BPP 1905 LXXXIV, pp. 3–28.

87.   Pember-Reeves, M., *About a Pound a Week* (London 1913).

88.   I have taken the figures for food consumption of those earning 25–30s. and the cheapest foodstuffs in each city.

	Bristol (*Midlands England*)	*Dublin* (*Ireland*)
Bread	30.96 lbs	40.82 lbs
Meat[a]	6.30 lbs	4.32 lbs
Bacon	1.76 lb	1.32 lbs
Milk	4.82 pints	12.95 pints
Cheese	0.80 lbs	0.07 lbs
Butter	1.16 lbs	2.18 lbs
Potatoes	11.91 lbs	29.36 lbs
Tea	0.52 lbs	0.65 lbs
Sugar	4.53 lbs	6.50 lbs

[a] Meat, equal quantities of imported rib beef, imported leg of Lamb and local leg of pork.

89.   De Rousiers, P., *The Labour Question in Britain* (London 1896), p. 20.

90.   Engels, F. 'Conditions of the Working Class in England'; Burnett, *Plenty and Want*, pp. 70–1.

91.   Cadbury, E. et al., *Women's Work and Wages* (London 1908), pp. 232–3; Pember-Reeves, *Pound a Week*, pp. 94–103; Bowley, *Manual of Statistics*, p. 168.

92.   Clarke, A., *The Effects of the Factory System* (London 1913), p. 50.

93.   Imports of foodstuffs into the Port of Bristol Docks Committee Reports (1913 & 1925).

	1880	*1914*	*1925*
Grains (tons)	317 232	910 642	998 725
Flour, Meal (tons)	10 097	44 343	73 820
Sugar (tons)	14 547	89 220	56 552
Bacon, Ham (tons)	7 836	8 051*	257
Butter (tons)	1 192	408*	2 322
Cheese (tons)	6 387	10 033*	10 033
Lard (tons)	958	9 121*	7 341
Frozen Meat (tons)	0	1 818*	4 692
Livestock – Cattle	9 709	10 130	3 493
Sheep	25 323	988	410
Pigs		156	2*

* = 1913.

94.   Burnett, *Plenty and Want*, p. 131; Perren, R., *The Meat Trade in Britain 1840–1940* (London 1978), chapter 10.

95. Board of Trade, Working Class Rents, Housing and Retail Prices (1905 & 1906).
96. Burnett, *Plenty and Want*, p. 136.
97. Jackson, E., *A Study in Democracy* (Manchester 1911), p. 153.
98. Burnett, *Plenty and Want*, p. 125.
99. Value of foodstuffs imported into the UK. Minutes of Bristol City Docks Committee, Vol. 9 BRO, Unregistered:

	1858	*1868*	*1878*
(A)	£1 390 068	£2 689 496	£6 012 564
(B)	£20 164 811	£39 432 624	£63 536 322
(C)	£4 898 592	£13 277 683	£30 144 013

(A) = Livestock (cattle, sheep and pigs).
(B) = Corn, grain and flour.
(C) = Dead meat, bacon, cheese & provisions.

100. Food Imports and Exports from Belfast, *Annual Reports of Belfast Harbour Board*

		1880	*1914*	*1925*
Wheat	Imp	13 292	75 534	83 770
(tons)	Exp	4	2 147	11 987
Flour/meal	Imp		102 102	93 553
(tons)	Exp		17 833	6 873
Sugar	Imp	20 378	35 211	34 360
(tons)	Exp	55	296	62
Bacon/Ham	Imp		3 074	4 244
(tons)	Exp		12 267	8 072
Butter	Imp		1 770	3 448
(tons)	Exp		3 051	1 248
Cheese	Imp	638	1 067	1 647
(tons)	Exp	37	20	110
Lard	Imp		1 395	1 960
(tons)	Exp		1 703	371
Beef	Imp		1 814	1 320
(tons)	Exp		807	8
Cattle	Imp	863	1 829	44
(live)	Exp	91 485	151 437	112 662
Sheep	Imp	2 563	13 534	5 390
(live)	Exp	21 455	20 734	47 143
Pigs	Imp	74	3	9
(live)	Exp	28 445	6 269	962

101. Registered pupils and attendance in Bristol schools

	Registered	*Attendance (average daily)*	*% Attendance*
1880–84	30 195	22 319	73.9
1885–89	33 943	25 984	76.6

1890–94	36 974	29 418	79.6
1895–99	46 093	38 337	83.2
1900–04	61 217	52 325	85.5
1905–09	62 271	55 262	88.7
1910–14	59 419	52 946	89.1
1915–19	58 977	50 938	86.4
1920–24	57 074	49 845	87.3

1881–1891 – Annual Reports of Bristol School Board.
1892–1893 – Handbook of Bristol School Board.
1894–1902 – Annual Report of Bristol School Board.
1903–1925 – Annual Report of the Education Committee.

102. Results of Proceedings taken against Children absent from school. Annual Reports of School Board (1881–6).

103. Report of His Majesty's Inspector of Schools, Board of Education, on Primary Education in Ireland. [Cd 1981] BPP 1904 XX, p. 2.

104. Inspector of Factories and Workshops (1901) [Cd 1112] BPP 1902 XII, p. 147.

105. Farren, S., *The Politics of Irish Education 1920–65* (Belfast 1995), p. 25.

106. Minute Book of the Belfast branch of the Irish National Teachers Association, 31 March 1914 PRONI D1285/1–3.

107. Fabian Society, *Facts About Bristol*, p. 12.

108. Fabian Society, *Facts About Bristol*, pp. 11–12; Annual Report of Bristol Education Committee (1914) p. 31.

109. Annual Report of Bristol Education Committee (1914–16); *Reasons for leaving Bristol schools*

	1912	1913	1914	1915
To secondary school	693	703	672	689
To employment,				
a. by age (14)	4684	4906	5052	4855
b. Labour cert	173	214	148	145
c. Exempted	306	242	241	471
Deceased	136	132	120	144
Emigration etc.	3377	3216	2992	2712
Removed (illness)	6	14	10	7
	9375	9427	9235	9021

110. Annual Reports, Bristol Education Committee (1914) pp. 14–15.

111. Fabian Society, *Facts about Bristol*, p. 12.

112. Annual Report, Bristol Education Committee, (1914) pp. 14–15.

113. Van Boys and Warehouse Boys Committee [Cd 6886 & 6887] BPP 1913 XXXIII Appen LXXIV.

114. Clarke, *Effects of Factory System*, p. 61.

115. Minutes of Belfast Trades Council, 2 June 1910.

116. Ibid., 7 July 1910.

117. Large, D. & Whitfield, R., *The Bristol Trades Council 1873–1973* (Bristol 1973), p. 13.

118. Turner, M., *A History of the Workers' Educational Association – Western District 1911–86* (Bristol 1987), p. 11.
119. Wearmouth, R.F., *Methodism and Trade Unionism* (London 1955), p. 13; Cole, G.D.H., *A Short History of the Working Class Movement 1789–1947* (London 1966), pp. 173, 248.
120. Wall, J., *Autumn Unemployment* (manuscript) 1911–12, John Wall Papers, BRO 37886 (62).
121. Lovell, J., *Stevedores and Dockers* (London 1969), p. 32.
122. Royal Commission on the Poor Law.
123. Patterson, H., *Class Conflict and Sectarianism* (Belfast 1980) pp. 53–4.
124. Pugsley, A.J., 'Modern Growth of Cities: the Economic Growth of Bristol' *Bristol Times and Mirror* 5 June 1922.
125. Minute Books of the Bristol Distress Committee, BRO 04967 28 April 1915; Minute Book of Belfast Distress Committee. BCH Unlisted.
126. Daly, M., *Dublin*, (Cork 1984), p. 3.
127. O'Connor, U., *Brendan Behan* (London 1970), p. 14.
128. Civic Federation, *Public Utilities*, Vol. 3, p. 699.
129. Daly, *Dublin*, p. 174.
130. Connolly, 'Belfast and its Problems', p. 227.
131. Civic Federation, *Public Utilities*, Vol. 1, p. 448.
132. Report of the Departmental Committee to Enquire into the Housing Conditions of the Working Classes of Dublin. [Cd 7273] BPP 1914 XIX, p. 3.
133. Wright, *Disturbed Dublin*, p. 29.
134. Statistical Tables and Charts, p. 46.
135. Board of Trade, Working Class Rents, Housing and Prices (1908) p. 560; Census of Ireland 1901, p. 561:

Dublin tenement rents 1908 and housing 1901

	1 Room	2 Rooms	3 Rooms	4 Rooms	5 Rooms +
Occupying	24.7	21.0	10.3	10.1	33.9
Rents weekly	2s.–3s.	3s.–4s. 6d.	4s.–6s.	6s.–8s.	8s.–10s.

136. Report of the Committee Appointed to Enquire into the Public Health of the City of Dublin [Cd 243 & 244] BPP 1900 XXXIX, pp. 2–3.
137. Redmond, S. *The Irish Municipal Employees Trade Union* 1883–1983 (Dublin 1985), p. 5.
138. Dublin Public Health Enquiry, p. 69.
139. Rents, Housing and Prices (1913), p. 561.
140. Belfast Health Commission (1908), pp. 13, 21.
141. Report of the Board of Local Government Medical Officer on Infant and Child Mortality.
142. Gogarty, O., 'It Isn't that Time of Year at all', *Collected Works* (London 1989), p. 236.
143. Belfast Health Commission, p. 32. (See table with footnote 43.)
144. Daly, *Dublin*, p. 268.

145. Poor Law Reform in Ireland (1906), pp. 166–9.
146. Details of the quantity of food are listed at reference 88. The prices of these commodities would be as follows

	Dublin	Bristol	Belfast A	Belfast B
Bread	4s. 1d.	4s. 1d.	4s. 1d.	4s. 8d.
Meat	2s. 3d.	3s. 0d.	3s. 8d.	2s. 5d.
Bacon	1s. 2d.	10d.	11d.	1s. 2d.
Milk	2s. 2d.	7d.	6d.	1s. 4d.
Cheese	½d.	6d.	7d.	1d.
Butter	1s. 7d.	1s. 3d.	1s. 5d.	2s. 9d.
Potatoes	1s. 0d.	5d.	5d.	1s. 0d.
Tea	1s. 1d.	9d.	1s. 0d.	1s. 1d.
Sugar	1s. 1d.	9d.	9d.	1s. 1d.
	15s. 5d.	12s. 3d.	13s. 4d.	15s. 7d.

147. Daly, *Dublin*, pp. 134–6.
148. *The W.E.A. Handbook 1918* (London 1920), p. 319.
149. Board of Trade Reports, Standard Time Rates of Wages.
150. Royal Commission on the Poor Law; Cyril Jackson's Report on conditions in Ireland [Cd 4630] BPP 1909 XXXVIII, pp. 5–6.
151. Wright, *Disturbed Dublin*, p. 33.
152. Royal Commission on the Poor Law, p. 29.
153. The records of the Dublin Distress Committee are not at this time (Jan 1996) available to the public.

Winter of	Reported unemployed in		
	Belfast	Bristol	Dublin
1905–6	928 (B+C)	2900 (A)	546 or 1900 (C)
1906–7		1772 (A)	1987 (C)
1907–8		1392 (A)	
1908–9	3620 (B)	2967 (A)	3299 (D)
1909–10	1959 (B)	2175 (A)	
1910–11	678 (B)	1188 (A)	3116 (D)
1911–12	* (B)	1030 (A)	2827 (D)
1912–13	* (B)	502 (A)	2650 (D)
1913–14	* (B)	423 (A)	2983 (D)
1914–15	* (B)	297 (A)	3173 (D)

* In these years Belfast Distress Committee did not meet.
(A) Minutes of the Bristol Distress Committee.
(B) Minutes of the Belfast Distress Committee.
(C) Royal Commission on Poor Laws: Ireland.
(D) Annual Reports Local Government Board: Ireland.

154. Inter-Departmental Committee on Physical Degeneration [Cd 2175, 2210, 2186] BPP 1904 XXXII.
155. Oliver, T., *The Health of the Workers* (London 1925), p. 54.

9 SECTARIANISM

1. Belfast Riots Commission 1886 [Cd 4925] BPP 1887 XVIII p. 4.
2. Ibid., Questions 1503–8.
3. *Annual Report of the Belfast Chamber of Commerce* y/e 15.2.1893, pp. 19–26.
4. Budge, I. & O'Leary, C., *Belfast Approach to Crisis* (London 1973), pp. 91–5.
5. MacMaolan, S., *I mBeal Feirsde domh* (Dublin), pp 223–6. Translated from the Irish by Gordon McCoy of the Department of Anthropology, Queen's University, Belfast Spring 1993.
6. McCarthy, M.J.F., *Five Years in Ireland* (Dublin 1901), pp. 126–7.
7. Ibid., p. 205.
8. Bardon, J., *A History of Ulster* (Belfast 1992), p. 218.
9. Budge & O'Leary, *Belfast*, p. 35:

	Catholics	% Population
1784	1 092	8
1808	4 000	16
1834	19 712	32
1861	41 406	33.9
1871	55 575	31.9
1881	59 975	28.8
1891	67 378	26.3
1901	84 992	24.3
1911	93 243	24.1
1926	95 682	23

10. Miller, D., *Peep o' Day Boys and Defenders* (Belfast 1990); Bardon, *History of Ulster*, p. 218; Foster, R.F., *Modern Ireland* (London 1988), pp. 271–3.
11. Budge & O'Leary, *Approach to Crisis*, p. 8.
12. Bardon, *History of Ulster*, p. 280.
13. Budge & O'Leary, *Approach to Crisis*, pp. 12–13; Hereward, S., *Orangism in Ireland and Britain 1795–1836* (London 1966), pp. 60, 77, 83.
14. Budge & O'Leary, *Approach to Crisis*, pp. 92–3.
15. Patterson, H., *Class Conflict and Sectarianism* (Belfast 1980), p. XIV.
16. Royal Arch Purple Order, *History of the Royal Arch Purple Order* (Belfast 1993), p. 118.
17. Cunningham, J., *Particulars of my Life* (manuscript) PRONI D1288/1A.
18. Harris, R., *Prejudice and Tolerance in Ulster: a Study of Neighbours and 'Strangers' in a Border Community (Manchester* 1972), pp. 194–5.
19. Budge & O'Leary, *Approach to Crisis*, p. 89.
20. Thompson, E.P., *Making of the English Working Class* (Harmondsworth 1968), pp. 469–85.
21. Dougan, D., *The History of North East Shipbuilding* (London 1968), pp. 36–7.
22. Lynch, M., *Scotland: A New History* (London 1994), p. 395.

23. Taplin, E., *The Dockers Union* (Leicester 1985), p. 23.
24. Coats, K. & Topham, T., *The History of the Transport and General Workers Union*, Vol. 1 Book 2 (Oxford 1991), pp. 541–6.
25. Bundock, C.J., *The Story of the National Union of Printing Bookbinding and Paper Workers* (Oxford 1959), p. 57.
26. Coughan, R.M., 'Ethno-Nationalism and the Cultural Division of Labour in Nineteenth Century Belfast' (PhD State University of New York 1981).
27. Census Ireland:

Percentage of work force in specific trades listed as Catholic at each census

	1891	*1901*	*1911*
Shipyard trades			
Ship, boat or barge builder	7.9	7.5	7.8
Shipwright	12.2	5.7	6.7
Sailmaker	6.7	13.2	11.0
'Amphibious' trades			
Carpenter/joiner	16.8	22.7	12.6
Plumber	12.0	11.6	11.8
Cabinet maker	21.0	19.9	17.0
Painter/glazier	26.0	21.4	20.0
Engineering trades			
Engine/machine maker	14.8	10.0	9.0
Fitter/turner	12.2	11.2	13.4
Boilermaker	15.3	9.9	8.5
Blacksmith	17.5	18.6	16.7
Unskilled occupations			
General labourer	37.0	32.0	33.0
Dock, harbour, wharfage	42.5	42.0	39.6
Coal-heaver	38.8	28.7	14.0
Catholics as % male Labour	**25.9**	**23.5**	**23.4**

28. Kenna, G.B., *Facts and Figures of the Belfast Pogrom 1920–22* (Dublin 1922), p. 125.

Employment of Catholics in public bodies 1892

	Members		*Paid Officials*	
	P	C	P	C
Belfast Corporation	40	0	89	2
Harbour Board	22	0	37	0
Water Commissioners	15	1	7	0
Poor Law Board	43	1	91	3
Asylum Board	19	3	65	8

29. Ibid., p. 126.
30. Belfast Riot Commission, Questions 7582–7597.

31. Kenna, *Facts and Figures*, p. 20.
32. Moss, M. & Hume, J.R., *Shipbuilders to the World* (Belfast 1986), p. 225; Stewart, A.T.Q., *Ulster Crisis* (London 1979), pp. 100, 208; Farrell, M., *Northern Ireland: the Orange State* (London 1980), pp. 28–9; Johnson, D.S. 'Sir George Smith Clark' *Dictionary of National Biography*.
33. Budge & O'Leary, *Approach to Crisis*, pp. 93–4.
34. Belfast Riot Commission, Question 74.
35. Ibid., Questions 7585–7594.
36. Patterson, *Class Conflict and Sectarianism*, p. xiv
37. Hume & Moss, *Shipbuilders*, p. 225.
38. Harland & Wolff Papers, PRONI D2805, 27 August 1920.
39. Kenna, *Belfast Pogrom*, pp. 9–11.
40. McCartney, C., 'Civil Strife and the Growth of Trade Union Unity: the case of Ireland' *Government and Opposition*, Vol. 8 (1973) Pt4, p. 414.
41. McElborough, R., 'My Years in the Gas Industry and my Fight with the Trade Unions' PRONI D770/1/1, p. 48.
42. Ibid., p. 60.
43. Belfast Labour Representation Committee Address *Delivered by William Walker to the Irish Trades Union Congress, 23 May 1904.*
44. Cunningham, *Particulars.*
45. Budge & O'Leary, *Approach to Crisis*, p. 89.
46. Boyd, A., *Holy War in Belfast* (Tralee 1970), p. 174.
47. *Belfast Newsletter*, 19 January 1886, quoted in Gibbon, P., *The Origins of Ulster Unionism* (Manchester 1975), p. 126.
48. Walker, W.M., *Juteopolis: Dundee and its Textile Workers* (Edinburgh 1978), pp. 114–47.
49. Pollard, S., *History of Labour in Sheffield* (Liverpool 1959), p. 91.
50. Lovell, J., *Stevedores and Dockers* (London 1968), pp. 57–8, and 'The Irish and the London Docks', *Labour History* Vol. 35 (1973), pp. 16–17.
51. Kidder, W., *The Old Trade Unions* (London 1931), pp. 125–6, 149.
52. Gainer, B., *The Alien Invasion* (London 1972), p. 212.
53. Chemesha, B., *History of Preston*, p. 224, quoted in Redford, A., *Labour Migration in England 1800–1830* (Manchester 1926), p. 140.
54. Ibid., p. 124–5.
55. Bryher, S., *An Account of the Labour and Socialist Movement in Bristol* (Bristol 1929), pp. 28–9; Atkinson, B., *Trade Unions in Bristol* (Bristol 1992), p. 8; Hobsbawm, E.J., *Labouring Men* (London 1976), p. 162.
56. Royal Commission on Labour: Agricultural Labourers [Cd 6894] BPP 1893–4 XXXVII.
57. Atkinson, *Trade Unions*, p. 24.
58. Ibid., p.1.
59. Minutes of the Bristol City Council Health Committee 30 July 1907.
60. Report of Inspector of Factories and Workshops 1892 [Cd 6978] BPP 1893–4 XVII, p. 113.
61. Wright, A., *Disturbed Dublin* (London 1914), pp. 35–6; Hobsbawm, *Labouring Men*, p. 46.
62. Annual Reports of the Education Committee of Bristol City Council 1913–22.

Started Secondary School	7 321	(8.3%)
Started Employment	53 165	(60.1%)
Deceased	1 390	(1.6%)
Emigrated/Moved District	26 382	(29.9%)
Withdrawn due to Illness	72	(0.1%)
Total 1913–22	88 330	

63. Lawrence, F.W., 'Local Variations in Wages' (1899). Quoted in Hobsbawm *Labouring Men*, p. 46.
64. Hobsbawm, *Labouring Men*, chapter 4; Leeson, R.A., *Travelling Brothers* (London 1979).
65. Shepherd, F., *Labour Unrest and some of its Causes* (Bristol 1912), p. 7.
66. Inter-Departmental Committee on Physical Degeneration [Cd 2175, 2210, 2186] BPP 1904 XXXII, p. 185.
67. Ibid., Question 2209.
68. Ibid., Question 10928.
69. O'Brian J.V., *Dear Old Dirty Dublin* (California 1982), pp. 215–16.
70. Daly, M., 'Social Structure of the Dublin Working Class 1871–1911' *Irish Historical Studies* XXIII No. 90 (Nov 1992), p. 123.
71. Maguire, M., 'The Organisation and Activism of Dublin's Protestant Working Class 1883–1935' *Irish Historical Studies* XXIX No. 113 (May 1994).
72. Daly, 'Social Structure of Dublin', p. 127.
73. Maguire, M., 'A Socio-Economic Analysis of the Dublin Protestant Working Class 1870–1926' *Irish Economic and Social History* XX (1993) pp. 35–59.
74. Maguire, 'Organisation and Activism', p. 65, and 'Socio-Economic Analysis', p. 35.
75. Arnold, M., 'The Incompatibles' *Irish Essays and Others* (London 1891), p. 27.
76. Ibid., pp. 24–5.
77. Billington, R.A., *The Protestant Crusade 1800–1860* (Chicago 1964), pp. 95, 113.
78. Protestant Reformation Society; Irish Church Missions Bristol and Clifton Auxiliary; Protestant League; Society for Promoting Christianity Among the Jews. *Sources: Arrowsmiths Dictionary of Bristol; Brights Bristol Directory.*
79. Wilks, G.H., *Bristol's Heathen Neighbours: The Story of the Bristol Itinerants Society* 1811–1911 (Bristol 1911).
80. Oliver, G., *Collections Illustrating the History of the Catholic Religion* (London 1857), pp. 108–15.
81. Anon, *Remarks on the Anti-Protestant and Democratic Tendency of the Reform Bill* (Bristol 1831).
82. *Bristol Christian Leader* (January 1892), p. 50.
83. Ibid., (May 1882), p. 165.
84. Shaw, G.B., *John Bull's Other Island*, p. 25.
85. *Bristol Christian Leader* (January 1892), p. 50.

86. Arnold, 'Incompatibles', pp. 24–5, 27.
87. Shaw, *Other Island*, p. 5.
88. *Bristol Christian Leader* (June 1892).
89. Ibid. (January 1892), p. 44.
90. Ibid. (July 1892), p. 282.
91. Bristol Chamber of Commerce, *Annual Report* (1899) p. 64.
92. *Western Daily Press*, 30 November 1910.
93. Ibid., 7 December 1918.
94. Ibid., 9 December 1918.
95. Bryher, *Labour and Socialist Movement*, p. 12.
96. Ibid., p. 55.
97. Gainer, B., *The Alien Invasion*, pp. 212–13.
98. Freedman, M., *A Minority in Britain: Social Studies of the Anglo-Jewish Community* (London 1955), p. 16.
99. Freedman, *Minority in Britain*, p. 44; Hymson, A.M., *History of the Jews in England* (London 1928), pp. 197, 241; Lipman, V.D., *Social History of the Jews in England* (London 1954), pp. 23 Ft 2; Pollins, H., *Economic History of the Jews in England* (London 1982), pp. 83–4.
100. Lipman, *Social History of Jews*, pp. 23, 171; Pollins, *Economic History of Jews*, p. 100.
101. Pollins, *Economic History of Jews*, p. 117.
102. *Bristol Observer*, 1 November 1913.
103. Inspector of Factories and Workshops (1880) [Cd 2825] BPP 1881 XXIII.
104. First Report of the Select Committee of the House of Lords on the Sweating Industry [Cd 361] BPP 1888 XX, Question 1061.
105. Reese, A., 'Jewish Ancestry and Records' *Journal of the Bristol and Avon Family History Society* No. 60 (June 1990), p. 6; Gartner, L.P., *The Jewish Immigrant in England* (London 1960), p. 30.
106. Webb, S. & B., 'Industrial Democracy' (1897), pp. 687–8, in Gartner, *Jewish Immigrant*, pp. 64–5.
107. Ibid., p. 65.
108. Emanuel, R.R., 'The History of Bristol Jewry' *Temple Local History Group Newsletter*, Vol. 4 (1988).
109. Report of the Select Committee on Emigration and Immigration (Foreigners) [Cd 311] BPP 1889 X p. 88.
110. *Arrowsmith's Dictionary of Bristol*, p. 259; *Wright's Directory* 1883–1917.
111. *Bristol Christian Leader* (April 1892), p. 140.
112. Hymson, *Jews in England*, pp. 139, 241.
113. Lipman, *Social History of the Jews*, p. 26; Pollins, *Economic History of the Jews*, p. 128.
114. Pollins, *Economic History of the Jews*, p. 132; Freedman, *Minority in Britain*, pp. 65–6.
115. Lipman, *Social History of the Jews*, p. 67; Freedman, *Minority in Britain*, pp. 65–6.
116. Volume and Effects of Recent Immigration from Eastern Europe into the United Kingdom [Cd 7406] BPP 1894 LXVIII, p. 17.
117. Committee on Physical Degeneration, Questions 11279–11285.

118. Valentine, J., *Irish Memories* (Bristol 1929), pp. 111–14.
119. Brymer, *Labour and Socialist Movement*, p. 11; Valentine, *Memories*, p. 13.
120. Valentine, *Memories*, pp. 13–15, 20–1, 29, 34, 52–4.
121. Buckland, P., *Irish Unionism 1885–1923* (Belfast 1973), pp. 294–5.
122. Ibid., pp. 301, 305, 306–7, 317–18.
123. Hereward, *Orangism*, p. 304.
124. Purple Order, *History of*, pp. 119–20.
125. *Arrowsmith's Dictionary of Bristol*, p. 19.
126. Powell, A.C. & Littleton J., *A History of Freemasonry in Bristol* (Bristol 1910), pp. 26, 51, 791–2, 876–9.
127. *Wills', Works Magazine*, February 1924, p. 258.
128. Minutes of the Bristol City Council Advisory Committee for the Relief of Distress. BRO 3879(1) 11 December 1919.

10 WAR AND REBELLION

1. Dangerfield, G., *The Strange Death of Liberal England* (London 1966).
2. Stewart, A.T.Q., *The Ulster Crisis* (London 1969); Beckett, J.C., *The Making of Modern Ireland 1603–1923* (London 1987) Chapter 23, pp. 419–34; Hoppen, K.T., *Ireland Since 1800* (London 1989), pp. 13–7; Lee, J.J., *Ireland 1912–1985* (Cambridge 1989), pp. 1–24; Travers, P., *Settlements and Divisions; Ireland 1870–1922* (Dublin 1988), pp. 125–35.
3. Bundock, C.J., *The Story of the National Union of Printing, Bookbinding and Paper Workers* (Oxford 1959), pp. 374–5.
4. Ibid.
5. Hyman, R., *The Workers Union* (Oxford 1971), pp. 63–4.
6. Minutes of Belfast Trades Council, 1 August 1912.
7. Ibid., 21 September 1912.
8. Cunningham, J., 'Particulars of my Life' (manuscript) PRONI C1288/1A.
9. Ibid., interview with Mrs Cunningham 1966.
10. Buckland, P., *Irish Unionism 1885–1923* (Belfast 1973), p. 307.
11. Beckett, *Modern Ireland* Chapter 22, pp. 419–34; Hoppen, *Ireland*, pp. 135–6; Lee, *Ireland*, pp. 18–24; Phoenix, E., *Northern Nationalism* (Belfast 1994), pp. 14–20; Travers, *Settlements and Divisions*, pp. 86–9.
12. Connolly, J., *Collected Works*, Vol. 1 (Dublin 1987): 'The Liberals and Ulster', pp. 377–90; 'North East Ulster', pp. 383–90; 'The First Hint of Partition', pp. 391.
13. Stone, G.F., *Bristol Chronology 1915: the City at War* (Bristol 1916), p. 3.
14. *Western Daily Press*, 9 February 1916.
15. Terraine, J., *Business in Great Waters: the U-boat Wars 1916–1945* (London 1989), pp. 39, 103, 129.
16. Sixth Annual Report of the Bristol Civic League, 31 December 1914, p. 30.

17. Farr, G., *Bristol Shipbuilding in the Nineteenth Century* (Bristol 1971), and *Shipbuilding in the Port of Bristol* (London 1977).
18. Stone, G.F. & Wells, C., *Bristol and the Great War* (Bristol 1920), pp. 266–8.
19. Lysaght, J. Ltd, *Lysaght 1857–1957*, pp. 12–13; Stone & Wells, *Great War*, p. 258.
20. Harvey, C. & Press, J., 'Industrial Change in the Economic Life of Bristol since 1800' in Harvey, C. & Press, J., *Studies in the Business History of Bristol* (Bristol 1988), pp. 22–3.
21. Stone & Wells, *Great War*, pp. 252–3.
22. Ibid., p. 256.
23. Stone, G. 'Rearmament, war and the performance of the Bristol Aeroplane Co.', in Harvey & Press, *Business History*, pp. 187–8; Stone & Wells, *Great War*, pp. 246–50.
24. Stone, *Chronology*, p. 4.
25. Annual Reports of the Bristol City Council Education Committee 1910–1925. It is possible to use the provision of school meals as an indicator of the general economic conditions within the city of Bristol.

Year	Meals provided
1910	340 501
1911	405 962
1912	433 625
1913	370 627
1914	282 152
1915	302 336
1916	51 669[a]
1917	27 662
1918	25 954
1919	21 731[b]
1920	16 585
1921	70 169[c]
1922	245 882[d]
1923	135 951[e]
1924	84 134[f]
1925	60 387

[a] Report noted improved industrial conditions.
[b] 75% of these meals to children of widows.
[c] Report notes lack of employment.
[d] Unemployment 'prevalent', 4089 children fed.
[e] During the year an agreement reached that no child whose parent in receipt of Poor Relief was eligible for school meals.
[f] First full year of effects of e.

26. Inspector of Factories and Workshops (1915) [Cd 8276] BPP 1916 IX, p. 5.
27. Stone, *Chronology*, p. 6–7.
28. Sir George White Papers, Returns to West of England Engineering Trades Employers Federation. BRO 35810/GW/T/28 Oct 1918.

29. Ibid.
30. Anon, *The Cobbler's Tale: G.B. Brittion and Sons* (Bristol 1963), p. 4.
31. Wills Papers, Management Committee Minutes, 29 October 1918, BRO 38169/M/6(c).
32. Large, D. & Whitfield, R., *The Bristol Trades Council* (Bristol 1973), pp. 13–14.
33. Bain, G.S., *The Growth of White-Collar Unionist* (Oxford 1970), pp. 11–14; Blackburn, R.M., *Union Character and Social Class* (London 1967), pp. 130–7; Hughes, F., *By Hand and Brain: The Story of the Clerical and Administrative Workers Union* (London 1953), p. 48; Jones, M., *Those Obstreperous Lassies: A History of the I.W.W.U.* (Dublin 1988), pp. 16–29; Hyman, R., *The Workers Union* (Oxford 1971), p. 112; Wrigley, C., 'Labour and Trade Unions in Great Britain' *ReFRESH* Vol. 13 (1991), pp. 1–4.
34. Large & Whitfield, *Trades Council*, p. 13.
35. Ibid., p. 14.
36. Newsletters of the Bristol ILP. These have been used as scraps for press cuttings. BRO 320/TC10/24 a + b.
37. Turner, M., *WEA Western District: 75 Years* (Bristol 1986), p. 14.
38. Connolly, J., 'A Continental Revolution' *Collected Works*, Vol. 2 (Dublin 1988), p. 39.
39. Allen, K., *The Politics of James Connolly* (London 1990), pp. 123–33; Desmond-Greaves, C., *The Life and Times of James Connolly* (London 1976), pp. 351–9; Pimley, A., 'The Working Class Movement in the Irish Revolution' Boyce, D.G., *The Revolution in Ireland 1879–1923* (Dublin 1988), pp. 204–5.
40. Connolly, 'Irish Worker, 5 Sept 1914' *Collected Works*, Vol. 2, p. 46.
41. Lee, *Ireland*, pp. 21–4; Phoenix, *Northern Nationalism*, pp. 16–21; Travers, *Settlements and Divisions*, pp. 84–91.
42. Press Cutting Files of Bristol Trades Council BRO 32080/TC8/2/48 & 32080/TC10/24 a–b.
43. Large & Whitfield, *Trades Council*, pp. 16–17.
44. Newsletter of the South Western Division of the N.C.F., BRO 32080/TC8/2/29.
45. Independent Labour Party, *Democracy and the War* (London 1918), p. 1.
46. Bristol Joint Advisory Committee for Conscientious Objectors, Newsletter 27 Aug 1916, BCL B32052.
47. Ibid., 15 June 1916, BCL B32050.
48. Ibid., late 1917, BCL B37051.
49. Inspector of Factories and Workshops (1914) [Cd 8051] BPP 1914–16 XXI p. 36; Inspector of Factories and Workshops (1915) [Cd 8276] BPP 1916 IX p. 7.
50. Moss, M. & Hume, J.R., *Shipbuilders to the World* (Belfast 1986), p. 175.
51. Cunningham, J., 'Particulars of my life' (manuscript) PRONI D1288/1A.
52. Report of the War Cabinet Committee on Women in Industry [Cd 135] BPP 1919 XXXI Pt II, p. 115.
53. Harland & Wolff Papers, PRONI D2805, 28 August 1917.

54. Kenna, G.B., *Facts and Figures of the Belfast Pogrom* (Dublin 1922), p. 32.
55. Harland & Wolff Papers, PRONI D2805, 31 July 1916.
56. Patterson, H., *Class, Conflict and Sectarianism* (Belfast 1980), pp. 92–3; O'Connor, E., *A Labour History of Ireland 1824–1960* (Dublin 1992), p. 94.
57. Paybooks of the Dublin Laundry Co Ltd, 20/12/1913 & 21/12/1918.

	1913		1918	
	F	M	F	M
30s. +	0	3	0	7
25–29s.	0	0	0	7
20–24s.	0	2	3	2
15–19s.	1	12	65	0
10–14s.	50	1	24	3
5–9s.	91	8	12	7
under 5s.	19	0	0	0

58. Dudley-Edwards, R., *Atlas of Irish History* (London 1973), p. 75:

	Civilians	Government	Insurgents
Killed	300	136	76
Wounded	2000	400	120

There is some dispute about the exact casualty list, Lee in *Ireland 1912–85* suggests a figure of 400 killed and 3000 wounded while Foster in *Modern Ireland* says 450 killed and 2614 wounded.
59. Caulfield, M., *The Easter Rebellion* (London 1965), p. 257; O'Broin, *Dublin Castle*, p. 180.
60. Shaw, G.B., *John Bull's Other Island* (London 1931), p. 65.
61. Kenna, *Pogrom*, p. 33; Bowman, T., 'Composing Division: the Recruitment of Ulster and National Volunteers into the British Army in 1914' *Causeway* (Spring 1995), pp. 24–9.
62. Travers, *Settlements and Divisions*, pp. 108–11.
63. Stone & Wells, *Great War*, p. 116.
64. Kennedy, P., *The Rise and Fall of British Naval Mastery* (London 1991), pp. 307–8.
65. Oliver, T., *The Health of the Workers* (London 1925), p. 54.
66. *Western Daily Press*, 20 March 1924.
67. Johnson, D. *The Interwar Economy in Ireland* (Dublin 1989), pp. 4–5.
68. Patterson, *Class & Conflict* chapter 5, pp. 92–114.
69. Morgan, *Labour & Partition*, pp. 229–49; Patterson, *Class & Conflict*, pp. 92–114.
70. Clinton, A., *The Trade Union Rank and File* (Manchester 1977), p. 116.
71. Moss, M. & Hume, J.R., *Shipbuilders to the World* (Belfast 1986), pp. 209–10; Morgan, *Labour & Partition*, pp. 224–5; Patterson, *Class & Conflict*, pp. 108–9.
72. Lee, *Ireland*, pp. 40–1.

73. Bower-Bell, J., *The Secret Army* (New York 1970); chapters 1 & 2, pp. 3–28; Cougan, T.P., *The I.R.A.* (Glasgow 1987) chapter 1, pp. 15–59.
74. Townshend, C., *The British Campaign in Ireland 1919–1921* (Oxford 1978).
75. Mitchell, A., 'Labour and the National Struggle' *Capuchin Annual* (1971), pp. 262, 265.
76. Thornley, D., 'Development of the Irish Labour Movement' *Christus Rex*, Vol. 18 (1964) pp. 17, 19.
77. Irish Labour Party and Trades Union Congress, *A Handbook for Rebels: A Guide to Successful Defiance of the British Government (Dublin 1918); Who Burnt Cork? A tale of Arson, Loot and Murder* (Dublin 1921).
78. Gallagher, M., 'Socialism and the Nationalist Tradition in Ireland', *Eire-Ireland* 12 (1977), pp. 97–102; Mitchell, A., 'William O'Brian, 1881–1968, and the Irish Labour Movement' *Studies* 60 (1971), pp. 321–4; Rumpf, E. & Hepburn, A.C. *Nationalism and Socialism in Twentith-Century Ireland* (Liverpool 1977), pp. 10–3, 62.
79. Schneider, F.D., 'British Labour and Ireland 1918–1921' *Review of Politics*, Vol. 40 (1979), pp. 369–91.
80. Henderson, A., *Labour and Ireland* (London 1919), p. 7.
81. Shaw, G.B., *Irish Nationalism and Labour Internationalism* (London 1920), p. 9.
82. *Report of the Labour Commission to Ireland* (London 1921), pp. 2–3.
83. Ibid., pp. 6–7.
84. Patterson, *Class & Conflict* pp. 102, 111–12.
85. Ulster Unionist Labour Association *Labour Commission on Ireland: Analysis and Criticism* (Belfast 1921).
86. Morgan, A., *Labour and Partition* (London 1991), p. 267.
87. Patterson, *Class & Conflict*, pp. 115–142.
88. G.B. Kenna was a pseudonym used by Fr John Hassan, a Catholic priest living in Belfast at the time. By the time *Facts and Figures of the Belfast Pogrom* was ready to be released the conditions in the city had improved considerably. Hassan decided that he did not want to provoke any further ill feeling so had most copies destroyed. The copy I have used is in the Collection of the Belfast Society for the Propagation of Knowledge (Linen Hall Library).
89. Kenna, *Pogrom*, p. 19.
90. Morgan, *Labour and Partition*, pp. 269–70.
91. Kenna, *Pogrom*, pp. 106–16.
92. Higgenbottom, S., *Our Society's History* (Manchester 1939), pp. 226–9.
93. Hezlet, A., *The 'B' Specials* (London 1972), pp. 28–9.
94. Farrell, M., *Arming the Protestants* (London 1983).
95. Press Cutting from Unknown Source, 8 February 1921 Fry's Archives 913.3–001083.
96. Records of Bristol Constabulary, BRO 34908(46)b Report of Constable Cecil Hodge, 13 September 1921.
97. Ibid., Evidence of J. Harper, 17 September 1921.
98. Ibid., Evidence of Charles Harris, 3 October 1921.
99. Ibid., J. Freely, Police Inspector, 30 September 1921.

100. Minutes of the Bristol City Council Advisory Committee for the Relief of Distress, 27 January 1921; *Western Daily Press* 'The Kings Roll', 20 March 1921.
101. Bristol Association for Industrial Research: Unemployment a Suggested Remedy for Immediate Application BRO 11172(9).
102. *Daily Express*, 20 September 1921.
103. *Bristol Times and Mirror*, 21 June 1922.
104. *Daily Express*, 3 February 1923; Dividends paid by Bristol brewers:

	1919	1920	1921
Bristol Brewery Co.	16%	16%	16%
Bristol United Brewery	15%	15%	16.25%

105. Briefing Papers for the Visit of the Right Honourable Neville Chamberlain MP Minister of Health 1 October 1925, BRO 11173(10).
106. Minutes of the Bristol City Council Housing of the Working Classes Sub-Committee, 30 October 1914.
107. Sixth Annual Report of the Bristol Civic League, 31 December 1914, p. 22.
108. Report of the Bristol City Engineer (1925–6) BRO 35510:

Houses erected and available in Bristol

Year	Houses erected	Houses empty
1906	1372	
1907	1239	
1908	859	
1909	454	4800
1910	386	4750
1911	297	4650
1912	204	4500
1913	218	3400
1914	132	2600
1915	98	2580
1916	89	1670
1917	42	1025
1918	25	756
1919	72	530
1920	101	320
1921	248	220
1922	691	281
1923	361	204
1924	449	337
1925	1051	380

109. Housing of Working Classes Sub-Committee, 28 January 1920.
110. Patterson, *Class and Conflict*, p. 120.
111. Report of the Bristol Housing Famine Campaign (Bristol 1923), pp. 1, 2, 4.
112. Briefing Papers, Nevil Chamberlain, p. 4.
113. Report of City Engineer (1925–6).

114. Harland & Wolff Papers, 25 Oct 1921.

Rise in Retail Prices 1914–21:

	July 1914		Oct 1921	
	s.	d.	s.	d.
Bread (2 lb loaf)		$2\frac{1}{2}$		$6\frac{3}{4}$
Tea (lb average quality)	1	8	3	0
Potatoes (per stone)		8		10
Milk (quart)		$3\frac{1}{2}$		7
Buttermilk (quart)		$\frac{1}{2}$		$1\frac{1}{2}$
Condensed milk (average tin)		$4\frac{1}{2}$	1	$\frac{3}{4}$
Butter (lb)	1	0	2	0
Margarine (lb)		6		8
Sugar (lb)		2		6
Eggs (doz average)		$11\frac{1}{2}$	3	10
Oatmeal (stone)	2	0	3	3
Bacon (lb)		10	2	4
Beef (lb average)		$9\frac{1}{2}$	1	8
Mutton (lb average)		9	2	2
Fish (lb average)		$5\frac{1}{2}$		11
Salt (packet)		$\frac{1}{2}$		2
Pepper (oz)		$\frac{3}{4}$		2
Mustard (tin)		1		$2\frac{1}{2}$
Baking soda		$\frac{3}{4}$		2
Matches (doz boxes)		2		11
Starch (lb)		3		6
Blue-bag		1		2

115. Harland & Wolff papers, 25 October 1922.

Cost of local government officers rations:

	July 1914		October 1921	
	s.	d.	s.	d.
2 × 2 lb loaves		5	1	$5\frac{1}{2}$
2.5 lbs of best beef	2	1	4	7
1 lb fish		3	1	0
10.5 pts of milk	1	$3\frac{3}{4}$	3	1
6 oz of tea		9	1	$1\frac{1}{2}$
12 oz of sugar		$1\frac{1}{2}$		$4\frac{1}{2}$
2 lb of rice		4	1	0
10.5 lb of potatoes		$3\frac{3}{4}$		9
7 eggs		$5\frac{1}{2}$	2	4
$\frac{3}{4}$ lb of jam		$2\frac{1}{2}$		$7\frac{1}{2}$
Total	6s.	$2\frac{3}{4}$d.	16s.	0d.

116. *Daily Mail*, 14 February 1922.
117. Harland & Wolff papers, 1 September 1919.

Increase in tool costs (patternmakers)

	Pre-War	1918
Stanley plane No. 7	16s. 0d.	£1.8s. 0d.
Stanley plane No. 4	9s. 9d.	£1.1s. 0d.
Wooden plane (Jack)	4s. 9d.	10s. 6d.
Set of chisels	15s. 3d.	£1.7s. 1d.
Combination square	8s. 0d.	12s. 6d.
Hand saw	6s. 6d.	13s. 0d.
Tenon saw	5s. 6d.	10s. 10d.

118. Report of the City of Bristol Public Assistance Committee for y/e 31 March 1933, p. 46; Devlin, P. *Yes We Have No Bananas* (Belfast 1981), p. 84.
119. Minutes of Bristol Health Committee, Re-construction Sub-Committee, 29 June 1922.

11 CONCLUSION

1. Report of an Enquiry by the Board of Trade into Working Class Rents, Housing and Retail Prices [Cd 3864] BPP 1908 CVII.

Town	A	B	C	D
Belfast	349 180	28.9	43.7	17.1
Bristol	328 945	22.9	42.8	15.9
Dublin	290 000	23.0	37.5	58.3
Glasgow	776 000	26.2	31.0	25.7
Manchester	543 872	26.3	37.7	21.6
Newcastle	215 328	22.9	22.7	69.0
Sheffield	380 795	25.8	23.6	46.0

   A = Population 1901.
   B = % Population, employed
   (excluding professions & commercial).
   C = % of B female.
   D = % of C employed in domestic service.

2. Morton, H.V., *In Search of Ireland* (London 1930), pp. 252–3.
3. Morton, H.V., *In Search of England* (London 1931), pp. 154–5.
4. Morton, *Ireland*, p. 6.
5. Craig, M.J., 'Ballad to Traditional Refrain'. By kind permission of Maurice James Craig and the Lilliput Press Ltd, Dublin.
6. Bristol Development Board, *Progressive Bristol* (Bristol 1930), p. 17; *Commercial* 1 March 1928, 'The wide range of the industries of Bristol'.
7. Morton, *Ireland*, p. 8.

8. Ibid., p. 9.
9. *Waxie's Dargle*, traditional song.
10. Pugsley, A.J., 'Modern Growth in Cities: the Economic Development of Bristol' *Bristol Times and Mirror*, 5 June 1922.
11. Meakin, B., *Model Factories and Villages* (London 1905), pp. 153, 191, 193, 196, 272, 276, 297.
12. Working class rents, housing and retail prices (1905)

Town	% of Population living in		
	1 Room	*5 + Rooms*	*Overcrowded*
Northampton	0.3	86.9	0.7
Bristol	1.6	74.3	3.6
Nottingham	0.4	71.7	3.7
Coventry	0.2	67.0	4.8
Manchester	0.8	51.3	6.3
Rochdale	0.3	36.3	7.3
Oldham	0.2	30.6	7.4
Liverpool	2.7	64.2	7.9
Belfast	0.4	59.4	8.3
Sheffield	0.4	53.6	9.5
St Helens	0.2	50.1	10.9
Merthyr Tydfil	0.2	52.8	12.2
Wigan	0.1	46.8	13.4
Halifax	2.2	44.6	14.5
Bradford	1.2	37.0	14.6
Londonderry	3.3	46.8	16.8
Plymouth	8.9	38.8	20.2
Waterford	3.2	43.9	20.6
Cork	5.1	41.7	23.5
Sunderland	4.6	28.1	30.1
Limerick	8.7	37.4	31.7
South Shields	4.3	21.2	32.4
Gateshead	5.2	19.0	34.6
Dublin	24.7	33.9	40.6

13. Working class rents housing and retail prices (shillings/pence)

Town	*A*	*B*	*C*	*D*	*E*
London	92.0%	7/6–10/6	6.7	46.0	16.1
Edinburgh	103.0%	7/2– 9/9	8.9	25.7	*
Dublin	1.3%	6/0– 8/0	24.7	33.9	40.6
Belfast	224%	3/0– 5/0	0.4	59.4	8.3
Birmingham	115%	5/0– 6/0	0.3	54.9	10.3
Cardiff	711%	5/0– 6/0	0.7	76.3	2.9
Bristol	114%	4/0– 5/0	1.6	74.3	3.6
Barrow	5658%	5/6– 6/0	0.6	71.5	10.1

A = Population growth 1851–1901.
B = Cost of four-room accommodation.
C = % population living in 1 room.

$D = \%$ population living in $5+$ rooms.
$E = \%$ population living 'overcrowded'.
* Scottish 'overcrowding' is not calculated in same way, but described as 'acute' in some districts of this city.

Bibliography

LOCATION OF MATERIAL

Belfast City Hall	BCH
Belfast Harbour Commissioners Library	BHC
Bristol Central Library	BCL
Bristol Co-Operative Society Archives	BCS
Bristol Record Office	BRO
Cadbury Archives	CAB
Dublin Civil Archive	DCA
Dublin Port and Docks Authority	DPD
Irish National Archives	INA
Linen Hall Library, Belfast	LH
National University of Ireland	NUI
Public Record Office of Northern Ireland	PRONI
Queen's University of Belfast	QUB
Workers' Educational Association Bristol	WEAB
Working Class Movement Library	WCML

PRIMARY SOURCES

(i) Private Papers

Butler Miss R.F., Notes on Bristol Industries. BRO 14760

Cunningham, J., Papers relating to his life. PRONI Ref D1288/1A

Sheppard, F., Papers relating to trade unions and Labour Party in Bristol. BRO 12452

Hanna-Bell, S., Interviews with 1907 Strikers PRONI Ref D3358/1

Wall, J., Papers relating to Labour Party, Co-operative Movement and socialist groups in Bristol, BRO 37886

Webb, S., Extracts from Minutes of the Bristol Trades Council, BRO 32080/ TC1/20

Williams, F.G., Papers relating to Teachers Union in Bristol, BRO 38773

(ii) Institutional Papers

Belfast Chamber of Commerce, *Annual Reports*, (1878–1907). LH N3200

Belfast City Council, Minutes of Distress Committee. BCH Unlisted

Belfast Flax Spinners Association, file of correspondence with trade unions (1919–1930s). Was PRONI D2279 now unlisted

Belfast Branch of United Operative Plumbers Association Minute Books and Membership records. PRONI D1050/5/2/ 1–7, D1050/5/1/ 1–3

Belfast Trade Council, Council and Executive Committee Minutes, LH unlisted

Belfast Harbour Board, *Annual Reports*, (1880–1925). BHC unlisted
Bristol Constabulary Records, BRO. Ref. 34908
Bristol Chamber of Commerce, *Annual Reports*, BRO 38605/A
Bristol Charity Organisation Society, *Annual Reports*. BRO 35510
Bristol City Council, Minutes and Annual Reports of various Committees. BRO
Bristol Civic League, *Annual Report y/e 31 Dec 1914*. BRO 35510
Bristol Joint Advisory Committee for Conscientious Objectors. BCL B32050, B32051, B32052
Bristol Teachers Association Records. BRO 32225
Bristol Trades Council, Records. BRO 36126, 32080
Bristol Trade Union Movement, Papers relating. BRO 27161
Bristol Typographical Society, Records. BRO 34463
British Parliamentary Papers. QUB
Co-operative Congress, *Annual Reports*. BCS unlisted
Harland & Wolff Papers. PRONI D2805
Irish National Teachers Association (Belfast Branch). PRONI D1285/1–3
Irish Protestant National Teachers Union, Minute Book. PRONI D517
National Union of Teachers, Records. BRO 40439
Scottish Council of Women's Trades, Erwin Report on Sweated Industries in Belfast 1910. PRONI D1326/26/70
WEA, Western District, *Annual Reports*. WEAB unlisted
Wills, W.D. & H.O., Company Archives. BRO 38169

(iii)   Newspapers and Other Publications

Belfast Telegraph
Belfast Newsletter
Bristol Observer
Bristol Times and Mirror
Western Daily Press
Bristol Christian Leader

(iv)   Directories and Similar

Belfast and Ulster Trades Directory (1880–1920)
Lloyd's Register of Shipping (1880–1925)
J. Wright and Co.'s (Mathew's) Bristol and Clifton Directory (1880–1900)
Wright's Bristol Directory (1901–1925)

(v)   Books

Anon, *Bristol Sweated Industries Exhibition Handbook* (Bristol 1908)
Anon, *Souvenir of the Opening of Kingsley Hall* (Bristol 1911)
Anon, *Remarks upon the Anti-Protestant and Democratic Tendency of the Reform Bill* (Bristol 1831)
Arnold, M., *Irish Essays and Others* (London 1891)
Arrowsmith & Co., *Dictionary of Bristol* (Bristol 1906)

Askwith, G., *Industrial Problems and Disputes* (London 1920)
Bax, E.B., *Essays in Socialism: New and Old* (London 1907)
Bowley, A.L., *An Elementary Manual of Statistics* (London 1915)
Bristol Socialist Society, *Liberty Fayre Souvenir* (Bristol 1911)
Bristol Adult School Union, *Facts of Bristol's Social Life* (Bristol 1914)
Bristol City Council, *Bristol as it is Today, Illustrated Handbook and Guide* (Bristol 1905)
Cadbury, E. Matheson, M.C. and Shann, G., *Women's Work and Wages* (London 1908)
Clarke, A., *The Effects of the Factory System* (London 1913)
Connolly, J., *Collected Works*, 2 vols (Dublin, 1987 & 1988)
Cook, A., *Bristol Hovels* (Bristol 1907)
Cummings, D.C., *A Historical Survey of the Boilermakers and Iron and Steel Ship Builders Society* (Robinson & Co. 1905)
De Rousiers, P., *The Labour Question in Britain* (London 1896)
Fabian Society, *Facts about Bristol; Fabian Tract No. 18* (London 1891)
Henderson, A., *Labour and Ireland* (London 1919)
Independent Labour Party, *Democracy and the War* (London 1918)
Jackson, E., *A Study in Democracy: Industrial Co-operation in Bristol* (Manchester 1911)
Jones, T., *First Annual Trades Union Directory, 1861* (reprint Farnborough 1991)
Kenna, G.B., *Facts and Figures of the Belfast Pogrom* (Dublin 1922)
Irish Labour Party, *Who Burned Cork?* (Dublin 1921)
——, *A Handbook for Rebels. A Guide to Successful Defiance of the British Government* (Dublin 1918)
Labour Party, *Report of the Labour Commission to Ireland* (London 1920)
Ludlow, F., *Trades and Sketches of Old and New Bristol* (Bristol 1890)
Mansbridge, A., *An Adventure in Working Class Education* (London 1920)
McCarthy, M.J.F., *Five Years in Ireland 1895–1900* (Dublin 1901)
Meakin, B., *Model Factories and Villages* (London 1905)
National Civic Federation, *Municipal and Private Operation of Public Utilities* 3 Vol (New York 1907)
Oliver, G., *Collections Illustrating the History of the Catholic Religion* (London 1857)
Oliver, T., *Dangerous Trades* (London 1902)
——, *The Health of the Workers* (London 1925)
Pease, E.R., *A History of Socialism* (London 1913)
——, *A History of the Fabian Society* (London 1918)
Postgate, R., *The Builders History* (London 1923)
Powell, A.C. & Littlejohn, S., *A History of Freemasonry in Bristol* (Bristol 1910)
Reeves, M.P., *Round About a Pound a Week* (London 1913) (1979, Virago edition)
Ryan, W.P., *The Irish Labour Movement from the Twenties to our own Day* (Dublin 1919)
Shaw, G.B., *John Bull's Other Island* (London 1912, 1931 standard edition used)
——, *Irish Nationalism and Labour Internationalism* (London 1920)
Sheppard, F., *Labour Unrest and its Causes* (Bristol 1912)
Stone, G.F., *Bristol Chronology 1915* (Bristol 1916)

Stone, G. & Wells, C., *Bristol and the Great War* (Bristol 1920)
Tressell, R., *The Ragged Trousered Philantropist 1911* (London 1955)
Ulster Unionist Labour Association, *Labour Commission on Ireland: Analysis and Criticism* (Belfast 1921)
Way, J.P., *A Short History of Old Bristol Pottery and Porcelain* (Bristol undated 1920s)
Webb, S & B., *History of Trade Unionism* (London 1920)
Wells, C., *Short History of the Port of Bristol* (Bristol 1909)
Wicks, G.H., *Bristol's Heathen Neighbours: the Story of the Bristol Itinerant Society* (Bristol 1911)
Workers Education Association, *W.E.A. Handbook 1918* (London 1920)
Wright, A., *Disturbed Dublin: the Story of the Great Strike of 1913–14* (London 1914)

(vi) Articles

Anon, 'Work in Bristol: A Series of Sketches of the Chief Manufactures in the city', *Bristol Times and Mirror* Various Issues (1883)
Pugsley, A.J., 'Modern Growth in Cities: the Economic Development of Bristol', *Bristol Times & Mirror* 5 June 1922

SECONDARY SOURCES

(i) Books and Pamphlets

Anon, *Cobblers Tale: A History of the Firm of G.B. Brittion and Sons* (Bristol 1951)
Akinson, B., *Trades Unions in Bristol* (Bristol 1992)
Anderson, G., *Victorian Clerks* (Manchester 1976)
Backstrom, P.N., *Christian Socialism and Co-operation in Victorian England* (London 1974)
Bagwell, P.S., *The Railwaymen* (London 1963)
Bailey, V., *Forged in Fire: the History of the Fire Brigades Union* (London 1992)
Bain, G.S., *The Growth of White-Collar Unionism* (Oxford 1970)
Bardon, J., *Belfast an Illustrated History* (Belfast 1982)
——, *A History of Ulster* (Belfast 1992)
Beattie, G., *We are the People* (London 1993)
Beckett, J.C. & Glasscock, R.E., *Belfast: Origin and Growth of an Industrial City* (Belfast 1967)
Beckett, J.C. et al., *Belfast: the Making of the City* (Belfast 1983)
Beckett, J.C., *Making of Modern Ireland 1603–1923* (London 1987)
Belfast Trades Council, *Souvenir of the Trades Union Congress at the Grosvenor Hall* (Belfast 1929)
Bettey, J.H., *Bristol Observed* (Bristol 1986)
Billington, R.A., *The Protestant Crusade 1800–1860* (Chicago 1964)
Blackburn, R.M., *Union Charter and Social Class* (London 1967)

Bowyer-Bell, J., *The Secret Army* (New York 1974)

Boyce, D.G., *Nineteenth Century Ireland* (Dublin 1990)

——, *The Revolution in Ireland 1879–1923* (Dublin 1988)

Boyd, A., *The Rise of the Irish Trade Unions* (Tralee 1972)

——, *Holy War in Belfast* (Tralee 1970)

Boyle, J.W., *The Irish Labour Movement in the Nineteenth Century* (Washington 1988)

Bristol Broadsides, *Placards and Pin Money* (Bristol 1986)

Bristol Development Board, *Progressive Bristol* (Bristol 1929)

Brown, G., *The Industrial Syndicalist* (Nottingham 1974)

Bryher, S., *An Account of the Labour and Socialist Movement in Bristol* (Bristol 1929)

Buckland, P., *Ulster Unionism 1885–1923* (Belfast 1973)

Buchanan, A. & Cossons, N., *Industrial Archaeology of the Bristol Region* (Bristol 1969)

Budge, I. & O'Leary, C., *Belfast Approach to Crisis* (London 1973)

Bundock, C.J., *The Story of the National Union of Printing, Bookbinding and Paper Workers*, (Oxford 1959)

Burnett, J., *Plenty and Want* (Harmondsworth 1968)

——, *A Social History of Housing 1815–1970* (Newton Abbot 1978)

Burgess, K., *The Challenge of Labour: Shaping British Society* (London 1980)

Bythell, D., *The Sweated Trades: Outwork in Nineteenth Century Britain* (London 1978)

Caulfield, M., *The Easter Rebellion* (London 1965)

Clarkson, J.D., *Labour and Nationalism in Ireland* (New York 1926)

Clegg, H.A., *General Union* (Oxford 1954)

Clegg, H.A., *A History of the British Trade Unions since 1889*, Vol. 2 (Oxford, 1985)

Clegg, H.A. Fox, A. & Thompson, A.F., *A History of the British Trade Unions since 1889*, Vol. 1 (Oxford, 1964)

Clinton, A., *The Trade Union Rank and File* (Manchester 1977)

Coates, K. & Topham, T., *The History of the Transport and General Workers Union* Vol. 1 (Oxford 1991)

Cody, S. O'Dowd, D. & Rigney, P., *The Parliament of Labour: 100 years of the Dublin Council of Trade Unions* (Dublin 1986)

Coe, W.E., *The Engineering Industry of the North of Ireland* (Newton Abbot 1969)

Cole, G.D.H., *A Short History of the British Working Class Movement 1789–1947* (London 1966)

Connelly, T.J., *The Woodworkers* (Manchester 1960)

Cougan, T.P., *The I.R.A.* (Glasgow 1987)

Cullen, L.M., *An Economic History of Ireland since 1660* (London 1978)

Daly, M.E., *Dublin: The Deposed Capital* (Cork 1984)

Dangerfield, G., *The Strange Death of Liberal England* (London 1966)

Desmond-Greaves, C., *Life and Times of James Connolly* (London 1976)

Devlin, P., *Yes We Have No Bananas* (Belfast 1981)

Dougan, D., *The History of North East Shipbuilding* (London 1968)

——, *The Shipwrights* (1972)

Dudley-Edwards, R., *James Connolly* (Dublin 1981)

Dudley-Edwards, R., *Atlas of Irish History* (London 1973)
Farr, G., *Bristol Shipbuilding in the Nineteenth Century* (Bristol 1971)
——, *Shipbuilding in the Port of Bristol* (London 1977)
Farrell, M., *Arming the Protestants* (London 1983)
Farren, S., *The Politics of Irish Education* (Belfast 1995)
Fielding, S., *Class and Ethnicity* (Manchester 1993)
Finnegan, F., *Poverty and Prejudice* (Cork 1982)
Foster, R., *Modern Ireland* (London 1988)
Fox, A., *A History of the National Union of Boot and Shoe Operatives* (Oxford 1958)
Freedman M. (ed.), *A Minority in Britain: Social Studies of the Anglo-Jewish Community* (London 1955)
French, J.O., *Plumbers in Unity* (London 1965)
Fyrth, H.J. & Collins, H., *The Foundry Workers: a Trade Union History* (Manchester 1959)
Gainer, B., *The Alien Invasion* (London 1972)
Gartner, L.P., *The Jewish Immigrant in England 1870–1914* (London 1960)
Gaughan, J.A., *Thomas Johnson 1872–1968* (Dublin 1980)
Gibbon, P., *The Origins of Ulster Unionism* (Manchester 1975)
Gogarty, O., *'Sackville Street' Collected Works* (London 1989)
Gray, J., *City in Revolt* (Belfast 1985)
Gray, R., *Labour Aristocracy in Nineteenth Century Britain* (London 1981)
Gray, R., *The Labour Aristocracy in Victorian Edinburgh* (Oxford 1976)
Harkness, D. & O'Dowd, M., *The Town in Ireland* (Belfast 1981)
Harris, R., *Prejudice and Tolerance in Ulster* (Manchester 1972)
Harvey, C. & Press, J., *Studies in the Business History of Bristol* (Bristol 1988)
——, *Sir George White of Bristol* (Bristol 1989)
Hearn, M., *Below Stairs* (Dublin 1993)
Hereward, S., *Orangism in Ireland and Britain* (London 1966)
Hezlet, A., *The 'B' Specials* (London 1972)
Hilton, G.W., *The Truck System* (Cambridge 1960)
Higgenbottom, A., *Our Society's History* (Manchester 1939)
Hobsbawm, E.J., *Labouring Men* (London 1976)
Hoffman, P.C., *They Also Serve: the Story of the Shopworker* (London 1949)
Holton, R., *British Syndicalism 1900–1914* (London 1976)
Hoppen, K.T., *Ireland since 1800* (London 1989)
Howell, B., *The Police in Victorian Bristol* (Bristol 1989)
Hughes, F., *By Hand and Brain: the Story of the Clerical and Administrative Workers Union* (London 1953)
Hunt, E.H., *British Labour History 1815–1914* (Atlantic Heights 1982)
——, *Regional Wage Variations in Britain 1815–1914* (Oxford 1973)
Hyman, R., *The Workers Union* (Oxford 1971)
——, *Strikes* (Glasgow 1978)
Hymson, A.M., *A History of the Jews in England* (London 1928)
Jefferys, J.B., *The Story of the Engineers* (London 1945)
Jennings B., *Knowledge is Power: a Short History of the W.E.A.* (Hull 1979)
Johnson, D., *The Interwar Economy of Ireland* (Dublin 1989)
Johnson, P. (ed), *20th Century Britain: Economic, Social and Cultural Change* (Harlow 1994)

Jones, M., *Those Obstreperous Lassies: a History of the I.W.W.U.* (Dublin 1988)

Kennedy, L. & Ollerenshaw, P., *An Economic History of Ulster 1820–1914* (Manchester 1987)

Kennedy, P., *The Rise and Fall of British Naval Mastery* (London 1991)

Keogh, D., *The Rise of the Irish Working Class* (Belfast 1982)

Kidd, A.T., *History of the Tin-Plate Workers and Sheet Metal Workers and Braziers Society.* (London 1949)

Kiddier, W., *The Old Trade Unions* (London 1931)

Large, D. & Round, F., *Public Health in Mid-Victorian Bristol* (Bristol 1977)

Large, D. & Whitfield,R., *The Bristol Trades Council* (Bristol 1973)

Lee, J.J., *Ireland 1912–1985* (Cambridge 1989)

Leeson, R.A., *Travelling Brothers* (London 1980)

Levy, C. (ed.), *Socialism and the Intelligentsia 1880–1914* (London 1987)

Lipman, V.D., *Social History of the Jews in England* (London 1954)

Lovell, J., *British Trade Unions 1875–1933* (London 1979)

——, *Stevedores and Dockers* (London 1969)

Lynch, M., *Scotland a New History* (London 1994)

Lysaght Ltd, *Lysaght 1857–1957* (Bristol 1957)

Marsh, A. & Ryan, V., *Historical Directory of Trade Unions* 4 vols (Aldershot, 1980, 1984, 1987, 1989)

McCutcheon, J., *The Industrial Archaeology of Northern Ireland* (Cranbury 1980)

McGrath, P., *A Bristol Miscellany* (Bristol 1985)

McKee, A., *Belfast Trades Council: the First Hundred Years 1881–1981* (Belfast 1983)

McKillop, N., *The Lighted Flame: a History of ASLEF* (London 1950)

McMaolan, S., *I mBeal Feirsde domh* (Dublin)

McNeilly, N., *Exactly Fifty Years* (Belfast 1973)

Merrigan, M., *Eagle or Cuckoo, the Story of the A.T.G.W.U. in Ireland* (Dublin 1989)

Messenger, B., *Picking up the Linen Threads* (Belfast 1980)

Miller, D., *Peep o' Day Boys and Defenders* (Belfast 1990)

Mitchell, A., *Labour in Irish Politics 1890–1930* (Dublin 1974)

Mitchell, B.R. & Deane, P., *Abstract of British Historical Statistics* (Cambridge 1962)

More, C., *Skill and the English Working Class 1870–1914* (London 1980)

Morgan, A., *Labour and Partition* (London 1991)

Morgan, A. & Purdy, B. *Ireland: Divided Nation Divided Class* (London 1980)

Mortimer, J.E., *A History of the Association of Engineering and Shipbuilding Draughtsmen* (London 1960)

——, *History of the Boilermakers Society* (2 vols, London, 1973 & 1982)

Morton, H.V., *In Search of Ireland* (London 1930)

——, *In Search of England* (London 1931)

Moss, M. & Hume, J.R., *Shipbuilders to the World* (Belfast 1986)

Mosses, W., *A History of the Patternmakers Association 1872–1922* (1927)

Musson, A.E., *The Typographical Association: Origins and History up to 1949* (Oxford 1954)

O'Brian, J., *Dear Dirty Dublin: a City in Distress 1899–1916* (University of California 1982)

O'Broin, L., *Dublin Castle and the 1916 Rising* (Dublin 1966)

O'Connor, E., *Syndicalism in Ireland* (Cork 1988)

——, *A Labour History of Ireland* (Dublin 1992)

O'Connor, U., *Oliver St John Gogarty* (London 1963)

——, *Brendan Behan* (London 1970)

O'Grada, C., *Ireland an Economic History* (Oxford 1994)

Owens, R.C., *Smashing Times: a History of the Irish Women's Suffrage Movement 1889–1922* (Dublin 1984)

Patterson, H., *Class, Conflict and Sectarianism* (Belfast 1980)

Pelling, H., *A History of British Trade Unionism* (Harmondsworth 1976)

Perren, R., *The Meat Trade in Britain 1840* (London 1978)

Phelps-Brown, E.H., *The Growth of British Industrial Relations* (London 1959)

Phoenix, E., *Northern Nationalism* (Belfast 1994)

Pollard, S. & Robertson, P., *The British Shipbuilding Industry 1870–1914* (Harvard 1979)

Pollard, S., *A History of Labour in Sheffield* (Liverpool 1959)

Pollins, H., *Economic History of the Jews in England* (London 1982)

Port of Bristol Authority, *Facts and Figures Relating to the Port and its Docks* (Bristol 1928)

——, *Port of Bristol: History, Trade and Facilities* (Bristol 1959)

Powell, L.H., *The Shipping Federation* (London 1950)

Price, R., *Masters, Unions and Men* (Cambridge 1980)

Redford, A., *Labour Migration in England 1800–50* (Manchester 1926)

Redmond, S., *Irish Municipal Employees Trade Union 1883–1893* (Dublin 1985)

Reid, A.J., *Social Classes and Social Relations in Britain 1850–1914* (London 1992)

Rolt, L.T.C., *A Hunslett Hundred* (Dawlish 1964)

Royal Arch Purple Order, *History of the Royal Arch Purple Order* (Belfast 1993)

Rumpf, E. & Hepburn, A.C., *Nationalism and Socialism in Twentieth-Century Ireland* (Liverpool 1977)

Somerville, J., *Christopher Thomas: Soapmaker of Bristol* (1991)

Stevens, W.C., *The Story of the E.T.U.* (1952)

Stewart, A.T.Q., *The Ulster Crisis* (London 1969)

Stewart, M. & Hunter, L., *The Needle is Threaded: the History of an Industry* (London 1964)

Sturmthal, A., *White Collar Trade Union* (London 1966)

Sweetman, R. & Simmons, C., *The Port of Belfast* (Belfast 1985)

Taplin, E., *The Dockers Union* (Leicester 1985)

Terraine, J., *Business in Great Waters: the U-boat Wars 1916–1945* (London 1989)

Thompson, E.P., *The Making of the English Working Class* (Harmondsworth 1968)

Totton, M., *Founded in Brass: the First Hundred Years of the National Society of Metal Mechanics* (1972)

Townshend, C., *The British Campaign in Ireland 1919–21* (Oxford 1978)

Travers, P., *Settlements and Divisions: Ireland 1870–1922* (Dublin 1988)

Tuckett, A., *The Blacksmith's History* (London 1974)

Turner, M., *A History of the Workers Education Association Western District 1911–86* (Bristol 1987)

Valintine, J., *Irish Memories* (Bristol 1929)

Wainwright, E., *Trade Unions* (London 1984)

Walker, W.M., *Juteopolis: Dundee and its Textile Workers 1885–1923* (Edinburgh 1979)

Wearmouth R.F., *Methodisism and Trade Unions* (London 1959)

Whitaker, W.B., *Victorian and Edwardian Shopworkers* (Newton Abbot 1973)

Wrigley, C., *Some Aspects of the Labour Market in Britain 1870–1914* (Brighton 1982)

(ii) Articles

Anon, 'The Wide Range of the Industries of Bristol', *Commercial* 1 March 1928

Anon, 'The Chocolate Age', *Fry's Works Magazine*, Bi-centennial Issue 1928

Child, J., 'Quaker Employers and Industrial Relations', *Sociology Review* 12 (1964), pp. 293–315

Daly, M., 'Social Structure of the Dublin Working Class', *Irish Historical Studies*, XXIII No. 90 (1982), pp. 121–33

Emanuel, R.R., 'The History of Bristol Jewry', *Temple Local History Group Newsletter*, Vol. 4 (1988)

Gallagher, M., 'Socialism and the Nationalist Tradition in Ireland', *Eire-Ireland*, 12 (1977), pp. 63–102

Kenny, B., 'The Growth of the Irish Transport and General Workers Union: a Geographer's View', *Saothar* 12 (1987), pp. 78–84

Lee, M.J., 'Peckett and Sons Ltd: a Brief Memoir' *Industrial Railway Record*, 53, April 1974, pp. 190–5

Lovell, J., 'Employers and Craft Unionism a Programme of Action for British Shipbuilding 1902–5', *Business History*, 34 (1992), pp. 38–58

——, 'The Irish and the London Dockers', *Bulletin of the Society for the Study of Labour History*, 35 (1977), pp. 16–18

Maguire, M., 'The Organisation and Activism of Dublin's Protestant Working Class', *Irish Historical Studies* XXXIX (May 1994), pp. 65–87

——, 'A Socio-Economic Analysis of the Dublin Protestant Working Class', *Irish Economic and Social History* XX (1993), pp. 35–59

McCarthy, C., 'The Impact of Larkinism on the Irish Working Class', *Bulletin of the Society for the Study of Labour History*, 35 (1977), pp. 12–16

——, 'Civil Strife and the Growth of Trade Union Unity: the Case of Ireland', *Government and Opposition*, Vol. 8 (1973), pp. 407–431

McHugh, J., 'Belfast Labour Dispute and Riots of 1907', *International Review of Social History*, 22 (1977), pp. 1–20

McInevney, M., 'The Irish Labour Movement', *Hibernia*, March (1963), pp. 6, 12, 16

Mitchell, A., 'William O'Brian 1881–1968 and the Irish Labour Movement', *Studies (Ireland)*, 60 (1971), pp. 311–31

——, 'Labour and the National Struggle', *Capuchin Annual* (1971), pp. 261–88

Mitchell, A., 'The Irish Labour Movement and the Foundation of the Irish Free State', *Capuchin Annual* (1972), pp. 326–74

Reese, A., 'Jewish Ancestry and Records', *Journal of the Bristol and Avon Family History Society*, No. 60 (June 1990), p. 6

Schneider, F.D., 'British Labour and Ireland 1918–1921', *Review of Politics*, 40 (1978), pp. 368–91

Thornley, D., 'The Development of the Irish Labour Movement', *Christus Rex*, 18 (1964), pp. 7–21

Weedon, C., 'The Bristol Bottlemakers: the Rise and Fall of an Industry', *Chemistry and Industry*, June (1978), pp. 375–81

——, 'The Bristol Glass Industry: Its Rise and Decline', *Glass Technology*, 24 No. 5 October (1983), pp. 240–246

Wrigley, C., 'Labour and Trade Unions in Great Britain' *ReFresh*, 13 (Autumn 1991), p. 1

(iii) Theses

Atkinson, B., 'The Bristol Labour Movement 1868–1906', Oxford DPhil., 1969

Blackenhorn, D.G., 'Cabinet Makers in Victorian Britain', Warwick MA., 1978

Coughlan, R.M., 'Ethno-nationalism and the Cultural Division of Labour in Nineteenth Century Belfast', University of New York DPhil., 1981

Fraser, W.H., 'Trades Councils in England and Scotland: 1858–1897', Sussex DPhil., 1967

Hewitt, F., 'Population and Urban Growth in East Bristol 1800–1914', Bristol DPhil., 1965

Hirsch, M., 'The Federation of Sailmakers of Great Britain and Ireland 1889–1922: a Craft Union in Crisis', Warwick MA, 1976

Judge, J.J., 'The Labour Movement in the Republic of Ireland' National University of Ireland DPhil., 1955

Pugsley, A.J., 'Some Contributions towards the study of the Economic Development of Bristol in the Eighteenth and Nineteenth Centuries', Bristol MA., 1921

Webb, D.J., The Changing Industrial Geography of the Port and City of Bristol since 1861: a Study in Port Function', London MA., 1967

(iv) Unpublished

Hutchinson, E., *Reminiscence*. Typed manuscript

McElborough Robert, *My Years in the Gas Industry and my Fight with the Trade Unions*. Handwritten manuscript. PRONI D770/1/1–4

Index